Praise for *The Ultimate Guide to Sex after Fifty*

"Living 'happily ever after' may be the stuff of fairy tale endings, but in this forthright and important book, Joan Price shows us how 'sexy ever after' can be a new beginning for the senior set."

—Ian Kerner,
New York Times bestselling author of *She Comes First*

"Thank you, Joan Price, sister warrior, for joining me in building an army of orgasmic vibrating women (and men) to change society's view of sexuality. The healing has begun."

—Betty Dodson, PhD sexologist and author of *Sex for One*

"Let this be your guide to juice and wisdom—at any age! Joan Price has written a frank, generous, inclusive book to remind us that sexual expression can become richer over time, with scores of ways to encourage a safe and delicious journey of discovery."

—Gina Ogden, PhD, LMFT, author of *The Return of Desire*

"Lots of people have questions about how sex works when we get older. And even if you don't think it's a topic that's relevant to your life now, it will be eventually, I hope. Nobody knows how to talk about the challenges and pleasures of sex after fifty better than Joan Price. She's created the most comprehensive, realistic, useful, and funny guide to relationships, dating, and sexuality I've ever found. There are lots of practical tips, positive information, and suggestions for things to think about so you can create an amazing sex life. Whether you're currently in a relationship or not, and whether you're over fifty yet or not, there's a lot here for you."

—Charlie Glickman, PhD, sexuality and relationship coach

"Joan Price's *The Ultimate Guide to Sex after Fifty* is not just a rule book for aging couples. It's a powerful, sexy reminder that getting older doesn't have to mean giving up a passionate love life. Price's advice and direction give us lots of things to look forward to. She also answers the questions that many of us may be afraid to ask. Sexy aging is possible. Anyone who hopes to stay hot and juicy and get older at the same time (everyone) should read this book."

—Dr. Tammy Nelson, author of *Getting the Sex You Want*

"Joan Price is a spirit among us. Her frankness is stunning, and it shimmers among all the cotton wool pronouncements about how we should be living out our sexual selves, but somehow don't. Her curiosity has led her to amass a trove of stories and facts which she shares generously, and her deep intelligence has formatted this knowledge in an accessible form. Among all the noise about sex that surrounds us daily, her simple truths slip into our lives shepherded by tolerance and compassion. And, while Joan addresses facts and feelings that so easily cause shame and regret, how is it that we always come away laughing? Viva Joan Price!"
—Ann Evans, author of *Daring to Date Again*

"*The Ultimate Guide to Sex after Fifty* is an absolute must-read for anyone who wants to maintain a vibrant erotic life in middle age and beyond. Joan Price is a treasure; in our youth-obsessed society, she's unyielding in her insistence that older people have just as much right to sexual pleasure as younger ones. Her *Ultimate Guide* is at once fierce, humorous, and deeply practical. This straightforward, comprehensive, and moving book also comes with an extensive resource guide."
—Mark A. Michaels and Patricia Johnson,
authors of *Partners in Passion*

"Joan Price is a rare treasure. She's America's senior sexpert with the knowing smile. Yes, you can still enjoy sex, you Boomers who've always loved sex. No need to stop now. Sore knees? Quirky libido? Let Joan show you a few work-arounds. Joan's connection is instantaneous. Her compassionate tone feels like a good friend over a hot cup of coffee. It's just what's needed for the sharing of intimate, essential details. Whether just curious or in need of answers, you'll find everything you're looking for and more in *The Ultimate Guide to Sex after Fifty*."
—Rae Padilla Francoeur,
author of *Free Fall: A Late-in-Life Love Affair*

"Way to go, Joan Price! If you're over fifty, you need to read this book. If you're over fifty and not having great sex, you should find out more about what's holding you back and how to get past it. This is exactly what *The Ultimate Guide to Sex after Fifty* will help you find out. Whether you have issues in your relationship or if sex is painful, if you have erectile issues or you find yourself thrown back into the dating world after fifty, this book will help you find your way. You deserve to have great sex and this book can show you the way!"
—Dr. Jen Landa,
author of the bestseller *The Sex Drive Solution for Women*

The Ultimate Guide to Sex after Fifty

How to Maintain—or Regain—
a Spicy, Satisfying Sex Life

JOAN PRICE

CLEiS
PRESS

Published in the United States by Cleis Press,
an imprint of Start Midnight, LLC,
609 Greenwich St., Sixth Floor, New York, New York 10014.

Printed in the United States.
Cover design: Scott Idleman/Blink
Cover illustration: Sharon Dominick/Getty Images
Text design: Frank Wiedemann

First Edition.
10 9 8 7 6 5 4 3 2 1

Trade paper ISBN: 978-1-62778-096-4
E-book ISBN: 978-1-62778-110-7

Library of Congress Cataloging-in-Publication Data is available.

To access the index, please visit my website, www.joanprice.com. *The Ultimate Guide to Sex after Fifty* book page will have a link to an index you can print out.

The Ultimate Guide to Sex after Fifty is dedicated to the memory of my beloved husband, Robert Rice, who taught me how to give and receive love fully during our seven years together. The love, intimacy, and sexual passion that we discovered together were the best of our lives. I continue this work in Robert's honor, in memory of our great love.

TABLE OF CONTENTS

INTRODUCTION

What were you taught about older-age sex?

Nothing?

I wasn't taught anything about it either. Like most young people, I figured that at a certain age, I'd *know* it was time to let go of the sexual delights that dominated my thoughts and actions to that point and relax into being, I don't know—old?

I'm seventy as I write this, and though my sexuality is no longer driven by hormones, it's still a strong, solid part of who I am. It's calmer, less urgent, less driven—but still joyful and an essential part of my vitality and my sense of myself. You may experience your sexuality differently—there isn't one right way.

Part of embracing our sexuality across the lifespan means

redefining what sex means at different stages of our lives. I celebrated my sexuality in my late fifties and early sixties with my beloved Robert, who was my lover and then my husband. I celebrate it now, widowed—as many of us are—with drawers full of sex toys and occasional lusty dates. Things change. We change. But with knowledge and creativity, sex can remain a part of who we are.

I've assembled the topics, concerns, and questions that readers of my books and blog told me they want addressed. I wrote *The Ultimate Guide to Sex after Fifty* to give you clear and reliable information, action tips, and helpful resources. Whether you have a vibrant sex life now or an unfulfilling one that you'd like to fix—or even if you're just curious about what other people might be experiencing—this book will be a real resource for you now and through the years ahead.

The population over fifty is the largest in our history. We're healthier, more aware, more active, and more vocal than any previous older generation. Thanks to ongoing medical discoveries, the Sexual Revolution, and the Internet, we are also sexier than past generations of seniors. We're living and loving in aging bodies, and finally we're talking out loud about it.

I wrote this book to affirm that yes, the generation that many called the Love Generation is still interested in getting it on. How we do it might look and feel different, but our sexuality is ageless if we want it to be. We are the generation that takes credit for discovering clitoral orgasms, vibrators, and Viagra, and there's no stopping our thirst for knowledge and pleasure now.

This book is aimed primarily at readers over fifty, though

I welcome younger readers, too. I've had younger people tell me, "I want to know what to expect," and "I want to know what to do now to make sure I can enjoy sex for a very long time."

We of the boomer-and-beyond generation want information about the sexual changes, questions, and concerns we're experiencing. *The Ultimate Guide to Sex after Fifty* offers straightforward, nonjudgmental information and immediately useful tips, spiced with comments from my readers. I hope you'll let me know how this book helps you by emailing me at joan@joanprice.com—I'd love to hear from you. Please also visit my blog, www.NakedAtOurAge.com, where we'll keep talking about sex and aging.

Joan Price
Sebastopol, California

BUSTING THE MYTHS
ABOUT SEX AND AGING

How's your sex life? Choose all that apply:

1. Amazing. I never knew sex could be this great at my age.

2. Different, but satisfying in its own way.

3. Okay on my own, but I sure would like to share it with a partner.

4. Frustrating and unsatisfying. I wish I knew how to fix it.

5. What sex life?

6. I think I remember sex.

I get emails and whispered confidences all the time from women and men age fifty to eighty-plus, recounting hot sex with a new lover or sweet sex with an older one. And I also get tons of questions about decreased desire, vaginal pain, and erectile dysfunction, as well as "what happened to my sex life?"

It's a myth that at a certain age, we have to clamp down what shreds are left of our frayed sexuality. But we may need to redefine it. Aging is all about change. Our bodies change. Our relationships change. Medical conditions and medications affect our sexual responsiveness. Crap happens. We may lose a partner. Everything that affects us physically and emotionally affects us sexually. Embracing our sexuality doesn't mean everything stays juicy and sparkling.

But here's the good news that I need you to know: *All our sexual challenges have solutions.* I'm not going to sugarcoat the problems, but I assure you that solutions exist. If your sex life is anything but joyous, please keep reading. A problem is a beginning stage, not an ending. Let's get the problems out into the open candidly, and then start filling in the knowledge gaps so that you know what to do about them.

WHAT IS SEX TO YOU NOW?

To me, being sexual at this time of life means:

- Enjoying arousal and orgasm, with or without a partner

- Having a zesty, sex-positive frame of mind

- Being open to new possibilities

- Giving pleasure to this body that is capable of great delights

- Making a commitment to myself to be sexually aware and healthy

What does it mean to you? Let's talk about it.

I know that's not easy. Our upbringing, religious heritage, and ageist society want us to be quiet about sex—preferably not do it or think about it anymore. The media largely ignores us—or, strangely, makes it a news story when they discover that we are still lusty. Our medical professionals buy into the myth that we're past sex, rarely talking to us about the sexual side effects of our medical conditions or treatments.

Listen, our generation has changed a lot of beliefs and behavior in our culture already. Now let's change this. Let's ask questions, seek answers, and joyously assert our right to lifelong sexual pleasure. Let's bust the myths about sex and aging.

Our culture needs a wake-up call. What can the young aspire to if we don't show them that aging is not a prison sentence? Just because I've had a lot of birthdays doesn't mean my libido died. Wrinkles and gravity do not erase the person, they accentuate!

SOCIETY'S MYTH

Every element of our media landscape screams that old is not where anyone wants to be.

We live in a youth-focused culture, where we are viewed as pathetic and laughable if we are—or want to be—sexually active at our age. It's what I call the *ick factor*—that aversion to the sexuality of older adults.

We see society's ageist stereotypes in the media, where we seldom view a sexually active woman past menopause. We do see older men portrayed as eager to stay sexual, but they're usually objects of derision—no one wants them, unless they have enough money that potential mates will overlook how unappealing they are.

If we believe what we see in all the forms of media, we are either invisible or perverts. Ha! Little do they know. We have a great time and it's just lovely.

We hear this stereotype in jokes about dirty old men, geezers, cougars, and pathetic, sex-starved women trying to seduce anyone from the pizza delivery boy to their own sad, aging husbands. The message is, "That's disgusting." We're supposed to laugh at cartoons of women with sagging skin and boobs down to here and men with downward-pointing penises and their teeth in a jar.

Why do we accept society's ageist trap? We've fought against discrimination and prejudice our whole lives—where's our battle cry now?

I once taught a sex education class to thirteen-year-olds. We showed the class some line drawings of various pairings, and one was of a grey-haired couple simply lying in bed in an embrace.

"Yuck! That could be my grandmother," said one young man.

"Why would you want to deny the comfort of sex to your grandmother?" I answered. "She has lost so much in her life. At the least, she should have some physical pleasure."

He was wide-eyed. "I never thought of it that way," he said.

OUR OWN MISCONCEPTIONS

I used to think that if we all banded together and refuted the ick factor, we'd change society. We'd lead the parade of women and men proclaiming our right to joyful sex, and soon everyone would acknowledge that we can be sexy at any age. We'd celebrate aging, rather than bemoaning it.

I didn't realize that many of us in our generation have *internalized* society's stereotype. Many of us truly believe that we're no longer sexually vital and attractive if we have wrinkles, sags, and age spots, and we don't have easy arousal, lubrication, or erections. We look in the mirror and grimace.

With this attitude pummeled into us, some of us give up on sex. We're too embarrassed to ask questions or seek information. We don't talk to our doctors about sexual problems. Most important: *we don't realize that a sexual problem is a challenge that we can overcome with new knowledge, creativity, and maybe a new outlook.*

Do you believe any of these myths and stereotypes? I'll debunk them all in this book.

MYTH #1: People our age don't care about sex anymore.

Not only is there no biological necessity for us to give up on sex, there are many important health, intimacy, and pleasure-related reasons to stay sexually vibrant, either with a partner or solo. Many of us discover that sex can be better, in many ways, than it was during our youth.

> *I'm so annoyed with the media depiction of women over fifty with no libido. I call that B.S. Bring on the adventure and don't forget the toys!*

MYTH #2: Sex at our age ought to be the same as it used to be, and if it's not, it's the end of sexual pleasure.

No, it's not the same. What we like, how we like it, even our erogenous zones or the partner we desire may have shifted.

We may have thought that penetration was "real sex" in the past, and now orgasms come from fingers, tongues, and toys. Rather than despair what we feel we've lost, let's rejoice that we're still capable of this amazing sexual pleasure. Let's go on a creative journey to rediscover our *new* sexual selves—and that goes for those of us who are without a partner, too.

> *As a woman nearly sixty, I can say with certainty that there are days when I feel like that "hot thang" who stopped traffic back in the day—other days I feel like the detour sign.*

MYTH #3: If I'm not feeling the drive to have sex anymore, it's not worth the bother, so I might as well just let it go.
If you don't care much about sex anymore, and you don't miss it when you don't do it, that's a reason to go after *more* sex, not less. You'll learn so many ways that regular arousal and orgasms are good for health that your head will spin. And the more you do it, the more you'll enjoy it and want to keep doing it. I hope you're smiling now, because this journey will be delightful!

> *I think it really is about attitude, communication, and courage—about claiming your right to have a sexual life for your whole life, with another or with yourself.*

33 REASONS WHY SEX IS GOOD FOR YOU

Sex—and by that we mean sexual activity and orgasm *with or without* a partner—does all these good things for your body and mind:

- Reduces stress
- Enhances mood
- Strengthens the immune system
- Helps fight infection and disease
- Lowers diastolic blood pressure
- Burns calories
- Keeps sex organs healthy
- Improves blood flow
- Helps with sleep
- Aids in healing wounds
- Helps prevent vaginal atrophy
- Relieves headaches and other body aches
- Boosts self-esteem
- Improves body image
- Relieves depression
- Reduces risk of heart disease
- Reduces risk of prostate cancer
- Reduces risk of dermatitis
- Relieves chronic pain

- Boosts testosterone and estrogen levels
- Strengthens the pelvic floor to prevent incontinence
- Increases blood flow to all regions of the brain, increasing mental acuity
- Produces phenethylamine, a natural amphetamine that may help reduce overeating and cravings for junk food and cigarettes
- Makes you feel more loving toward and bonded with your partner
- Revs up your creative energy
- Reduces cholesterol levels
- Makes your skin glow
- Relaxes you
- Enhances quality of life
- May improve longevity
- Makes you look younger
- Makes you happier
- Feels really good

MYTH #4: If I don't have a partner and I don't feel the urge to pleasure myself on my own, there's no reason to masturbate. Many women of our generation are still uncomfortable with masturbation, seeing it as a poor stepsister to "real" sex. (Men don't usually fall for this myth.) The truth is that an orgasm a week—with or without a partner—keeps our sexual selves healthy, and can be utterly delightful.

> I don't have a partner right now. I learned that I can really enjoy sex by myself. I used to think that masturbation was a crappy substitute for the real thing, but if the real thing isn't available, I realize that a hands-on solution can be great fun!

MYTH #5: A man who can't have a dependable erection cannot satisfy his partner or enjoy sex himself.

Many men are victims of what I call the "I am my penis" myth. Once you expand your understanding of the kind of sexual enjoyment you can give and receive, a whole new world opens. Indeed, men are capable of orgasms without erection or ejaculation—something few men know until they experience it for themselves. Sex can be immensely pleasurable with an open mind and a commitment to exploration, creativity, and communication.

> My fiancé of three years is seventy-two and has ED, but with the special love we have, he pleases me orally so much that I reach my peak of satisfaction beyond belief. His not getting an erection doesn't bother us. We just love each other every way we can. I love him so much.

MYTH #6: Dating again at our age is too depressing and hopeless.

So many single boomers and seniors tell me that they'd rather be alone than try to navigate today's world of online dating, misadventures, rejections, weirdos, bores, and people who can't stop talking about their grandchildren or former partners. We can put the fun into dating again (honest!) with an upbeat attitude, new guidelines, and strategies for dealing with the situations you'll face. And of course we'll discuss when and how to get sexual again and how much fun that can be.

> *I am fifty-six, in a new relationship after twenty-one years of marriage and five years of widowhood. My new partner was married to a woman who would have no sex of any description, and then he was on his own for twenty-one years. He is the most sensual, gentle, and loving man I could possibly want, and he is enjoying our full and happy sex life, finally, at sixty-four years of age and after a forty-year love drought.*

MYTH #7: Being a sexually active, single senior carries no risk of pregnancy, so we don't have to use barrier protection. Wishful thinking! I'm going to have to burst your bubble and startle you with some scary statistics about the growing sexually transmitted disease (STD) rates among our generation—even in assisted-living facilities. I encourage you to be smart as well as sexy by using barrier protection always, with everyone, until or unless you're in an exclusive relationship, and you've both been tested.

> *STDs can change your life in a minute, and from my perspective, it is not worth the risk for a few moments of pleasure in exchange for a lifetime disease.*

MYTH #8: We'll decide to give up sex when we're [fill in the blank] years old.

Sexual pleasure can be ours our whole lives through. We'll have to adapt to changing bodies, changing situations, and changing sensations, yes. So let's look at it in new ways, explore our new sexuality, and smile through the journey.

I think that as the boomers effected major changes in civil rights, the women's movement, and gay rights, we will also have to cut a new path to acceptance of sexuality throughout the lifespan. I don't care what younger people think of my wanting a sexual life after fifty—it's because of all of us who are willing to be open now that it will become normalized for them when they age.

2

WHAT'S HAPPENING TO MY BODY?

I need to communicate with my partner about what is going on with my body and explain it isn't the same as it used to be. I just don't know where to begin.

"My body feels like an alien being," you tell me. "I want my old self back!" We spent decades figuring out who we were sexually, what turned us on, what touch or rhythm brought us to orgasm, and how to please a partner. Now it feels like we have to learn this all over again.

Aging affects sex in a gazillion ways: physical comfort, emotional needs, body image, and what we need for sexual arousal and pleasure, to name a few. This is true whether we're having sex with someone new, a reunited lover from our past, or a longtime partner. It's not what we signed up for, but it's what we get with aging.

We may need stronger or lighter stimulation now, a gentler or rougher touch, slower or faster rhythm, and lots more time. Sometimes we don't even know what we need, and we mistakenly think that if sex as we knew it no longer works for us, we're doomed to a sexless future. Not true! We just have to rediscover what turns us on now and makes our body respond. Think of it as a wonderful journey of discovery.

Sex has always been good, but things have changed in a big way. No more "movie quickies"—those hot moments of tossing each other onto the bed and going for it. It takes time and patience. Penetration is not the absolute entity of intimacy with my partner. A well-lubricated finger or vibrator can get things warmed up and even finished up.

Maybe we're not automatically and mindlessly turned on the way we used to be when the hormones took center stage and sang the "Hallelujah" chorus. We may not go through the day aroused, but we are "arousable." If we look at aging as a series of *changes*, not *deficiencies*, we'll be better able to cope and find ways to keep sex (and all those other parts of life) enjoyable.

Instead of focusing on what *doesn't* work, let's focus on what *does* work, and make that special, such as:

- Plan sex for the time of day when you are most energetic and in the mood for sex. If you're too tired for sex at night, enjoy a morning or afternoon delight. If energy is a problem, try resting or napping first.

- Have sex before a meal—not after one. When our diminished blood flow is working on digestion, there isn't enough to arouse the genitals. You'll have more energy and better arousal before eating.

- If a medical condition is making sex problematic, plan your sex dates for the times that your medication is working best to ease the condition while leaving you lively. Ask your doctor about the timing of your medications—is there a way to modify the schedule for better sexual response and comfort?

I have to be careful and not play into that old, competitive shtick of "Oh, you think that's bad? I've got this, that, and the other ailment!" because invariably there's always someone a lot worse off. So long as I can still get up and move—and occasionally enjoy whatever sexual stimulation I can manage—I'm not going to complain.

- Celebrate the deliciousness of long, slow arousal. Rather than wishing orgasm came faster, enjoy the slow-moving ride. That goes for men as well as women.

- So what if you're not lubricating well enough for sex—apply lubricant to make your genitals juicy again. (More about lubricants later in this chapter.)

- If stiff joints interfere with your enjoyment of sex, try a shower or a bath to loosen up. Swimming, tai chi, yoga, Pilates, and other kinds of gentle exercise also benefit joints.

- Try new positions if a position you used to love is no longer comfortable. If one position is the best way for you to reach orgasm but you can't stay in it comfortably for a long enough time, try starting in another position and finishing with your favorite.

- If you're partnered, emphasize intimacy. Kiss, laugh, and touch each other a lot. Express your love and attraction for your partner as part of your interaction all the time, not just when you want or are having sex.

My beloved husband and I had the most amazing sex life, which endured up to his seventy-ninth year when he became ill. We mourned the loss of it for the years remaining, but even then, the touch of his hand on my stomach sent thrills through me.

- Whether you're single or partnered, relish the capacity of your body to enjoy sensual pleasure and indulge yourself regularly on your own (see chapter 4, Sex with Yourself and Toys).

- If you used to love frequent sex and now it's not often that you're feeling well enough, celebrate when it does happen and make it magic.

We now treat sex like a very tasty treat—we nibble away at it, rather than dump the whole box of chocolates on the table at once.

WOMEN AND BODY IMAGE

We've been married thirty years. The other day I said, "I wish my stomach was flat so I could be sexier for you," and he said, "Well, I wish I had a twelve-inch dick, but it ain't gonna happen!" That made me feel so good.

In a study of 1,789 women ages fifty and above, only 12 percent said that they were satisfied with their bodies.[1] That means that 88 percent of us are not! Half of the satisfied 12 percent still found things they didn't like.[2] We're never *really* satisfied.

> *The overemphasis on youth and young, perfect, unlined bodies in our society has made us too self-critical. I know that I certainly struggle with this in my life, and this results in more inhibitions when I'm having sex.*

When have we women ever loved our bodies? Didn't most of us fret about body size and shape since we were teenagers? Yet when we look at photos of ourselves as young women, or even ten years ago, we marvel now at how good we looked then. Could we see it at the time? No way.

Please, if your female partner is self-conscious about her body, give her truthful compliments that emphasize the features that you find sexy and alluring. What turns you on about her? Say it out loud. Never, even in anger or mindlessness, utter a hurtful comment that she will never be able to forget.

> *I'm nervous and feel judged by my partner when I'm naked. I know, because he told me so, that he liked me more when I was younger. That comment really hurt me.*

Although men may appear to be less sensitive about their bodies, some have body image concerns and many are anxious about whether their penises will perform (more about that later). Let's be kind and loving to each other. Describing what turns you on about your partner's body goes a lot further than pointing out defects.

Instead of seeing sex with a partner as an embarrassing reveal of our (or our partner's) body's flaws, let's see it instead as an opportunity to give and receive pleasure, an affirmation of intimacy, a celebration that we can still feel sexual joy.

I was married to my wife for forty-two years. When it came to our lovemaking times together, I never noticed that she had gotten old. She always looked like the nineteen-year-old girl that I married many years ago.

LESSONS FROM MY LINGERIE SHOOT

"I'm photographing *real women* in lingerie," Ruth Lefkowitz told me shortly before my sixty-sixth birthday. "Would you be willing to model?" Not that I was shy, but I had worn lingerie only for intimate times with a lover, never for a photography session, and I wasn't feeling confident that my body looked as good as it used to. But whose does? And if you can't do something new and scary at our age, when can you do it?

I loved the experience, and I loved the results (which you can see on my blog—put LINGERIE SHOOT in the search box). In fact, I enjoyed it so much that two years later, I did it again for my sixty-eighth birthday. Here's what I learned both times:

- We are much more attractive than we think.

- Sexy lingerie can make our bodies look amazing, whatever our shape, size, age.

- A self-assured, racy attitude is our sexiest attribute.

- It can be really fun to flaunt pretty underwear in front of a camera!

We can choose to just say no to society's view that older women's bodies are no longer sexy. These are the bodies that we live in. They are capable of giving us extraordinary pleasure. Let's finally give ourselves permission to fling away our insecurities about body image. I'm not telling you to hire a boudoir photographer and take your clothes off if this doesn't appeal to you—but I do recommend it if it intrigues you!

AGE-RELATED SEXUAL CHANGES[3]

These changes are all normal. You may not experience all of these, but they are very common as we age.

Female bodies:
- Reduced levels of estrogen and testosterone

- Less blood flow to the genitals

- Decreased genital lubrication

- Thinning of vaginal tissues

- Decreased elasticity and expansion of vagina

- Decreased sexual desire, libido

- Decreased clitoral sensitivity

- Slower arousal

- Longer arousal needed for orgasm

- Inability to reach orgasm

- Less intense orgasms

Male bodies:
- Difficulty achieving and/or maintaining erection

- Erections are less hard

- Reduced testosterone

- Decreased sexual desire, libido

- Less blood flow to the penis

- Decreased penile sensitivity

- Longer arousal needed for orgasm

- Less forceful ejaculation, less semen

- Less intense orgasms

- More time needed after erection before getting aroused again

Additional problems that are not specifically sexual can impact our sexual enjoyment, too: loss of flexibility, arthritis, fatigue, lack of stamina, bad health. (You'll read more about medical conditions and sex in future chapters.)

These challenges are not cause for doom and gloom. Learn what's going on and what you can expect, and make sexual pleasure a priority during this new stage of life. Sex may take a different form than it used to, but you do *not* have to give it up. Sex is an important part of our health, well-being, pleasure, and intimacy.

> *Since officially hitting menopause at fifty, I feel more in control of my sexuality. While it does take me longer to get aroused and achieve orgasm, I find that I am highly satisfied when I do. I imagine it's like running a marathon and reaching the finish line.*

COMMUNICATING OUR CHANGES

Did you notice how many of the sex and aging changes I listed are the same or similar in both male and female bodies? At this time of life, we're more alike than different. Often partners of men do not realize that their guys are often embarrassed to talk about their changes and their new need for extended stimulation. A good first step, whatever your gender: talk to each other.

Here's a sample opener: "I'm finding that my sexual responses are changing as I age. Are yours? Could we explore different things that might feel good to us now?"

Communicate with your health professionals as well as your partner. Tell your doctor what's interfering with your sexual enjoyment and comfort, and ask if changing your medications might let you be more sexually responsive. There might be an easy fix if you're not shy about asking. Do *not* experiment on your own with decreasing, increasing, adding, or discontinuing medications—you could do yourself real harm (see chapter 8, You and Your Doctor, for more).

It's helpful to involve a sex therapist if you haven't had sex for a while, and you're having trouble opening to each other sexually again. The therapist can teach you both communications tools, help you get to and resolve the real issues, and start you on the path to regain sexual and emotional intimacy.

A sex therapist can also teach you how to do sensate focus exercises, where you focus your awareness on the physical sensations of touching and being touched without genital-oriented goals. Sensate focus helps couples reestablish intimacy when they've been derailed by physical or relationship changes, lack of communication, mismatched desire, or problems engaging in the kind of sexual interactions they're used to. Some couples find that their sex lives improve dramatically by putting the effort into these simple exercises for enjoying the sensations of the moment, with no expectations, no requirements, and no goals.

WHEN YOU NEED MORE STIMULATION

Whatever your gender, it's likely that you need more stimulation to get fully aroused. Extra time might do the trick—a slow, touch-filled afternoon in bed rather than a rushed and frustrating quickie before work or at the end of a tiring day. But you may find that even with all the time in the world, your body is barely responding. It feels like those nerve endings that used to quiver with every touch on your skin are now hidden deep inside—you just don't feel as much. Try these for an extra zing of sensation:

Sex toys. Learn more about sex toys in chapter 4, Sex with Yourself and Toys, and by visiting a local, women-friendly sex shop. *Women-friendly* doesn't mean *women only*—it means the store is a clean, well-lighted place where people of all genders and orientations feel welcome, with knowledgeable and helpful staff, and often an educational focus. My blog, www.NakedatOurAge.com, has links to several retailers that I endorse.

Clitoral arousal gels. These have ingredients that relax blood vessels to allow for more blood flow to the genitals, creating greater arousal and ease of reaching orgasm. They also stimulate sensation with ingredients that cause a warm and tingly feeling. Of course our experiences will vary—a product that feels fabulously tingly to one woman might feel unpleasantly burning to another, or not register much of any sensation to a third. Apply just a tiny drop first, then add more after a few minutes if you like it and want more intensity.

Personally, I love these. Ingredients like peppermint oil, sweet almond oil, menthol, arginine, and niacin (vitamin B3) give me a sensation that's somewhere between a tingle and almost a sting—but a good sting. There are arousal gels that are subtle, though my aging body prefers strong ones like Wet's wOw Max, Pure Pleasure Arousal Gel by Blossom Organics, JO Volt 12V, and Stimulating O Gel by Sliquid Organics. Others have recommended Sensuva's On Arousal

Oil and Intense Clitoral Gel from Intimate Organics. Many sex stores sell sampler packs, so you can experiment and discover which works best for you.

Check the ingredients, though. Avoid products with PEG-8 and propylene glycol if you want to use the gel during oral sex, because your partner might get sick from swallowing it.[4] Avoid products with L-arginine if you have herpes[5], heart problems, diabetes, or breast cancer.[6] Always check the packaging for additional cautions.

G-spot stimulation. We came of age before anyone had heard of the Gräfenberg spot, more commonly known as the G-spot. (I thank sex researcher Beverly Whipple for her fine work in this area.) If you have a vagina and haven't found your G-spot, I invite you to explore. Lubricate one or two fingers (a partner's helping hand often works better than your own), insert shallowly in your vagina, palm facing your belly, curving the fingers. Stroke or tap toward the front of the vaginal wall with a beckoning or "come hither" motion. The owner of the fingers may feel a spongy or slightly ridged spot, or the spot may be elusive until the vagina owner feels a special surge of pleasure. Some women insist that the G-spot doesn't exist (at least in their bodies), but many of us get great pleasure from having that area stimulated. Some women experience female ejaculation, often called *squirting*, from strong G-spot stimulation.

P-spot stimulation. The P-spot—the prostate—is an intense pleasure center for a man, capable of giving him gratifying sensations and strong orgasms. Some call it the "male

G-spot." Gay and bisexual men have long known about the pleasures of anal penetration. Many straight men are now discovering that prostate stimulation is enjoyable and doesn't imply anything about one's sexual orientation—it means that the man is open-minded enough to be receptive to this strong source of pleasure. (See sidebar: Prostate Massage).

I told her about wanting to have her pleasure my "G-spot" also. She had never heard about a man's prostate as a stimulation area, and I instructed her how this works and how to do it. We explored it all. She thought she might hurt me, but through talks and the use of lubes, we experienced this together. She was surprised at how explosive an orgasm this was for me.

Try a new flavor of sex. In chapter 6, Stretching Boundaries, you'll read about ways folks of our age use fantasy, erotica, relationship variety, and kink to intensify their sex lives. Some of these ways might tickle your fancy; others won't. Be open-minded about learning, let your fantasies roam, and see where they take you. Adding the spice of fantasy—even (especially?) if you're imagining something you wouldn't do in real life—can ignite your delight.

Watch your partner. If it doesn't feel too invasive, ask your partner if you can watch how he or she self-pleasures, and show your partner the same. The results might bring you more ideas—and stimulation—than you imagined.

After multiple surgeries, I am covered with scars, am over-weight, and can't wear a bra, so the girls are really heading south. My husband still has a very active sex drive. As children of the seventies, I always thought we were very open about sex, and we discussed and tried many of our fantasies over the years. But things have changed. Finally we talked about his frustration, my inability to believe he could desire this body, and what we could do now that intercourse is no longer an option.

Recently after some serious foreplay and mutual mastur-bation, it became obvious that he was not going to bring me to climax because I am taking large doses of painkillers. He said, "You do it."

As I lay back on the couch and began, this wonderful man watched as I reached with one hand around my belly to the mound I can't even see anymore and cupped my breast with the other. He became even more excited and said, "God, if I can watch you come like this, it'll be the highlight of my year!"

I still get tears in my eyes as I write this.

If you're partnered, share your discoveries with your lover once you've figured out some new techniques or products that you like. Many couples give up on sex when the old ways don't work, not realizing that a new way of doing things can bring back the zest and intimacy.

PROSTATE MASSAGE
By Charlie Glickman, PhD

Most men and their partners have only heard about the health concerns that affect prostates. But prostates have a lot more to offer than that!

Prostate massage can feel amazing, whether on its own or along with other kinds of sexual stimulation. Some men describe it as "the feeling like the first part of an orgasm." That's because the prostate squeezes during ejaculation, but instead of that sensation lasting just a few seconds, prostate massage can go as long as you want.

The easiest way to reach the prostate is through anal penetration. Simply slip on a glove for easy cleanup, get some lubricant on a finger, insert it about 3 to 4 inches (7.5–10 cm), and curve your finger toward the navel. (If your fingers are shorter than that, you can insert all the way and then press further in. The flexibility of the pelvic floor will allow for deeper penetration.)

The prostate will feel like a ripe plum. Stroke, don't poke! Try making circles, the "come hither" motion, or tapping with your fingertip. You can combine it with penis stimulation, or alternate, as you both prefer. Use firm pressure but not too hard. Think of spreading butter on toast—not too little, not too much.

Since prostates often get larger as men age, it's usually easier to find on older guys. And some men find that massage helps with symptoms of BPH (benign prostatic hyperplasia, a noncancerous enlargement of the prostate gland, a common occurrence in older men), so there can even be some wellness benefits from it.

For the record, doctors are trained to not make prostate exams feel good, because they don't want to be accused of sexual harassment. So don't let your experiences with a doctor get in your way of enjoying yourself.

—Charlie Glickman, PhD, is coauthor, with Aislinn Emirzian, of *The Ultimate Guide to Prostate Pleasure: Erotic Exploration for Men and Their Partners*, which includes overcoming common concerns, massage tips, positions, using toys, and prostate health.

LOVING LUBE

Lubricant can enhance the joy of two bodies rubbing together (or one body rubbing itself or an object), whatever the age of those bodies. At our age, adding lube is usually a necessity. Older women experience less natural lubrication, often not enough for comfortable penetration or even genital touching. Pair that with thinning vaginal tissues, and sex that used to make you go "Ooh!" can make you go "Ow!" Lubricants are always necessary for anal sex.

We're lucky to be living in an age where lubricants for sex are plentiful, safe, easy to find, inexpensive, and varied for every need or desire. Some lubricants feel like natural lubrication. Others are slick and slippery. Some are thick and help cushion delicate tissues. You can find organic lubricants; cooling, warming, or stimulating lubricants; lubes with flavors and scents; and that's just the beginning.

You'll see lubricants on the shelf at your local drugstore, but those choices are limited and many have harmful ingredients. I suggest buying from a women-friendly sexuality shop, either local or online, such as those recommended on my blog, www.NakedatOurAge.com. They have the greatest variety for every preference imaginable and are careful to carry only products that meet their quality and safety standards.

You may get dizzy figuring out which lubricant to buy, once you see the variety available. Try small samplers so you can decide on some favorites. Here are the different types of lube and some points to keep in mind from sex educators Megan Andelloux, CSE, IF, and Clinical Sexologist[7]; Jennifer Pritchett, MS, owner of The Smitten Kitten; and Sarah Mueller, lube specialist at The Smitten Kitten[8]:

Water-based lubes are compatible with latex condoms and all sex toys. However, many drugstore-brand water-based lubricants contain ingredients such as parabens, propylene glycol, glycerin, and hard preservatives that can exacerbate pelvic pain conditions like vulvodynia and dyspareunia. These ingredients can damage the cells of the vagina and rectum, leaving you more vulnerable to infections, including HIV. This is especially important for an aging vagina or rectum because the tissues are commonly more delicate and fragile. To avoid these ingredients, seek out high-quality, organic, water-based lubes from a reputable, education-based retailer.

Silicone lubricants are best for sensitive genitals, last much longer than water-based lubes, and are fine with condoms. They keep their slickness in water. They are recommended for anal play. Don't use silicone lube with silicone or Cyber-Skin sex toys. Silicone lube is flammable if it comes in direct contact with a flame, so don't be clumsy with a lit candle.[9]

Hybrid lubes are a blend of water-based and silicone, safe with condoms, dental dams, and latex gloves, and usually compatible with silicone sex toys. They last longer than regular water-based lubricants and are less likely to get tacky. Choose a hybrid lubricant that does not contain parabens, propylene glycol, or glycerin (see above, water-based lubes),

Warming and cooling lubricants are not recommended if you have pelvic pain. The warming lubes can cause a burning sensation—only use them if you already know you like them. Many of us like the cooling lubes, which are less irritating, but they are still to be avoided with pelvic pain.

Petroleum-based lubes, such as mineral oil or Vaseline, are okay for external male masturbation, but are hazardous when used internally for vaginal or anal play. Petroleum-based products irritate the vagina and rectal lining and will not clear out of the body easily, promoting harmful bacterial growth that will likely result in a trip to the doctor to treat bacterial vaginosis or a resulting yeast infection. These oils will break down latex barriers such as condoms, dental dams, and gloves, and will stain fabric.

Food oils and other plant-based oils are usually not recommended, especially if you are prone to bacterial vaginosis or yeast infections, because they accelerate bacteria growth in the vagina and are not easily flushed out. However, sex educators are divided about recommending coconut oil, which many people report enjoying without ill effects. Oil-based lubricants will break down condoms and stain fabric.

Saliva does not provide enough cushioning or slickness for our needs and dries up quickly.

Bottom line: get a lubricant made explicitly for sex play— you'll be surprised at how much it improves sex with yourself, with a partner, and/or with a sex toy.

KEGELS FOR WOMEN

I've been doing Kegel exercises the way a physical therapist taught me: (1) lying on the floor with knees bent and (2) making sure to fully relax as well as contract the muscles. I do a set of ten every morning. I can happily say that my occasional stress incontinence has disappeared completely, and I have stronger orgasmic contractions than I used to, which prolongs the pleasure of climaxing. For a few minutes and no cost, I'd say that's a great investment!

The PC (pubococcygeus) muscles are the muscles that contract during orgasm. Regular pelvic floor workouts, aka Kegel exercises, lead to more enjoyable sex: easier arousal, stronger orgasms, more pleasure. If that's not enough, strengthening the pelvic floor muscles also protects against urinary incontinence. (Ah, now I have your attention!)

You've probably heard, "Do your Kegels," but you may not have been told how to do them most effectively. Here are step-by-step instructions for women from Myrtle Wilhite, MD, MS, and co-owner of A Woman's Touch Sexuality Resource Center (www.sexualityresources.com):

1. Lie down on your back in a comfortable place with your knees bent, feet flat. Lying down takes the weight off your pelvic floor and leads to earlier success. Have your Kegel tool (if you are using one) and lubricant with you.

- If you're using a tool, such as Betty's Vaginal Barbell by created by Betty Dodson, the Stone Exercise Egg, or the Energie Exerciser, coat it with lubricant and insert it into your vagina until it comfortably slips into place just behind the pubic bone. You can't push it in too far; it cannot get lost inside of you.

- If you're using your finger(s), wash your hands first, then coat your finger(s) with lubricant. Next, insert your finger(s) about two inches into your vagina.

- You can also practice Kegels with nothing inside your vagina.

2. Contract your pelvic floor muscles. It will feel like you're pulling up and in toward your belly button. Don't push out, unless specifically advised by a health care provider. If you're using a tool, you should feel it rise a bit. If you're using your finger, you should feel a gentle tightening around the finger. Relax your leg, buttock, and abdominal muscles and breathe normally throughout the exercise.

3. Hold the lift for a count of five. If you're using a tool, you can add resistance by pulling gently on it as you continue using your muscles to pull the tool inward and upward. Remember to breathe!

4. Relax your muscles.

5. Important: After each contraction, take a deep belly breath. Inhale deeply and gently blow out the air while you relax your pelvis completely. This deep relaxation is just as important as the other steps, because the deep belly breath relaxes the muscles that are not under your conscious control.

"Pay equal attention to the contraction *and* the relaxation of the muscles that surround the vagina in particular," says sex educator and counselor Ellen Barnard, MSSW, co-owner of A Woman's Touch. "Otherwise you may find that these muscles are stiff and inflexible, which will also get in the way of comfortable penetration when you are ready to have it."

The deep relaxation phase is often omitted when we're told how to do our Kegels, but they're as important to practice as the contraction. Many women of our age, especially after a period of celibacy, experience what feels like tightening or shrinking of the vaginal opening, because the muscles don't fully release. This can interfere with our enjoyment of penetrative sex. Regular Kegel exercises can help relax the vaginal opening.

You can practice your Kegels without tools or fingers, even on the go: standing in the grocery line, driving, walking, working at your desk, during your Pilates or yoga class. If you're doing them in public, be sure you've mastered the part about not contracting your buttocks, or anyone standing behind you will see what you're doing!

KEGELS FOR MEN

I do Kegel exercises while driving and have found they benefit my orgasms. At age sixty-seven, while the volume of semen has diminished with age, my orgasmic contractions remain stronger than ever.

Kegels aren't just for women. The muscles located in the perineum, the area between the scrotum and the anus, contract during a man's orgasm. Kegel exercises can make sex more pleasurable for men with age-related, less intense orgasms. "By strengthening the muscles of the perineum, you will pump more blood to this vital area, achieve greater ejaculatory control, and increase the intensity of your orgasms," says urologist Dudley S. Danoff, MD, FACS, author of *Penis Power: The Ultimate Guide to Male Sexual Health.*

"Pelvic Floor Health for Men," an online brochure from A Woman's Touch (www.a-womans-touch.com/documents/ PelvicFloorMen12.pdf), offers complete instructions for doing Kegels and lists these benefits for men:

- Helps maintain erections through strong pelvic floor muscle tone that holds the blood in the penis more effectively.

- Orgasms feel bigger and stronger when the pelvic floor muscles are strong.

- More forceful ejaculations.

- Keeps urine inside the bladder at moments of unexpected belly pressure (laughing, coughing, lifting, sneezing, jumping).

- Keeps stool inside the rectum until you consciously relax your pelvic floor to allow it to pass.

To find the right muscles, imagine pulling your testicles into your body. Hold the contraction as you count to five, then release completely (don't push out, just relax the muscles). Your penis will rise as you tighten the muscles and fall as you relax them.

As a man doing Kegels, I had to learn not just to clench low—like I'm squeezing my butthole—because that's working a different area of the pelvic floor. Instead men have to concentrate a little higher—using the muscles that stop urine flow midstream. My pelvic floor therapist described it as retracting the "turtle's head."

UNDER A BLACK CLOUD

Do you wish you had the motivation to get in shape, have more sex, enjoy sex more, and accomplish your goals, but it's all too difficult? Occasional sadness is part of our lives, but if you're almost always gloomy and feel powerless to make changes, you may be suffering from depression.

Exercise is a proven antidepressant, and even ten minutes of exercise can alter your mood. Go for a brisk walk, dance in the living room, or get on that treadmill or exercise bike that's been gathering dust. You'll see that it lifts your mood.

But if you're too depressed to try to make improvements, or if your depression doesn't lift or returns with a vengeance, please talk to a therapist who will help you figure out what's going on. Talk therapy may be all you need, or a combination of talk therapy and an antidepressant might be the ticket.

Even if you usually feel good about yourself, if a recent loss has you spiraling in grief, you may be suffering from situational depression. I'm usually the most upbeat and energetic person you'll ever meet, but this happened to me when Robert died. I couldn't stop crying in private and in public. It took a combination of counselors and a temporary course of antidepressants to get me functioning normally again. I'm grateful to them for getting me back on track.

I implore you not to white-knuckle your

depression—it's not likely to get better on its own, and you'll just prolong it by not seeking help. I know it's hard to explore options when you feel bad about yourself and the future looks bleak, but you *can* get help and feel better. Show a trusted friend or medical professional this section and ask for help getting started.

SEX FURNITURE

Aren't we lucky! Special cushions, chairs, loungers, and other appurtenances that we lie on, sit in, or otherwise use for support are now made specifically for sex. These often let us modify or circumvent the problems that were stopping us from enjoying our favorite sex acts and positions. Some folks may use sex furniture for novelty—many use it out of necessity.

Robert and I used to laugh about how decrepit we felt trying to get into sexual positions that felt fine a decade before. I wouldn't say either of us bragged about being sexual gymnasts in our youth, but at least our desires weren't foiled by our abilities to get our bodies in the positions we liked best—until our sixties. With his bad back, my arthritic knees and neck, and the length of time we needed, we had to be careful what we tried, and generally we relied on the few positions that caused no discomfort. (Changing positions often might be a solution for you—for us, it interrupted the buildup.)

We were overjoyed to discover the Wedge, a special cushion made for sex. It's smooth and comfortable and keeps its firm shape so one person's hips are elevated and the back is well supported during the missionary position, oral sex, partner kneeling, partner standing at the side of the bed, and many other positions. The Wedge is made by Liberator (www.liber ator.com), which makes sex furniture of many shapes and sizes.

Clinical sexologist Dr. Marylou Naccarato (www.Dr Marylou.com) has designed the Love Bench™ to enable a variety of sexual positions and adaptations for people with limited mobility in hips and knees. It can be custom ordered to meet your individual measurements. Other brands of sex furniture are Love Bumper (www.lovebumper.com) in Canada and Intimate Furniture (www.intimatefurniture.com), both recommended by sex educators whom I respect. Though I haven't had occasion to try it, the Tantra Chair (www.tantra chair.com) is real furniture: a full-sized, *S*-shaped chaise longue that allows for endless possibilities of sexual positions. IntimateRider (www.intimaterider.com) makes a gliding chair for sex, designed for men with spinal cord injuries. It's also useful for people of any orientation or gender who have other mobility and balance limitations, such as Parkinson's, multiple sclerosis, and amputation, according to Jennifer Pritchett, MS, owner of Smitten Kitten. "It also works great for bondage!" she tells me.

WEIGHT

I have been in love with a man for over thirty-one years. For the past three years we have been just friends, no sex. I have been very ill, in and out of hospitals. I put on a lot of weight due to medication. I truly believe that my man is turned off by my weight and does not want to explore the possibility of having sex. I have no one to touch me, hold me, kiss me. I ache for that in my life. How can I approach him regarding this overweight issue?

Just as society and the media tell us that we're only sexy if we're young, we're also bludgeoned with the notion that we're only sexy if we're slim. I have the pleasure of knowing some lusciously curvaceous women who revel in their bodies. They feel sexy and exude confidence. Rather than hide under shapeless clothing, they flaunt their bodacious cleavage, curvy hips, and sexy attitude. Their partners appreciate their curves and their sensuality.

I often hear from women who feel that their weight is their enemy. They feel unhealthy, undesirable, and unhappy. They may be depressed, which is part of a vicious cycle—they're depressed, so they eat more and exercise less, they gain more weight, they get more depressed. They have sex in the dark wearing oversized T-shirts, if they have sex at all. When sex stops, if it was there to begin with, that's cause for more depression.

How do you break out of that cycle? First, say *no* to society's view of larger bodies as unworthy of sexual pleasure and attention. Say *no* to your own view of your weight as a reason that you're unentitled to express your sexuality. Say *no* to that voice in your head that clamps you down when you feel like a sexual being.

> *I just met up with a boyfriend from thirty-five years ago. I'm sixty, he's sixty-five. He said, "You were unhealthily skinny when I knew you—no breasts, no passion. Now, you have huge breasts, and you're smoking hot." Sex was great. Who knew it could be this way?*

EXERCISE AND SEX

Want to know the best, most effective, and least expensive remedy for a sagging sex life? Exercise. Seriously! You don't have to join a gym (unless you enjoy gyms), invest in expensive equipment, or even get sweaty. Just enjoy physical activity that raises your heart rate (even a little!) and works your muscles. Immediately, you'll have more energy, and your joints will feel lubricated. The increased blood flow to the heart and muscles will go to the genitals, too, making sexual arousal easier, faster, and stronger.

The downside? Let me think... Nope, can't think of a downside.

Here's another bonus: exercise improves sexual function if you're taking antidepressants, especially if you exercise just before sex. A 2013 study of women who reported problems with libido and orgasm as side effects from antidepressants reported that when they engaged in thirty minutes of moderately intense exercise right before sex, they experienced significantly stronger libido and better sexual function overall.[10] One more good reason to exercise!

If exercise hurts, try a different kind of exercise. A certified personal trainer who is used to working with people your age and with your medical condition would be a good start. You don't have to sign up for the rest of your life; just tell your trainer that you'd like a few sessions to design a program that works for you and to make sure you're doing it correctly. If you can't afford a personal trainer, try a senior exercise class at your local health club or senior center, but inquire whether the leader is certified, and watch a class first to make sure the leader individualizes exercises for class members.

You think you hate exercise? That just means that you haven't found the kind of physical activity that you enjoy. Instead of thinking *exercise*, think *movement*. Do you like dancing? Hiking? Swimming? Playing with children? Walking your dog?

Hubby has some energy level issues, so evenings and nights are no longer the right time for sex. However, he swims (gently) three or four times a week. He loves swimming, and afterward—he is convinced of this—he says, "My blood is really flowing," so it's a good time for romance. Sounds good to me. If he wants to have sex in the afternoon after swimming, I'm there!

If your life feels too busy to set aside exercise time, focus on making the things you do anyway more physically active. Walk over to a neighbor's house or coworker's office instead of emailing or phoning. Wash the car by hand instead of using the drive-through. I pulled together three hundred painless, fun ideas for making your daily life more active in *The Anytime, Anywhere Exercise Book: 300+ Quick and Easy Exercises You Can Do Whenever You Want!* (Order it directly from me by emailing joan@joanprice.com; tell me you read about it in *The Ultimate Guide to Sex after Fifty,* and I'll give you free shipping.)

> *I am a 59-year-old lesbian. I've always struggled with weight but was really attractive into my forties. Last winter I fell, breaking both my ankle and leg. I gained twenty pounds. What a huge difference that has made in my appearance and self-esteem. But I am walking now for exercise and beginning to work on myself—for myself! I wish everyone could know the importance of this.*

3

GETTING YOUR MOJO BACK

I used to be eager for sex, easily aroused. My desire dipped after menopause and now barely exists. I can go weeks or more without desiring sex or thinking much about it. The funny thing is, if I get started, I like it, but it's so hard to get in the mood.

The number one sex problem that I hear from women is the lack of desire for sex. They do still enjoy sex once they get started, they tell me, but they're seldom in the mood ahead of time. It isn't just a problem for women—many men also report decreased desire—but for women, it's the primary complaint. The problem is that if we wait for the mood and don't make sexual pleasure a priority, we'll rarely have sex.

There are lots of reasons that you may be feeling decreased desire, but let's cut to a solution that works first, and figure out the reasons afterward:

Instead of waiting for the mood, start getting yourself sexually aroused—on your own, with a partner, or with a vibrator. Just do it. The physiological arousal will trigger the emotional desire.

That's the *opposite* of the way it used to work! When we were younger, our hormone-induced sex drive bombarded our brain and body with desire—especially during our most fertile times. This was simple biology. A glance, a thought, a murmur, a fantasy, or a touch sparked the mood. Once in the mood, we opened ourselves to the pleasures of physiological arousal. We got turned on, our arousal built, and we crashed joyously into orgasm.

But now, this all works the other way around. Instead of waiting forever for the mood to strike, we can *induce* the mood by letting ourselves get physiologically aroused as the *first step*. Arousal will lead to mood and desire, instead of vice versa.

Here are your new mantras:

- Desire follows action.

- Use it, don't lose it.

- Just do it.

"You may have just saved my marriage," a woman told me after I gave this suggestion at a presentation. Try it—you may feel the same!

WHAT TO DO INSTEAD OF WAITING TO BE IN THE MOOD

I can't emphasize enough how important it is to approach our sexuality in this new way: Relax, start getting physically aroused, emotional arousal will happen, and voila, we'll be in the mood. So the key is to commit to regular sex, partnered or solo.

How does this translate to real life? Here are some tips:

- Schedule sex dates with your partner and/or with yourself.

- Create rituals with your partner that signal sex would be welcome.

- Allow plenty of time for warm up.

- Make sex a habit. The more you do it, the more you'll want to do it.

SOME OF THE MYRIAD REASONS FOR LOW SEXUAL DESIRE

Hormone imbalances

Job stress or job loss

Financial problems

Relationship stress

Conflicts with partner

Relationship staleness

Lack of sexual variety

Illness

Side effect of medication

Depression

Anger

Grief

Guilt, shame

Fear of unleashing unacceptable emotions

Distrust or fear of partner

Discovery of partner's infidelity

Boredom

Clamping down unfulfilled desires

Abuse or past history of abuse

Autoimmune problems

Metabolic imbalances

Lack of exercise

Poor eating choices

Overuse of alcohol or recreational drugs

Low self-esteem

Self-image as unattractive

Lack of senior sex education

Lack of communication

Lover who doesn't understand how to please

No longer attracted to partner

Not having a sexual partner

Not having regular arousal and orgasm (partnered or solo)

Societal message that older people don't have sex or enjoy it

WHY DOES DESIRE GO AWAY?

Our bodies still need touch and sexual release to deeply connect us as partners, but we don't always have the same biological prompt—a sexual urge, an instinctual nudge, or an outright horny feeling. A woman with low desire is like a Porsche with a tank full of gas and a broken starter.

—Laurie Watson,
certified sex therapist and author of *Wanting Sex Again:
How to Rediscover Your Desire and Heal a Sexless Marriage*

When you first fall in love, you're so filled with lust, interest, and excitement that you barely notice any difficulties. After years with the same partner, it's not unusual for sexual expression to seem less important, happen less often, and feel less satisfying than it used to. Reality sets in, the high wears off, and you need to work on keeping your relationship sexy. Our hormonal deficits compound the challenges.

But sex is worth nurturing. It's a big part of intimacy; it helps you stay bonded and strengthens your love and closeness. Even if you feel as if sex has flown the coop in your relationship, it's not too late to get it back. Understanding it is the first step.

When one of you doesn't want sex, it's important to find out what's going on for the less desirous partner. First, make sure there isn't something physical at the root of it, especially if the drop in desire is accompanied by decreased arousal once you get started. Heart disease, for example, can first show up this way. Get checked out before making assumptions.

If the body is working, but the desire isn't there, what can you do to bring romance, fantasy, and newness back into your relationship?

Remember how you couldn't keep your hands off each other when you were first dating? It didn't matter whether you were in the ice cream shop, in class, or sitting in the car with your parents; you had to squeeze in close to each other and share furtive touches. Bring back that sense of "gotta touch you" with non-goal-oriented touching, entwined arms, brushing against each other. It's best to confer about this rather than surprise your partner, especially if it's been decades since the "gotta touch you" era of your relationship.)

When you want a more active sex life and your partner doesn't seem as enthusiastic, be careful to be gentle, loving, and positive when you open up the conversation to avoid putting your mate on the defensive. Express your feelings in a tender, loving, and respectful way, and invite your partner to express his or her feelings honestly to you. You're lovers, not adversaries.

I'm a queer woman, sixty-six. In my thirties and forties, I preferred to be single. Not celibate, but single. If I got involved with a woman, an affair was unlikely to last longer than three months. When that initial intense attraction started to fade, so did my willingness to spend time on the relationship. In my fifties I met someone with whom the sexual connection was so strong, just the memory of when it was its hottest—and the hope of recapturing that early feeling—has kept me engaged for many years.

TOO MUCH TOGETHERNESS?

When you were first sexual with your partner, you craved each other when you were apart. If you're never apart anymore, how can you crave each other? If all your experiences happen together, how can you bring anything new to each other?

A major libido killer can be too much time together with your partner, especially if you're both retired and spending your days and nights together. To spark your libido, you need time apart and new experiences on your own.

Your relationship will benefit, emotionally and sexually, if you bring mystery, surprise, and excitement back into your lives. Pursue independent adventures. Join a group that does activities you enjoy separately. Go to your high school reunion on your own. Participate in a sport or learn a dance style that has always interested you.

Just to be clear, "pursue independent adventures" is *not* code for "have an affair." An affair does rev up sexual desire in the person having it—that's undeniable—and it often results in feeling more passion for the primary partner as well. But if it's cheating—when your partner doesn't know and would be devastated to find out—an affair can shatter your relationship.

(If your relationship agreement allows for outside lovers, or if you'd be willing to give each other a hall pass for an adventure once in a while that will light fires at home as well as away, see chapter 6, Stretching Boundaries, for more about open relationships.)

HOW DOES STRESS IMPACT SEX?

Stress tells your brain that you're in danger, triggering the fight-or-flight response that can shut down libido and sexual pleasure. Physiologically, the stress hormones make your blood vessels constrict, interfering with male erection, male and female arousal, and female lubrication. It also takes away the desire for sex,[11] decreases genital arousal, and increases distraction during sex.[12] Not good.

If you're experiencing low libido, look at ways to shut out stress. Exercising before sex is a powerful way to let stress dissipate. Then relax—maybe a long bath or a nap. Put yourself in an environment that nurtures you and feels sexy, with no distractions. Then just do it, and let your arousal fire up your desire.

EROTICA AND PORN

We're a loving couple in our sixties with an extra bedroom we call our "erotica room." It has a couch, a futon, and handicap rails mounted on the wall above the futon to hold onto. Our erotic videos and DVDs are there. The walls are decorated with erotic posters. A shelf holds lubricants and our toys; a bookshelf houses our erotic books. A lock on the door prevents accidental discovery by houseguests and visitors. We still make love in the master bedroom. But it's a treat to go to the erotica room to enjoy sensual pleasure. Having that room at the ready is a delicious treat.

UNFILLED DESIRES: AN ESCORT SPEAKS OUT

I am an escort. I have a heart for my older gentlemen friends. Most have partners that they adore and admire, but their partner's interest in physical intimacy has ebbed away over the years. The men appreciate the physical intimacy I offer. I like being the person who reminds them that they can be sensual, sexy, receive pleasure, and give pleasure as well.

The wives of a couple of my older friends know about their playtime with me and are supportive of having those needs for physical intimacy met. Most gentlemen, however, keep it private, because they think that it would hurt their partner to know. With me, there isn't the risk of the sort of emotional entanglements that would happen if they had an affair instead.

I think a lot of older gentlemen have absorbed this absurd notion that there is an expiration date on their desire for physical intimacy. I am saying to them, "Yes, you are sexy," "Yes, it's okay to want that," "Yes, you can please me sexually, and I want to please you, too," and, "No, you are not a bad guy."

To me, this is better than quietly suffering for want of sexual intimacy and fostering resentment toward an otherwise wonderful partner. Our sexuality and its expression are one of the most important aspects of our humanity. Being older doesn't change that.

We often need a little extra push to put us in a sexy frame of mind and to nudge our arousal centers awake. Reading erotica and/or watching porn can be exciting ways to stimulate our brain and start the tingle down below. Erotica and porn let you vicariously experience sexual situations, encounters, styles, and adventures that live in your secret fantasy life—plus some that have never occurred to you.

Don't panic if you get aroused by a sexual scene that you'd never want to do in real life. Getting turned on by a scene about being tied up or having sex with a stranger, a boss, the pizza delivery boy (or girl), or a son's best friend does *not* necessarily mean that you really want any of these scenarios to actually happen.

That's the point—you can experience a scene vicariously, let it make you squirm (in a good way), and get sexually charged without any actual forbidden behavior. That's likely what accounts for the runaway popularity of *Fifty Shades of Grey*. Millions of women read that book, and most of them aren't debating leaving their husbands to be dominated by a kinky billionaire. (At least, I don't think so.)

DESIRE IN A PILL?

A variety of drugs to treat low desire in women (known as Hypoactive Sexual Desire Disorder or HSDD) are being investigated in clinical trials. No drug has been approved at the time of this writing. Could such a drug really work? Do we even want it?

Desire is complicated and individual. There isn't just one

cause or reason. Sex educators are wary of the medicalization of female desire—throw a pill at it, let the drug companies make money. What about the side effects?

Ellen Barnard, co-owner of A Woman's Touch and one of my favorite sex educators, had plenty to say about this topic. You can read her entire response on my blog, and here is her conclusion:

> The bottom line is that drugs do best when there is a single, knowable cause for a symptom, and the drug directly addresses that cause by reducing or removing it. Sexual desire is complicated, varies a lot from person to person, and has many moving parts. The idea that a drug could be developed to change desire is pretty far-fetched once you understand it that way, and one of our biggest fears is that you end up with a drug that has pretty wide effects and some nasty, unintended side effects. We would prefer to address desire issues in ways that give individuals more control and more understanding of their mind and body connections, so that they can do their own problem solving and not be reliant on a pill or a doctor.[13]

SEXY FROM THE INSIDE OUT

If you miss sex—or your partner does—you can bring back the joy with some new strategies. Creative, sexy aging includes accepting the emotional changes as well as the physical changes, then moving beyond them to create the sexy new you that is both possible and a worthy goal. Sexiness comes from inside you—believe in it, and make it so. (Imagine sexy Patrick Stewart as Jean-Luc Picard, from *Star Trek: The Next Generation*, telling you that!)

We have the power to revitalize our capacity for sexual desire. Instead of shutting down our desire and joy of sex by avoiding sexual situations, instead let's intensify both by grabbing every chance we get.

> *Sexual desire is energy—a sustainable resource that's available to all of us if we want it, even those of us who may not have it right now. Not just to lead us into steamier encounters but to reconnect us with ourselves and our partners, and to discover new sources of pleasure and joy.*
>
> —Gina Ogden
> in *The Return of Desire: A Guide to Rediscovering Your Sexual Passion*

SEX WITH YOURSELF
AND TOYS

On my Naked at Our Age Facebook page, I posted a photo of
a button that said,

> OLD PEOPLE HAVE SEX.
> GET OVER IT.

This post got a quick thumbs-up from most readers, but these
comments also appeared:

- *If we're lucky.*

- *One can only hope.*

- *I wish that was a true statement. Only for
  some.*

Staying sexual is within our own power. Although partner sex is wonderful, we're not all lucky enough to have a sexual partner at this time of our lives. That does not mean that we can't be sexual. We can still remain sexual with ourselves, our toys, our fantasies, and our memories. It's important for our health that we do so—and important for our quality of life. Please take this to heart.

> *I have not had a sexual partner for years. I greatly miss the closeness, the touch of someone else, and the feeling and excitement of giving and receiving. In the meantime masturbation allows me to be a sexual being. Accepting the new reality of practical matters of sexuality is a challenge—it takes me longer to respond and I have softer erections (if at all). But to be alive means we are sexual beings.*

SELF-EXPLORATION THROUGH SELF-PLEASURE

> *Touching yourself for pleasure involves all of you—how you think and feel as well as your physical sensations. When you masturbate, you take the responsibility for sexual pleasure literally into your own hands. In fact, sex therapists routinely prescribe it as homeplay for women who need to know more about their sexual responses—what they like, what they don't like, how they feel, how they can be independently sexual, and how they can gather crucial clues for their sexual partners.*

> —Gina Ogden
> in *The Return of Desire: A Guide to Rediscovering Your Sexual Passion*

I've heard people scoff at my recommendation to learn how to pleasure yourself, saying, "As if we haven't learned this by now!" But our bodies continue to change, and part of how we change with aging is how we respond sexually.

Often the ways we used to masturbate don't work so well anymore. Maybe we need more sensation, a different kind of touch, or so much time that we sometimes give up and rip into the ice cream instead. Rather than giving up, let's learn what does work and enjoy it.

Even if we have a partner, self-stimulation is still important. Pleasuring ourselves is the way to rediscover what turns us on as our bodies change. It's not fair to expect our partners to figure this out for us if we haven't figured it out for ourselves.

Solo sex is a way we can explore what pleases us *now* and what works to give us great orgasms. We can then share that information with our partners, if we have them, or continue to pleasure ourselves solo with heightened awareness. Here are some tips:

Choose the time of day when you feel most sexually responsive. Pay attention to how sexy you feel on waking, after coffee, or after you've gotten up and moved around a bit. Often the sexiest time is right after exercise. You probably won't feel aroused after a meal, when the blood flow is going to your digestive system, but you may feel sexy right before that meal. Medications or medical conditions may affect your responsiveness at different times of the day. When you feel the tingle, set aside time for yourself. If that's not possible—you're at work, for example—use your knowledge of your erotic clock to schedule alone time on your next free day.

> *I am a widower, almost ninety-two, who lost my beloved wife to Alzheimer's in 2008. I take solo sex seriously as a way to try and keep up my level of testosterone and perhaps even increase it. I do much walking and am now quite sure a session of self-pleasuring in the morning invigorates my walking sprees.*

Choose the ambience and preparation that give you the best combination of relaxation and arousal. You want to be relaxed enough to invite your sexuality to emerge without anxiety or distraction, but you don't want to be so relaxed that you fall into slumber. What works best for you? Sensual lighting? Music? In bed? In a bathtub? Outdoors? After a glass of wine? While reading erotica? Watching porn or a romantic movie? There are no right or wrong answers, just what's right for your body, your mind, your mood.

> *My ex-husband frequently played erotic videos, and they worked well to stimulate me, too. Problem was, I had none now and could not afford to acquire any. So I decided to use music and my own imagination to help get the juices flowing. It worked. I was heady with the newfound power. Just knowing how to pleasure myself opened a whole new world. I no longer felt dependent on the skills of a lover or a video—I became independently sexual.*

Explore your body slowly. Use self-pleasuring to learn about your erogenous zones and the kind of stimulation you like—and how these both might have changed, rather than racing to orgasm. You may learn that your breasts are less sensitive now, or more sensitive, or you like to pinch your nipples rather than caress them. You may learn that you like anal stimulation, or that there's a special spot on your neck or thigh that makes you shiver when touched just right. What position lets you stay relaxed and comfortable while enhancing the sensations? Do you like to lie still, or move? What kind of movement?

Experiment with different kinds of touch. Do you like touch that's light, firm, or varied? Gentle or rough? Whole hand or fingertips? As you get more aroused, how does your preferred kind of touch change? What rhythm do you like? What happens if you vary the rhythm? How does lubricant on the genitals or massage oil on other parts of your body enhance the sensations?

> *Having sex is like bridge. If you don't have a good partner, you'd better have a good hand.*
>
> —Mae West (also attributed to Woody Allen)

Try an assortment of sex toys. As I always say, a well-chosen, well-placed sex toy can be the difference between orgasm and no orgasm. It's sometimes that simple. With the right sex toy and the right fantasy, we can enjoy the pleasures that our bodies are capable of giving us throughout our lives. More

information on sex toys follows, and my blog www.Naked
AtOurAge.com has reviews of toys and tools that enhance sex
for our age group.

> *I've learned that I can have a fulfilling sex life with myself using
> toys and fantasy, and when I'm ready I might date again.*

THE DELIGHTS OF SEX TOYS

I admit it: vibrators are my best friends, sexually speaking.
Without vibrators at my age (seventy as I write this), I'd rarely
manage to have an orgasm—with or without a partner—
and I really like orgasms. I know our experiences are vastly
different—you may have easy orgasms and a toy-free way of
getting there. But many of us would rarely enjoy one of life's
greatest pleasures if we couldn't use our power tools.

As I've explained before, we don't have that hormonal
drive to the finish anymore, and less blood flows to the parts
that need it. Sex toys give us focused stimulation and blood
flow exactly where we need it, as strong as we need it. Even
if we start out thinking an orgasm is unlikely, the right sex
toy can surprise us. The more orgasms we have, the more
easily we reach orgasm the next time. So using a vibrator to
get us over the edge actually enhances sensitivity and ease of
reaching orgasm.

Sex toys are also wonderful for warm up before or during
sex with a partner. They're not just for solo sex. In fact,
sex toys are so valuable in numerous ways, I mention them
throughout this book, not just in this chapter.

I'd never owned a sex toy—now I have a drawer full. I had always felt that masturbation, erotica, porn, and sex toys were wrong and somehow damaging to a person and society in general. I'd never enjoyed or read erotica, and now I'll read it often to jump start things.

TYPES OF SEX TOYS

Before the 1970s, our sex toy options consisted of using "personal massagers" (wink, wink), penis-shaped (or sort of penis-shaped) dildos, or seeing the potential in a cucumber or an electric toothbrush. Now, there are so many different types, styles, shapes, and sizes of sex toys that describing them all would take half this book.

I think of these sensation-giving products as "tools" more than "toys," but I'll use the familiar vernacular so that you know what I'm talking about. Some sex toys are explicitly designed for female genitals, some for male genitals, and most can be used by any gender. You can use toys solo or with a partner watching or participating. I'll divide them roughly into these categories, though some toys overlap categories:

Vibrators run the gamut from light stimulation to turbo power tools. Usually designed for clitoral stimulation, they can be used on any part that feels good on any gendered body. Dual-action vibrators, often known as *rabbits* (some are actually shaped like rabbits), aim to stimulate both the vagina and clitoris, with varying degrees of success, depending on how well they fit your own dimensions.

Dildos are penetrative toys. They may be *realistic*, meaning phallus-shaped; curved to reach the G-spot; or molded into an artistic or whimsical design. Dildos don't necessarily vibrate, though some do. Strap-on dildos let women penetrate men anally (called *pegging*) or penetrate other women vaginally or anally. They also work for men who do not get erections but want to satisfy a partner who enjoys penetration. Double dildos, toys with a dildo at each end, allow penetration of two partners of whatever gender simultaneously.

Couples vibrators, like the We-Vibe, are designed to be used during heterosexual intercourse—the small, curved shape keeps one end in the vagina where both penis and G-spot come in contact with it, and the other end covers the clitoris.

Butt plugs are inserted in the rectum of either gender for anal stimulation. The anus has a high concentration of nerve endings.

Prostate massagers, such as the well-known Aneros brand toys, are designed specifically to stimulate a man's prostate gland (also known as the "P-spot" or "male G-spot"), which can be extremely pleasurable.

Cock rings can help keep blood from draining away from an erect penis, giving the erection more staying power. Most are made to fit over the penis and scrotum; others go around the base of the penis only.

Masturbation sleeves cover the penis snugly and enhance the male masturbatory experience. Some vibrate; others leave the motion to the user. The material and design may simulate sex with a vagina, mouth, or anus.

Accessories. A plaything doesn't have to go on or in your genitals to qualify as a sex toy. For BDSM play (see chapter 6, Stretching Boundaries), role-playing, or just extra stimulation, you may enjoy blindfolds, nipple clamps, restraints, paddles, or any other kind of gear that you use consensually to intensify sexual pleasure.

Explore, experiment, and enjoy! You'll find some toys that hit the spot—pun intended—and turn your yawn into screams of delight. With all sex toys, use plenty of lubricant.

CHOOSING YOUR SEX TOY

To narrow down what you're looking for from the thousands of toys available, start by answering these questions:

1. **What do you want the toy to do?** I know, "give me orgasms," but be more specific about how you expect it to work: "fit between two bodies to stimulate my clitoris during partner sex until I'm screaming with pleasure," or "be worn in a harness for pegging," or "let me paddle my partner while he is cuffed to the bedpost," for example.

2. **What body part do you want the toy to stimulate?** Clitoris? Vagina/G-spot? Penis? Prostate? Anus? Both clitoris and vagina? Nipples? Other nongenital body part?

3. **Describe what you do and don't want it to look like,** if you care about this. Some want a dildo to look like a penis. Others really *don't* want it to look like a penis.

4. **How should it feel?** Firm, flexible, cushiony?

5. **Should it vibrate?** If so, how strong does it need to be: whispery, light, medium, strong, extra-strong, super turbo power? Do you care how noisy it is?

6. **What size is too big, too small, just right,** if this is a penetrating toy?

7. **What mobility restrictions or other physical issues** do you need to consider?

8. **If this is a role-playing aid, what scene will you enact,** and what do you need to make the scene work?

9. **What else is important to you?**

It's good to get some sex toy education before making your choice. Thanks to the Internet, we can read reviews of sex toys from users—not just descriptions by the retailer, but actual reviews from bloggers who are candid about the pros and cons.

VISITING A SEX TOY STORE

I agree with doing online research, but I'd have to recommend touching, feeling and handling toys in a shop. Sometimes sizes or texture of toys can surprise. And you need to know if the vibrations are strong enough to work for you. If there's a female-owned/managed shop near you, go there. They are a growing breed and really keen to make sure you make the right choice for yourself.

You can order sex toys from a reputable retailer online (my blog links to several), or visit a well-stocked, well-lighted, women-welcome sex shop in person. Roam around, look at the toys on display, examine and touch them, turn them on (a good store will have samples that you can pick up and turn on), and ask questions of the well-trained and friendly staff whose job it is to know the products they're selling.

If you think that a store that sells sex toys must be dark and grungy with sticky floors and leering men in overcoats, your ideas are, fortunately, stuck way in the past. You *can* find sleazy shops if you like them, but if you're like me, you'll prefer the clean, bright, progressive, all-genders-welcome, education-based sex stores. They are often women-owned and women-run, and while they do not ignore the needs of men, they make sure that plenty—if not most—of the products are designed for a woman's pleasure. They even invite me to come speak to staff and customers, so they're actively and enthusiastically learning what our age group wants.

"But the workers in these stores are the age of my grandchildren!" some of you tell me. "I'd be horrified to talk about sex with them!" I get it, but I invite you to look at these remarkable young people in a different way. We mistakenly assume that if they're the age of our grandchildren, (a) they don't know much, and (b) we can't possibly talk about our sexual concerns with them.

But in reality, they're smart "sex nerds," meaning that they find sexuality a fascinating and intellectual topic and take their mission seriously to provide sex education to everyone. Believe me, there is nothing you can ask that will shock or surprise them. In fact, one young man told me, "My older customers often start with, 'I'll bet you've never heard this before'—and it's never true!"

These folks aren't just sales associates—they're sex educators. They have knowledge that will help us enrich our sex lives, and they're ever eager to learn more. When I work with the staff of these stores, their main question to me is always, "How can I help our older customers feel comfortable asking us questions?"

It's up to us to meet them with a smile and a question, and give them a chance to help us.

MEN LIKE SEX TOYS, TOO

I was diagnosed HIV+ at fifty-five. I'm now fifty-nine. My sex life was nonexistent the first year. I slowly began to enjoy masturbation again. It wasn't all I wanted, but I found ways to prolong my short moments of joy. Anal masturbation and prostate massage have greatly helped. I enjoy nipple play. I do these things to build up to climax, so foreplay can be an hour or longer before I ever reach for myself. My toys for anal play are vibrators and plugs that give me all-around pleasure.

Male bodies have similar issues as female bodies with different visible results—decreased blood flow and hormonal changes make it more difficult to get or sustain an erection. Men may need longer arousal time and extra stimulation.

There are sex toys made especially for penises, such as masturbation sleeves (vibrating and not), cock rings, and an exceptional vibrator called the Pulse that can be used for sexual pleasure even when an erection is difficult or not possible. For backdoor play, many men get huge pleasure from prostate stimulating toys and butt plugs (women enjoy butt plugs, too).

But you don't have to stick to sex toys made specifically for male bodies. Many vibrators, dildos, and butt plugs that are marketed to women give plenty of pleasure to a man's penis, testicles, perineum, anus, prostate, nipples, and anywhere else he's sensitive.

CAUTIONS FOR ANAL TOYS

Use only toys with a flared base for anal insertion to keep your pleasure device from being pulled in by the powerful sphincter muscles. You do *not* want to have to visit the emergency room or find yourself on (actual—I am not making them up) web pages like "Things I Have Fished Out of People's Butts"[14] or "10 Craziest Foreign Objects Found Stuck in a Rectum."[15]

Don't try to save money by using a household object. The ER costs much more than any toy you could buy. And you'll have to explain how the object got there.

If you're not sure that a toy or other object is safe for anal use, *do not use it.* If anal play is new to you, please visit an education-focused sex toy store, and ask a staff person to help you understand what and what not to put in your butt. Really, it's okay to ask them that—it's all part of their day job.

THE THREE OF YOU

I got married a month ago. I showed my husband my vibrator, telling him, "I want to introduce you to the lover I've had for thirty years, Bob: battery-operated-boyfriend."

Sex toys are no threat to a partnered sex life—in fact, they enhance it. Same-sex couples generally see all kinds of sex toys as acceptable, even *de rigueur*, during partner play. Many straight couples do, too, but those older than boomer age may not have ever used sex toys together in the past and may find them threatening. One or more of these misconceptions can interfere.

He thinks:

- If she's really turned on by me, she shouldn't need a sex toy when—hello!—here I am.

- If she needs a sex toy, I'm not enough for her.

She thinks:

- He'll feel inadequate if I bring my favorite vibrator into our sex play.

- If he uses a sex toy on himself, I'm not good/ desirable/arousing enough.

If you're a woman in a heterosexual relationship, you've probably found that on your own, you zing and sing, thanks to your trusty, vibrating bed buddy. But during partner sex, your clitoris—the center of your pleasure powerhouse—may not be getting enough attention. Even when he's careful to stimulate you *just so*, it takes more time, more touching, and more focus. Nothing wrong with that, but if you could speed things up and pretty much guarantee the optimal result, wouldn't that be a lovely addition to your sex play?

So you may find it very satisfying to have a ménage à trois—you, him, and your vibrator. Many vibrators now are small and unobtrusive enough to fit between two bodies and give the clitoris a buzz without getting in the way. Some are specifically designed as an adjunct to penis-in-vagina sex, sort of *U*-shaped with one part hugging your clitoris and the other against your G-spot alongside his penis in your vagina. (Intrigued? Try the We-Vibe.)

If you agree that this kind of threesome is just what your sex life needs, or, at least, is worth a try, how do you convince *him*? If you worry that he'll think you're saying that he's not enough anymore, or that you prefer plastic and silicone to the real thing, try this approach:

1. Introduce him to your favorite toy when you're starting your sex play—but not yet in the throes of passion. Run it over his nipples. If he likes that, hand it to him and let him experiment on himself.

2. Show him how you like to use it on yourself. Don't get carried away—at first—just let him see how you respond.

3. Let him hold it and arouse you with it. Give him plenty of feedback about what rhythm and pressure feel best. You might hold your hand on his to guide him.

4. Say something like, "I love how it feels when you're inside me. I'll bet it would be really arousing for me if we used a vibrator on my clitoris at the same time. Could we try it?" or "I love how you bring me to orgasm with your hand, but I worry about how long it takes me to reach orgasm. Can we add a vibrator to save you from carpal tunnel syndrome?"

Be patient if he seems a bit vibrator-adverse at first. You don't have to go through all of those steps at the same time. But chances are he'll realize not only how much you enjoy it, but how much the two of you will enjoy it together!

We go on an adventure every time I show him a new sex toy, and we use it together to get me warmed up, or I use it on myself for clitoral stimulation during intercourse. He's always open to learning what pleases me. He's a bit of a sex geek anyway, so learning about anything sexual interests him. Lucky me!

AVOIDING TOXIC TOYS

I love sex toys, and I want you to have the same enjoyment I do from them. Part of that enjoyment is confidence that what you're putting into or onto your delicate tissues will not burn, irritate, or leach harmful chemicals into your body. Yes, some will, so it's important either to educate yourself about the materials used in sex toys or—simpler—buy from retailers you trust that have a strict, safe toy policy.

Sex toys are not regulated. Shampoo and mascara are. Baby toys are. Even dog toys are. But sex toys can be made of any material, including hazardous ingredients such as cadmium, lead, toluene, PVC (polyvinyl chloride), and phthalates. Although no research grants have been awarded to investigate the long-term effects of using these toxic materials on or in our genitals, we do know that they are hazardous to our health. Phthalates, for example, used to chemically soften plastics, have been linked to a variety of health problems, from burning, itching, and irritation to reproductive organ damage and liver cancer.

Many toys—especially the cheaper ones—are porous, which means they can't be cleaned well enough to disinfect them. They can trap bacteria and viruses and spread disease.

Let's say you educate yourself on the materials that are body safe, such as medical-grade silicone, stainless steel, Pyrex glass, and ABS plastic. As if you didn't have enough to worry about, lack of regulation means the manufacturers can say their toys are made out of whatever substance they want to claim. Nothing stops a sleazy (or uninformed) manufacturer or retailer from labeling a "novelty item" as silicone when it isn't.

Some companies and sex bloggers do their own tests to determine what a toy is made of. But unless you want to invest a lot of time, energy, and money (buying sex toys you'll decide not to use), the best shortcut is to buy from the retailers with a reputation of emphasizing education and safety, who carry toys that have been proven to be body-safe, and who disclose materials openly.

Avoid "jelly" toys, smelly toys, and cheap toys. If you're buying a glass toy, don't buy one made in China, because certain chemicals and compounds like mercury are used in China to form and temper glass.

Be wary of transparent toys that advertise that they're made of silicone. Although silicone can be clear—such as in the making of contact lenses—a toy made this way would cost the manufacturer hundreds of dollars or more, and the cost to the consumer would be outlandishly expensive. That transparent dildo that cost you $30 is not silicone, even if the label claims it.

"Transparency is a good warning sign that a toy merits closer inspection," says Hannah Jorden, senior sex educator at Smitten Kitten. ("Senior" refers to seniority, not age. Jorden is young—and very smart and sex-nerdy.) Jorden explains:

"Jelly" toys are often crystal clear and have a glossy, wet look, like a LifeSaver candy that's been sucked on already. The surface can also feel tacky or greasy to the touch. Jelly is a kind of code word that many manufacturers use to

describe toys made of softened PVC—usually containing phthalates that sweat out or outgas a very noticeable fruity, plastic-y aroma.

However, there are also transparent toys made of elastomer, which is nontoxic but porous. Elastomer is just a word used to describe lots of different thermo-plasticized, rubbery substances. Clear, nontoxic elastomers are usually just a little firmer and not quite as clear looking as jelly. Because they're chemically stable, they shouldn't melt, sweat, or give off any scent.

Even though they're nontoxic, I'd still advise against using elastomer toys inside the body or around the urethral opening. Porous materials are fine for cock rings or masturbation sleeves, but I'd never recommend one for penetrative play. Porous toys can harbor bacteria and other micro-organisms deep inside and can never be completely sterilized. No matter how awesome a vibrator, dildo, or butt plug might feel, it's just not worth a yeast infection, UTI, or STI. I hate seeing porous toys marketed for internal use! Finding a brand of silicone toys you can trust is really the best way to go."

SAFE SEX TOY CHECKLIST

Are the sex toys you already own or are considering buying safe and healthy for your body? The Coalition Against Toxic Toys (www.badvibes.org), started by Smitten Kitten's Jennifer Pritchett, MS, an activist, educator, and nationally respected sex toy safety expert, issued this checklist for buying a nontoxic, body-safe sex toy: [16]

Body Friendly
Sex toys should be made of a medical or food-grade material that is hypoallergenic and safe for intimate contact. Unfortunately many sex toys are manufactured from industrial-quality materials, do not include accurate information about material quality, and are not proven safe for intimate contact. Often these novelties are referred to as "jelly."

The Smell Test™
The easiest way to discern if a sex toy is made from a safe material is through smell. Unsafe sex toys frequently have an obvious chemical or plastic smell. The odor is caused by the release of chemicals into the air through outgassing. Safe toy materials, in contrast, have no smell and do not leach chemicals into your body or the surrounding environment.

Nonporous
Porous materials can harbor micro-organisms,

such as bacteria, viruses, and fungi, which can cause infections despite even the most diligent cleaning efforts. Sex toys should be nonporous. Examples of safe, nonporous materials include: 100 percent silicone from a reputable manufacturer, glass, surgical steel, sealed ceramic, and medical-grade plastics.

Form and Function

Sex toys should be made by reputable companies that design and manufacture their toys to be used sexually, rather than as gag gifts or novelties. It is important that sex toys be used for their intended purposes, and safe use requires common sense. If you are not sure how a specific toy is designed to be used, ask a knowledgeable sex educator or sales associate.

JUST PUT A CONDOM ON IT?

If you have toys that you like but realize they don't pass the healthy toy test, I—along with many others—used to recommend that you put condoms on them. I still read that recommendation in books and on websites. I've learned, however, that condoms do not, in fact, create instant safe sex toys. Here's what Jennifer Pritchett, MS, told us:

Here's the thing: no one has ever tested condom efficacy against these toxic chemicals. These chemicals are so bad that if handled alone, you'd wear hazmat gear. I certainly wouldn't trust a condom for this purpose and consider it irresponsible for anyone to claim, "Just put a condom on it." Having said that, if you absolutely must continue using an old toxic toy, putting a condom on it is better than nothing. But, with all my heart, I implore people to get rid of those toys!

BUT THEY COST SO MUCH!

Body-safe toys are more expensive, because they cost more to manufacture. Medical-grade, well-tested materials cost more than the crappy stuff that you don't want inside your body or against your skin. You're paying for research and development and high-quality material that won't degrade, melt, leach nasty chemicals into your body, break, overheat, or burn. You're also paying for toys that deliver what they promise—and last.

Instead of buying cheap toys that put your health at risk and are likely to break or turn into goop on a hot day, go for the best ones that you can afford.

The missus and I spent $100 for our last vibrator. Worth it! A man spends $300 for a chain saw without a flinch. Since he doesn't spend a couple hours a day thinking about cutting wood, I don't see why he and his wood wouldn't invest good money in his woman, in their relationship, and her finishing well.

CAN SEX TOYS RUIN YOUR RELATIONSHIP?

My wife got a gigantic vibrator about a year ago. This is when the troubles started. I think it was a prelude to her loosening her sexual inhibitions. Well, now she's cheated on me with four guys that I know of, and in all probability countless others. Do you think that vibrators are a signal of loosening sexual inhibitions?

Sex toys do not wreck relationships. Sex toys don't turn women—or men—into wanton sex fiends. Sex toys don't turn faithful spouses into cheaters. Sex toys just make arousal and orgasm easier, that's all. Oh, yes, there's more to it than that—sex toys help alleviate frustration, anxiety, depression, and nervousness—but that's just because they facilitate orgasm, which has all those happy results.

If one person prefers a sex toy to the exclusion of the partner, it's a signal that there's a bigger problem in the relationship than sex toys.

It's possible that a partner's reliance on her vibrator means simply that she can't have an orgasm without it, or she worries that it will take forever. Talk to her about this without language that will be perceived as accusing or shaming her.

Tell her you'd like to learn how to use the vibrator with her during your lovemaking, if she's willing. Maybe you can use it with her for a while and then hand it to her to finish in the way she knows best. She might rather use the vibrator as a warm-up and invite you to participate. Or she might prefer that you just watch. (One couple told me they had an elabo-rate ritual where the husband hid and spied on his wife as she masturbated with her vibrator. It was completely consen-sual, but they both got mighty aroused by pretending that she didn't know he was there.)

However this scenario goes, you'll learn from it what she needs to reach orgasm. The vibrator can be your buddy, your assistant, and your show of generosity to your partner.

On the other hand, this reader wrote me in frustration because her husband insisted on using her toys together:

What would you suggest for a woman whose husband thinks sex toys are okay as long as he gets to use them on her? When does her need enter the picture?

Whether the issue is sex toys or anything else, you'll only get what you need when you stand up for it. In this case, the woman could say, "We'll use my toys together when we both want to, but I'll also use them privately whenever I want." A partner doesn't get to dictate what you do in private, and it's up to you to speak out loud and clearly. Otherwise, your partner may think that you're fine with the way things are. In this as in everything else, your partner's ability to read your mind has been wildly overrated.

WHY DO WE FEEL GUILTY?

Having no significant other, I satisfy my sexual needs by masturbating. I am a lesbian, cradle Catholic, ex-nun. Even at fifty-nine and well-educated, I still am plagued with guilt about masturbating. I'm not sure what makes me feel guilty. Masturbation was never mentioned in my home, or in twelve years of Catholic education. I never heard it mentioned or alluded to in the convent.

Many women our age resist self-pleasuring. Our paltry sex education was anything but pleasure-based. We were taught as children never to touch ourselves *down there*. Fortunately, our bodies usually insisted on teaching us, maybe with roaming fingers in the bathtub, a fantasy that surprised us with its intensity, or the shock of how good it felt to slide down the jungle gym pole or hump our pillow. But few of us escaped the notion that masturbation was wanton and wrong.

Here we are, fifty, sixty, seventy years later. If we haven't yet made peace with our wonderful capacity to give ourselves sexual pleasure, might it be time to do that?

Many women also feel that something is lacking in them—their desirability or their skill—if a male partner needs to masturbate or use a sex toy to get the stimulation he needs.

My partner has discussed sexual toys, which were certainly frowned on in my culture, and when he plays with himself while I am stimulating him, it really upsets me. I guess I have a long way to go in this new world of senior sexuality.

Whatever is going on with us or our partner, if we have one, self-pleasuring isn't the problem—it's often part of the solution. If this is a new idea for you, I hope you'll open your mind to it and shake off whatever guilt still remains from what you were taught many decades ago. We have the capability of choosing pleasure, and if it doesn't look the way we thought it would, let's just change our way of looking at it—and let's enjoy it!

Frankly I am on the side of those who think it's pretty hot when my man scratches his own itch!

CAN MASTURBATION ENHANCE YOUR RELATIONSHIP?

If you're in a sexual relationship, is there any reason to masturbate? Sure. The more we pleasure ourselves, the more sexually vibrant we remain, physically and emotionally, and that translates to better sex with a partner, too. Feeling comfortable with masturbation helps us accept our changing bodies, because we stay in touch—literally—with the sexual pleasure these bodies give us and how to access that pleasure.

Although I became sexually active as a teen in the seventies, and I was definitely aroused by the foreplay and sex, I was completely ignorant of female orgasms. It wasn't until a college boyfriend stimulated me manually and I reached orgasm that I found out what it was all about. It was a shocking revelation and very humorous to look back on. From that day forward, I made good use of masturbating and gained a lot more satisfaction out of my sexual encounters.

And if you're in a relationship that has become nonsexual or only sporadically sexual due to your partner's health problems, masturbation will help you keep your sexual self in shape. This will help your relationship, too—you'll feel more loving and less stressed if you're having regular orgasms.

Because my husband is seventy years old and has been dealing with bladder cancer, most of my orgasms are through masturbation.

On the physical level, masturbation increases blood flow to the genitals, keeping them responsive and healthy. Our pelvic floor muscles get a workout with every orgasm. Regular masturbation—at least once a week—helps us keep sex on the brain. That's a good thing, because at our age, without the hormonal urge, we can find ourselves *forgetting* about sex. Once we let weeks or even months pass without sexual arousal and orgasm, it becomes harder and harder to make it happen. Think of regular orgasms as *sex insurance.*

I'm sixty-six. About twelve years ago, my husband gave up on having sex with me due to his ED, probably related to his Type 2 Diabetes. At the time it didn't seem like a big deal to me since our sex life wasn't that great anyway. However, as time went on, I felt frustrated and missed the bonding and intimacy that come with good sex. I started reading romance and erotica stories and was surprised that they stimulated me. My libido woke up! I decided to take charge of my sleeping sexuality and began masturbating. While my current sex life isn't joyful in the sense of being able to lovingly share it with someone special, I do feel more satisfied and in control of my sexual needs.

SOLO: WORTH THE TROUBLE?

I hear, almost exclusively from women, "I don't want to do it myself; I want a partner to please me, or I'd rather do without," and "If I don't have a lover, masturbation isn't worth the trouble."

It's self-defeating to see masturbation as no more than a lousy substitute for partner sex. We're only depriving ourselves of the pleasure of arousal, the satisfaction of self-nurturing, and the high of sexual release. The key to enjoying solo sex is to celebrate the capacity for pleasure that our bodies still give us and that we can access completely on our own whenever we want.

Another good reason for regular self-pleasuring: you'll be ready, willing, and able if a new partner appears. For men and women, the more we arouse ourselves and give ourselves orgasms, the more easily we become aroused and orgasmic, despite our diminished hormones.

> *I believe the more orgasms we have, the more easily we reach orgasm the next time. So using a vibrator to get us over the edge actually enhances sensitivity and ease of reaching orgasm.*

If we don't continue to bring blood flow to the penis or vagina and clitoris, arousal becomes more difficult, and libido retreats along with our hormones. Penises have more difficulty becoming erect. Vaginas feel tighter, drier, and less flexible, and penetration may be painful or impossible. Orgasms become much more elusive.

It's a health thing—do it!

> *Now that I'm without a partner, I pleasure myself in all ways such as the sight of beautiful flowers and Tiffany lamps by my desk, the taste of French champagne and fresh raspberries, the feel of silk on my body, the scent of orange blossoms and jasmine recalling the south of France, and Jim Morrison singing, "I'm gonna love you till the stars fall from the sky…." And all this before I pull out my favorite toy!*

5

SEX WITH A LONGTIME PARTNER

As a queer woman, age sixty-six, I know very few people who escape what is known as lesbian bed death—mythically a seven-year sexual slump that couples rarely recover from. It's certainly not just a lesbian phenomenon. The only way to recover from waning arousal is to make an agreement to do so. We have to be conscious and explicit about making room for sex. We need to make and protect sexual dates. We must turn off all screens including TVs and phones. We need to check in with each other about obstacles—a creaky back or a tender bunion—and figure out how to work around them. We already know where and how our partner likes to be touched—we just have to create the private time to do it.

I was giving a talk about senior sex and romance at a Valentine's Day event a few years ago. My love affair with Robert was vibrant, strong, and sexy, and I punctuated my tips for keeping sex alive with anecdotes about our relationship. Most of the attendees were my age and older, and the response was warm and positive. During the question-and-answer period, though, one man who looked to be about seventy said, "Yeah, that's all very nice, but your relationship is still new. Would you sound as positive after forty years together?"

His comment brought home to me how little we talk about how to keep sex alive and vibrant after decades together. Maybe we can't keep our longtime relationship ablaze with lust the way it was when we first discovered each other, but we *can* keep it spicy and satisfying. It's up to us to nurture our partner's pleasure and our own. Sex together can deepen, get more intimate, and still stay at the top of things we love to do with each other, despite the decades together— or maybe because of them. But it's not automatic—it takes commitment.

As we celebrate thirty-five years, there have been ups and downs. The highs are longer and far more satisfying. The lows just suck.

Some of the most joyful emails I get from readers are from those who have figured out how to keep the sexuality alive in their relationships lasting thirty, forty, even fifty-plus years. They usually credit these habits:

- **Novelty:** keeping the element of surprise so that their partners never find them totally predictable.

- **Affection:** kissing and touching throughout the day, not just when they desire sex.

SURPRISE EACH OTHER

There's a powerful tendency in long-term relationships to favor the predictable over the unpredictable. Yet eroticism thrives on the unpredictable.... If we are to maintain desire with one person over time we must be able to bring a sense of unknown into a familiar space.... Eroticism is numbed by repetition. It thrives on the mysterious, the novel, and the unexpected.

—Esther Perel, in *Mating in Captivity: Unlocking Erotic Intelligence*

Think about it: when your relationship was new, you never knew what to expect from your lover. What romantic overture, while out on a date, would make you or your partner melt? What would cause your lover to gasp or shiver with pleasure in bed? Discovering how to please each other, both in and out of bed, was a thrill—and a major sexual turn-on.

It's easy to let activities that you enjoyed fall away when you get into a routine, and a long relationship is full of predictable routines.

When you were newly in love, what—besides sex—did you have fun doing with each other? Did you dance or bicycle together? Walk in the moonlight? See a foreign film and discuss it endlessly? Discuss this with your partner. Energize your relationship by bringing a favorite activity back into your life.

Maintaining an intimate relationship at this stage of life is a real challenge, because the issues of love, sex, aging, and just plain relating to each other are so different from when we were younger. It is these challenges that stymie aging couples. Yes, sex is important, but really, it is almost always, at base, about the relationship.

TIPS FOR RECAPTURING THE EXCITEMENT OF NEW LOVE

Share memories: Tell each other the story of how you met and fell in love. Describe what attracted you to your partner, what he or she said or did that was particularly endearing. Describe how you felt. Tell your partner how you knew you were in love.

Date night: Remember when you planned a date and anticipated it for days beforehand? Do that at least once a week. Don't do the predictable, such as dinner at your usual restaurant or a video at home. Go somewhere new. Dress sexier than usual.

Return to the scene: Take a trip to a place you used to make out, dance, or talk for hours, if this is feasible. Reenact the experience. If actually going there isn't possible, describe details of the scene in a way that brings it back. Act it out.

Leave sexy messages: Put a note beside your partner's toothbrush or send a text about a sexy thing you want to do.

Gift for no occasion: Buy a little gift for your partner for no reason at all, except to show your love. Gift wrap it and leave it on the pillow, or present it with a declaration of love.

Write a love letter: Nothing is more precious than a gift of your words expressing your love. Write what you find wonderful and sexy about your partner. Either read it aloud or leave it where your beloved will find it.

Golden oldies: Play the music you fell in love to. Sing along! Dance. Make fun of the lyrics—or act them out.

Relive the old times: "Ask yourself: when, in this relationship, did you feel the most erotically charged?" suggests therapist Barry McCarthy, PhD[17], author of several books about sex and desire. Then figure out what you can do to recapture that feeling. "What would be a really special scenario to create that for you?" McCarthy asks. "Sex isn't just about intercourse. It's about playful, erotic activities, without pressure."

It's not what you do in bed that's most important; it's what you do every day to keep your shared sensual life active.

SPICE IT UP

If something were to happen to both my husband and me, our children would find sex toys, vibrators, cock rings, oils, pills, and spicy DVDs when they had to clean the place out.

If your day-to-day relationship is satisfying, but in bed, it's easier to yawn than to orgasm, it's time to add some spice to that familiar flavor. Which of these ideas appeal to you?

Dress for disrobing: Invest in some silky, sexy lingerie. With a well-chosen garment that accentuates our best features, we look alluring. And we *feel* amazing, both emotionally and physically. This isn't for women only—silk bikini briefs or satin boxers for men are enticing, too!

Try a new toy or prop: Using a new vibrator or other sex toy together can be very hot. So can introducing a blindfold, light bondage, or the light touch of a feather. Experiment. If you don't like something that you thought would turn you on, you can laugh about it. And if you do like it, it's a new part of your repertoire.

A blindfold is a sex toy. Honest. And you don't even have to wash it after each use.

Read erotica or view porn together: Stroke each other as you read or watch, and imagine yourself part of the scene. Feel free to start getting frisky before you've finished the story or the film.

> *My hubby likes to see naked women on the Internet and in videos. Recently, I came across a few videos of women getting stimulated to orgasm while they were reading. This was a real turn-on for me, and I shared it with him. So, yeah, we had a great time shortly after that. Finding those videos and sharing them with him opened up new trust and understanding between us. After thirty-three years together, I didn't think it possible to grow any closer, but it happened!*

Pleasure each other in a new way: This can be as simple as changing who goes first (or more accurately, who *comes* first), or making love in a different position or in a different room. Or it can be more involved: try a new technique, go to a hotel overnight, or act out a fantasy scene.

> *We share fantasies and act them out. We have date night that is actually date afternoon. We share what we like and want. Sexy stories are really a fun turn-on. When we read them out loud to each other, great things happen!*

IS TANTRA FOR YOU?
By Mark A. Michaels and
Patricia Johnson

Tantra is an ancient Indian tradition that recognizes sexual energy as a source of personal and spiritual empowerment. Sexual energy refers to the life force, not just sexual activity. This life force exists within us regardless of age or ability. Classical Indian Tantra involves many elements, including a sexual ritual in which partners worship each other as embodiments of the divine; taboo breaking; and an approach to sexuality that embraces the entire mind-body-spirit complex.

All of these elements have significant implications for people over fifty. Developing an attitude of reverence and worship for each other and treating lovemaking as sacred can deepen and renew a long-term relationship both in and out of bed.

There's no need to embrace the whole tradition, wrap yourselves in exotic garb, or engage in elaborate rituals to do this. All it takes is a slight shift in awareness, a conscious recognition that you have chosen each other, and that you're honoring and respecting that choice. Recognizing sex as something special and important, regardless of your religious or spiritual beliefs, gives it new layers of meaning. This can be especially profound as we age and are less ruled by hormonal impulses.

In Tantric sex, the effort is to transform the surface of the skin into a massive genital. Focusing on the totality of your physical connection, whether or not any organs are penetrating or being penetrated, is increasingly valuable as we age. This makes it possible to remain erotically engaged, even when more conventional sexual activity is not an option.

—Mark A. Michaels and Patricia Johnson are coauthors of *Partners in Passion, Great Sex Made Simple, Tantra for Erotic Empowerment,* and *The Essence of Tantric Sexuality.*

My wife and I have been together for forty-four years. In our late forties, after twenty-four years of marriage, we hit a patch where sex was getting stale and perfunctory, so we made a conscious effort to experiment with new ideas. A couple who practiced Tantric sex shared ideas and resources with us, and we have been enthusiastic practitioners ever since. Tantra was a revelation for us. It strongly reinforces trust, love, and intimacy between partners. It is also simply amazing sex. Neither of us had ever experienced anything like the duration and intensity of a true Tantric full-body orgasm, the multiplicity of orgasms, or the deep bonding experience that Tantra creates.

SHOW AFFECTION

Some couples act like honeymooners, even though they've been together for many years. They're always kissing, holding hands, touching each other, and cuddling. Even when they're not touching, they're meeting each other's eyes, smiling at a shared secret, or laughing together.

Contrast that with couples who barely speak, look everywhere but at each other, and read the paper or talk on their phones when they're out to brunch.

Which kind of couple are you?

Make a point of showing affection habitually, not just when you're hoping to get sexual. Make that part of the way you relate in public and private. I'm not suggesting that you need to drape over each other or exchange sloppy kisses in public, but touching hands or exchanging pecks on the cheek can help you feel connected.

Robert and I held hands as we walked. We coined the term *restaurant kiss* for the quick kisses we exchanged in public. This started when we were seated at a restaurant, and one of us announced, "Restaurant kiss!" and deposited a quick kiss on the other's cheek. We made this a routine—indeed, a game—at every public outing, from coffee shops to doctors' waiting rooms.

Little public displays of attention communicate to your partner that you're in love and that it feels good to express that love physically. And if friends and strangers see you as two old folks in love, that's cool, too.

When your love was new, you told everyone who would

listen how wonderful your partner was. Do that now—when you're out with friends or at a party together, announce in your partner's hearing the many qualities that you love in him or her, or describe something that your partner did recently that warmed your heart.

What do we older men want? And why do we stop wanting? We want to be desired. We want passion. Like in the Cheap Trick song: "I want you to want me/I need you to need me." Honestly, we older guys would bring it more if older women showed us they wanted it more, wanted us more, wanted more passion in their lives.

APPRECIATE WHAT'S GOING RIGHT

At sixty-eight, married for seventeen years, I have more desire for my husband today than when we first had sex. He is overweight, on meds for high blood pressure, and occasionally loses erections, but he turns me on! The sound of his voice, the sight of his body, the gait of his walk, the touch of his hand on my arm, the hugs he shares, and his laughter and love have me captivated. When he offers all this, who cares about an erection? I am wet and ready; I want his body every day!

He has mastered his hands touching me, slowly and tenderly, and drives me into ecstasy with his lips and tongue on my clitoris! I also love to lay my head on his inner thigh, stroke his balls ever so lightly, and touch his penis, taking it into my warm wet mouth until he is drained. What incredible excitement. Could anyone else have this effect on me? Nope!

When things are going right during times of satisfying intimacy, what else is going on that makes those moments happen? How do you act? What do you bring to the relationship during those times that might be missing at other times?

Most relationships are sometimes good, sometimes not so good. Looking at what else is happening when it *is* good will help you make that happen more often. It's about setting the stage for the best to happen, instead of dreading the worst.

Even if your intimacy is only good 10 percent of the time, find ways to "accentuate the positive," as the old song said. If you love it when your partner brings you to an orgasm orally, but he or she only does that once in a blue moon these days, try saying something like, "You get me so excited when you go down on me—you're an incredibly hot lover." That is a lot more exciting for your lover to hear than, "You never go down on me anymore."

Whether you're expressing appreciation in the moment ("Umm, I love it when you touch me like that.") or during a nonsexual part of your daily life ("I'm still smiling remembering that orgasm you gave me." or "I know you're dressed to go out, but I can't help picturing your beautiful, naked body. I can't wait to see it again."), keep the sexual energy positive and complimentary. You'll feel more connected, less prone to irritation, and sexier.

As I joyfully approach my forty-eighth anniversary with the cherished love of my life, I hope all who read this will work to maintain the love connections they have, and not let temporary upsets come between you. "Grow old with me..." because the best really is yet to be, tomorrow and every day you share together.

SCHEDULE SEX DATES

Approaching our midsixties, we've pretty much bristled at the seemingly mechanical or staged approach to planning sex. But I've been reading about setting up hot scenes: planning, setting the stage. Well, why not. It's making an appointment for sex, right? Hey, we need it!

"You've got to be kidding," people tell me when I suggest that one important key to a sexually fulfilling, longtime relationship is scheduling sex dates at least once a week. "Sex should be spontaneous," they insist.

Spontaneity is vastly overrated at our age. When we no longer have the hormonal urge driving us to mate, sex isn't often the first thing on our minds. Maybe it isn't even in the top ten. It doesn't happen spontaneously anymore.

By scheduling a sex date, you make sure you carve time for it, and this insures that it really happens.

This also creates days of anticipation, where you fantasize about what you'll do together—a form of mental foreplay. Your brain is your major sex organ. When you focus your brain on the prospect of enjoying sex with your lover, you'll be that much more ready for it when the date arrives.

A common feature of couples who have a strong, vibrant, and pleasurable sex life is that they maintain a regular sexual connection. This means a steady pattern of sex regardless of what barriers may arise. Research verifies the value of regularity, whether twice a week or three times a month. When you know your pattern, good things happen.

—Michael E. Metz and Barry W. McCarthy in
Enduring Desire: Your Guide to Lifelong Intimacy

TRY SOMETHING NEW

Liven up your relationship by trying something completely new but that isn't so extreme that it would damage your relationship, your self-esteem, or your health if it turns out that you don't like it. It can be as simple as having sex in an unusual place or picking out a costume for the other to wear.

Or it can be something more daring, such as enacting a fantasy. Try describing the fantasy first while you're not having sex, and if you agree, describe it in juicy detail while you are having sex. If that's all good, then role-play it in private, acting out the parts. You can then decide whether to take the fantasy to the next stage, whatever that is, or just delight each other in private with storytelling or role-play.

Agree to stop the enactment immediately if either of you feels uncomfortable or gets upset. People who are into kinky play use a *safeword,* a word that you wouldn't ordinarily utter that conveys "Stop right now." You don't want to use the word *stop*, because you might want to use that word as part of the fantasy—a stranger seduction, for example, or a naughty schoolchild being punished by an angry teacher—without halting the action. A safeword like *juniper berry* or *doghouse* might work better, because you won't accidentally say it. Of course, make sure the word is one you'll remember. (For more about fantasies and enacting them, see chapter 6, Stretching Boundaries.)

If you try something and it doesn't turn you on the way you'd hoped, just laugh about it afterward and try something else. Make the exploration part of the fun.

My husband and I, both in our midfifties, were in a rut and busy, not spending much time together. We decided to make an extra-special effort to improve our relationship and our sex life. I read The Sex Diaries by Australian sex therapist Bettina Arndt. In this book, someone gave out a challenge to have sex every day for one year. We decided to challenge ourselves. I kept a record, and at the end of the twelve-month period, we had some type of sexual contact on 344 out of 365 days. My husband achieved eighty-eight orgasms, which is not bad for someone who thought he was "losing it." I had heaps more orgasms. We have never returned to the boring and intermittent state that we previously were in.

HAVE MORE SEX, WANT MORE SEX

Haven't you noticed that right after a delicious sexual inter-action, you say to yourself (or aloud), "Wow, why don't we do this more often?" The fact is that the more regularly you indulge in sex, the more you'll enjoy it, anticipate it, and crave it. Just by scheduling it, you're defeating that sexual inertia that often inserts itself into an otherwise loving relationship.

If slow arousal is your challenge, you'll also find that the regularity of scheduled sex dates will make you feel ready for sex more quickly. Partially, that's the brain at work, and it's also a physiological response to having regular sex. Arousal leads to more and better arousal. Orgasms beget orgasms.

"GGG"

> GGG stands for "good, giving, and game," as in, "good in bed," "giving pleasure without expectation of immediate reciprocation," and "game for anything—within reason." GGG is about both partners in a relationship being honest and open with each other about their sexual interests and making a good-faith effort to meet each other's needs.
>
> —Dan Savage in *American Savage: Insights, Slights, and Fights on Faith, Sex, Love, and Politics*

Sex columnist and activist Dan Savage popularized the term *GGG*, and it's a useful concept for our age group. The more generous we are in bed, the more sexual generosity we can expect. But in order to be "good, giving, and game" and break out of the rut of predictable and unsatisfying sex, you have to identify what needs are not being met.

If that's difficult to tell your partner, try this:

1. Each of you sit down with paper and pen and finish this sentence privately: "Three things I'd really like to explore with you are..."

2. You read aloud your first item to your partner, starting by saying, "One thing I'd really like to explore with you is..."

3. Your partner reads his or her first item the same way.

4. Continue alternating, reading the second item.

5. You may want to continue with the third, or keep that in reserve for another time, if you have enough exciting ideas on board already.

6. Discuss what turns you on about your partner's request and what you'd like to try together.

7. Decide how and when you'll put one of these requests into action.

I've always held to the Dan Savage principle of being GGG. Although for myself I would add another G: Grateful. The second G would stand for Generous as well as Giving. My bout of impotence taught me that attention, enthusiasm, and caring about my partner's pleasure help make up for other shortcomings.

WHEN YOU DON'T WANT THE SAME THING

Jake told me that after thirty years with his committed partner, Roger, their desires had gone in different directions. Jake was only aroused by oral sex and didn't like anal penetration—either giving or receiving it. Roger was only satisfied through prostate stimulation. The solution they discovered on their own is one I've suggested to many couples since then:

Agree that every other time, you'll have the kind of sex that you like the best. On the alternate sexual encounters, you'll do exactly what your partner prefers. When it's your partner's turn, all the focus is on her or him and vice versa when it's your turn. This allows both partners to focus on the one being pleasured the entire time, and it's deeply intimate. You don't have to worry about running out of energy to return the favor—that will happen next time.

This works for all kinds of differences. One couple told me that they each felt aroused at totally different times of the day. They were at an impasse, both feeling stressed and dissatisfied. When I suggested that they alternate time of day instead of trying to compromise, they were relieved and eager to try it out.

WHEN COMMUNICATION BREAKS DOWN

This chapter so far has presumed that you and your partner are on the same wavelength, maybe even reading this book together, and any changes you want to make are shared. But what if you're feeling alone in your quest for better sex? Maybe your partner is so predictable that you can't stand it—or so different that he or she seems like a stranger. What if you'd like more sex, or different sex, or different behavior outside of the bedroom?

> *How about women treat us like men and don't be afraid to tell us the truth. Gently would be okay, but we need truth here. I wish we guys put it out there that we want the truth more than we wanted nice strokes (pun, sure) all the time for our ego.*

Shouldn't our partner just *know* how to please us after all this time?

Actually, partners often think they're doing exactly what we want, because we haven't told them otherwise. Though we may be so in sync at times that we think we're reading each other's minds, we're not—we're responding to longstanding habits, knowledge of each other's responses over the years, and knowing how to read gestures and voice tones. Too bad that doesn't always transfer to the bedroom.

If the problems have been building for a long time, you may not even know what's wrong, how to fix it, or what to try next. Nothing will change unless you decide to speak up.

TALKING ABOUT SEX

Even after thirty-three years with the love of my life, it was and can be frustrating to discuss the most simple and yet intimate things.

If you've attempted to change things and your partner is unwilling or nonresponsive, or you don't know how to ask for what you want, here's some help.

It may be easy to joke about sex and discuss other people's sex lives, but when it comes to expressing our own deep sexual feelings and desires to our intimate partner, we often become shy and scared. What if we express what we really want, and our partner thinks we're disgusting?

We have to learn to talk out loud about ways we want to change our sexual interaction, especially when the old ways aren't working for us anymore. These Dos and Don'ts may be helpful:

Do: Plan ahead to have "the talk." You could say, "I would like to schedule a time when we can talk about how sex has changed for us. Can we do this tomorrow afternoon?"

Don't: Blurt out, "We need to talk about our miserable sex life now."

Do: Plan ahead what you want to say, and practice saying it.

Don't: Assume you'll say the right thing when the time comes.

Do: Choose a neutral, nonsexual place for the discussion, where you'll have privacy and be able to face each other. If you anticipate that your partner will be nervous or defensive, choose his or her most familiar and comfortable room.

Don't: Have the discussion in bed or in a public place.

Do: Express yourself lovingly, without anger.

Don't: Say something in the heat of the moment that you'll wish you could take back.

I just did something stupid and told my partner out of the blue that I didn't really like our sex—I wasn't enjoying it all that much. He is hurt and is not talking to me.

Do: Express how your request will benefit you both.

Don't: Come across as whiney or selfish.

Do: Clearly and specifically state the problem in "I" statements that express your experience and your desire, such as:

- I'm realizing that I need more stimulation to get aroused. Can we go longer/use a vibrator/kiss more/spend more time touching?

- I love how you stroke my clitoris, but I need more allover touching before I'm ready to be touched there.

- I worry that my erection won't last, and worrying just makes it worse. Can we talk about how to give each other pleasure that doesn't depend on my erection?

- I'm sensing that I'm not doing what you need to get aroused. Can you tell me what you'd like?

- I can't have sex comfortably without lubricant, and I'm embarrassed to stop you when I need it. Can we make it a part of our lovemaking from the beginning?

- I'm feeling pain during sex, and I'd like to figure out a way that I can have the enjoyment without the pain.

- I know I used to like a soft/hard/fast/slow touch, but now I need it softer/harder/faster/slower.

- When we make love after a meal, it's harder for me to get aroused. Can we plan a morning time instead?

Don't: Start your sentences with "You…" and express the problem as something your partner does wrong, like, "You don't know how I like to be touched" or "You never kiss me anymore."

Do: Present your request as something that you both need to work on together, without assigning fault.

Don't: Blame or accuse your partner, which will just make your partner withdraw or retaliate defensively.

One time we were talking about the changes, and I said that if he'd been nicer to me, we would have had lots more sex, and he said that if we'd had more sex, he would have been nicer. I shake my head at our foolishness and the wasted opportunities. I wish we could go back and redo those wasted years, but since that's not possible, we are enjoying the sex and the improved relationship that we have now.

Do: Speak slowly, in a normal tone and volume.

Don't: Race through your points or raise your voice.

Do: Really listen to what your partner has to say.

Don't: Think about the next point you want to make while your partner is speaking.

Do: Restate what your partner is saying to make sure you understand and to validate your partner's point of view. For example, say, "I think I understand that you're saying..." or "I hear that you would like me to..." and paraphrase what your partner just told you.

Don't: Assume you understand each other without checking it out.

Do: Come to a resolution together, such as "Let's both suggest what we can try to make this better."

Don't: Decide what should happen next without your partner's input.

Do: End your talk with an action plan for trying a new solution, such as "Let's make love next time without the goal of intercourse," or "Let's have sex in the morning instead of after dinner," or the playful "When we watch TV, let's kiss during the commercials."

Don't: Leave the conversation with nothing resolved unless you need time to think about the next step. In that case, schedule the next conversation.

If these talking techniques don't work to resolve the problems, or they seem overwhelming, or your partner says no to your wishes:

> **Do:** Consult a sex therapist or relationship counselor. This could be the best way to improve your relationship—maybe save it.

> **Don't:** Give up or decide your problems can't be solved.

I'm female, sixty-five, married to the same man for forty-five years. My relationship with my moody husband had not always been satisfying, and I often dreaded the nights he wanted sex. We'd go weeks and sometimes months without sex. I deeply regret now that I didn't realize how much a robust, active sex life would affect our entire marriage.

WHY SEEK COUNSELING?

Sometimes trying to solve this on your own just doesn't work. If you can't seem to talk about your relationship problems without one of you getting angry or withdrawn, or if you can't seem to make the discussion happen, a few sessions with a counselor, therapist, or sex therapist could make the difference between a permanent impasse and a renewed relationship.

These professionals are used to helping couples resolve issues just like yours—they're highly trained, skilled, and intuitive. They can hear what you're having trouble saying and help you express it to your partner. They can help you understand and overcome barriers. They can clear pathways that for you seem hidden in brambles or poison oak. They can teach you coping skills, discussion tools, and even sex techniques that you haven't figured out on your own.

If your partner won't agree to get counseling, go on your own. You'll learn tools and strategies that will improve your relationship and your feelings about it. And often after one person reports back about how valuable this is, the other will agree to go.

How to find a professional:

- Ask your doctor for a referral. Your HMO may have counselors and therapists available within your plan.

- Ask friends to recommend a local counselor or therapist—you'd be surprised how many of them have been helped by counseling in their own lives.

- Find a certified sex therapist in your area at www.aasect.org.

Long-term relationships can take you on a never-ending journey where something new, exciting, and sensual can be found around every corner. It can be the longest, most exhilarating ride in one's life.

6

STRETCHING BOUNDARIES

Fighting your sexuality is like holding your breath: it can be done, yes, but not for long (when it comes to your breath) and not forever (when it comes to your sexuality).

—Dan Savage in *American Savage: Insights, Slights, and Fights on Faith, Sex, Love, and Politics*

If you imagine stretching the boundaries of your current sexual behavior, what comes to mind? What fantasy sets your brain and body sizzling? If you could try anything at all, with no repercussions later, what would you try?

Which of these is most true for you?

1. I like the fantasy, but I wouldn't want to do it in real life. I'll keep it to myself and just use it to stimulate myself mentally.

2. Although I don't really want to do this, the fantasy is very stimulating, and I'd like to tell my lover about it.

3. I would love to try this in reality, but it's scary. What if I don't like it? What if I do harm to my relationship?

4. I absolutely need to do this in real life. I'm living a lie without it.

Most of us have developed a habitual way of having sex by now—what we do and with whom is an expected routine. This may be fine, indeed fabulous. (If so, feel free to skip this chapter or just skim it out of curiosity. The same if you're already fully into an alternative lifestyle that is all you want it to be, and you don't need beginner level advice.)

For many people our age, though, familiar sexual habits have become restrictive over time, even deadening. Our sexual sensations feel dulled, both physically and emotionally. We long for something different, yet we have the lessons of a lifetime to overcome if we step outside the boundaries we were taught.

Rather than smash your boundaries, start by stretching them an inch at a time. Stretching your boundaries doesn't mean you have to get all-out kinky (unless you want to) or pursue new lovers (unless you want to). You can take small steps that give you a buzz of excitement without committing to a huge change that you're not sure about.

My husband was a gentle, strong, self-reliant man—but once in a while, he liked to have me tie his hands to the bedposts and ravish him. The bondage was more role-playing and fantasy than actual bondage, because we only used satin ribbon tied in loose bows or Velcro cuffs he could pull out of. He never felt truly confined, by choice. Because of abuse in childhood, he would have panicked if he didn't have an easy and obvious escape.

STEP ONE: FANTASIZE

When you're pleasuring yourself or having sex with a partner, imagine a scenario that turns you on. Give yourself permission to fantasize whatever thoughts, images, or activities get your heart and genitals thumping. Give yourself a free pass to imagine whatever your brain needs to get revved up and send the message to your genitals.

Read erotica related to your fantasy. Watch porn if you enjoy it. Whatever you're imagining, you can be sure there are books and films about your specific turn-on. Immerse yourself in the world you're fantasizing.

No one has to know what you're imagining unless you decide to share it, and this first step may be the only step you need. If not...

STEP TWO: SHARE YOUR FANTASY

If your fantasy is very different from the sexual desires and behavior that your partner knows about you, or if the two of you are not used to being sexually open with each other, there might be two risks of describing or sharing your fantasy.

1. Your partner might find your favorite sexy scene distasteful and shame you, or worry that you'll forsake the relationship to pursue the fantasy.

2. The fantasy might seem less sexy to you once it's no longer a secret.

So you need to know yourself and your partner well and already be sexually communicative before deciding to proceed. If the process feels scary yet exciting, take it slowly so that you can evaluate each small step before you take any giant leaps. Start by just telling part of your fantasy, or asking your partner to read an erotic story that turns you on because a character has the same fantasy that you do. If you sense that your partner would feel inadequate compared to the lust object of your fantasies (especially if the lust object is considerably younger or an ex!), concentrate on the body parts or actions rather than the person whom you're imagining.

If that goes well, tell more, or narrate your fantasy as a delicious dirty story between the sheets. You might enjoy writing it as an erotic scene.

After that, if your partner is eager to participate in your

fantasy, maybe you'll want to role-play a scene, as Donna George Storey and her husband did:

> *"Look at that pretty pink pussy all spread wide," he murmurs. "They see you all naked and exposed. They're touching themselves as they watch, because they know how much you like to show off."...*
>
> *Suddenly they are not alone in the room. The bed is surrounded by glittering eyes. An entire hockey team of horny college boys taking a lesson in how to please a woman from the coach's wife.*
>
> —Donna George Storey in "Invitation to Lunch" in *Ageless Erotica*.

Voicing this inner world of fantasy might be all you need to stimulate your responsiveness and turn up the heat. If not—if you need to turn the fantasy into reality, exploring kink or an open relationship or both—educate yourself through books, videos, workshops, and talking to people who are already into that lifestyle. The rest of this chapter will deal with making your fantasy a reality.

> *I am a seventy-two-year-old man still very interested in sex, as is my sixty-seven-year-old wife. For about twenty years my wife has spanked me, and I am forever grateful that she will give me this, because it removes all of my stress, and I love her more because of it.*

If you have a fantasy that would be destructive or dangerous if you enacted it in real life—to you, your partner, your family, your career—yet you feel you must make it real to be fulfilled, please talk to a sex therapist first. This may save you heartbreak and other repercussions by looking at where this fantasy comes from and helping you weigh the pros and cons of taking it further.

ARE WE NATURALLY MONOGAMOUS?

No group-living nonhuman primate is monogamous, and adultery has been documented in every human culture studied—including those in which fornicators are routinely stoned to death. In light of all this bloody retribution, it's hard to see how monogamy comes "naturally" to our species.

—Christopher Ryan and Cacilda Jethá in
Sex at Dawn: The Prehistoric Origins of Modern Sexuality

Our society says that monogamy—being sexual exclusively with one committed partner—is right, moral, and what separates humans from animals. But is it truly natural for human beings? If so, why do we struggle so hard to remain monogamous, and so often fail? The book *Sex at Dawn*—which I highly recommend—makes a strong and well-researched case that human beings are not and never have been *naturally* monogamous.

We boomers and seniors have widely varying ideas about what is acceptable in a relationship, including whether or not it needs to be sexually exclusive. Which of these is yours?

- We promise strict monogamy, and breaking that promise would be grounds for ending the relationship.

- We're usually monogamous, but if the right occasion occurs, we have a pass to enjoy a fling, a threesome, or whatever else we've agreed might be delicious.

- One of us has permission to step out of the relationship to satisfy a particular kink or need that the other doesn't share.

- We're in an open relationship, where sex with others is expected and accepted.

- We're in polyamorous relationships with more than one partner.

Twelve years after our last threesome, we still have a sort of standing agreement that if the right opportunity presents itself, we are open to nonmonogamy. The rules for this, still in place, involve communication about who and where.

Personally, I've been monogamous, and I've been in nonexclusive sexual relationships. I'm capable of both, and having lived both ways, I don't condemn either—or find either unnatural.

I know the heady delights of variety: the thrill of discovering and undressing a new lover, and the excitement of responding to pleasure from an unfamiliar touch. I also know the unsurpassed ecstasy of being so deeply in love that I don't want anyone except this one person whom I love. I know the intimacy of freely chosen exclusivity.

Having done both, and realizing that I'm capable of being happy both ways, I've resisted the temptation to fall into "my way is right and any other way is wrong." I also acknowledge that what was right for us when we were younger may not be right for us now, and that something new might emerge for us or our partners that we need to look at with an open mind.

I'm not pushing you to do something you consider repugnant or immoral—I only encourage you to explore what's right for you and not condemn those who choose another path. I hope the information here empowers you to do exactly that.

I'm seventy-four, HIV positive, male, bisexual, and in a relationship with another man. We keep the spark going by having an open relationship. He has another male partner. We cuddle and make love, and although my energy is low, due to age and the toll taken by HIV drugs, the sparks often fly because we're both kinky, and I have a large whips and chains collection!

DO WOMEN WANT VARIETY, TOO?

By Carol Queen, PhD

Some women, far from being hardwired for monogamy, find erotic value in novelty. New partners can awaken a snoozing libido quicker than anything, an insight that men have acknowledged forever.

Sex with many people is actually the most functional form of sex education for many in our culture. In a society that doesn't value or take seriously the responsibility to teach about pleasure, many of us still derive our most profound understandings about our own sexuality on the hoof, in the street, on the prowl.

I'm not the only woman who ever found value in exploring the diversity of experience granted by multiple partners. If we all had access to safe space to explore this way, we'd understand that some people are more monogamous by nature, while some are more open, polyamorous, nonmonogamous, or whatever term you give it.

Give thought to what you want from sex, what you bring to it, and what it would mean to have it when you wanted it. I wonder if this would make the world a better place. It surely seems that way.

—Carol Queen, PhD,
(www.carolqueen.com) is a sexologist, activist, author,
and founder of the Center for Sex and Culture
(www.sexandculture.org) in San Francisco.

EXPLORING NONMONOGAMY

If you're currently in a relationship, the first thing to consider is how solid it is. Be honest about that. Adding extra variables to the mix requires a really good foundation, and if you're not in the right place for that, nonmonogamy is only going to make it worse. It's also important that both of you are on the same page in terms of why you want to explore opening your relationship and how.

—Charlie Glickman, PhD, www.charlieglickman.com

First, *nonmonogamy* is not a five-syllable word meaning *cheating*. Tristan Taormino, in her excellent book, *Opening Up: A Guide to Creating and Sustaining Open Relationships*, explains the difference this way:

Cheating involves lying, deception, and breaking a commitment previously made. For nonmonogamy to be successful, everyone must tell the truth and respect the rules agreed upon. Consensual nonmonogamy means that all parties involved have agreed to the arrangement.

An open relationship is pretty much the opposite of cheating, because everything is out in the open and agreed to by everyone involved. Some folks of our age have always had open relationships. Other couples started out as sexually exclusive, but they decided to expand because they wanted variety; one partner was unable or unwilling to provide the amount or kind of sex that the other needed; or one partner had a particular desire that the other didn't share. Some couples in open relationships find that sharing details about encounters with other lovers actually intensifies intimacy between the primary partners; others prefer a "don't ask, don't tell" agreement. There's no one-size-fits-all.

> Mostly having other relationships has been easy. We committed to maintaining our relationship. Not to say there hasn't been some minor jealousy. We talk openly about who else we are seeing—it is just easier to know. At times we have shared details of our sexual connections with others. We both prefer open, honest, direct communication.

If you're interested in expanding your relationship from monogamous to open, *Opening Up* should be your essential guidebook. Be sure to answer its self-evaluation questions near the beginning of the book. *Opening Up* covers different relationship styles to consider, questions to ask yourself and each other, how to negotiate, and the types of rules you'll need to agree upon.

RULES?!

Yes, rules. Arnie told me that he and Ray had been in a monogamous relationship for decades. Ray was older than Arnie, and his sex drive diminished while Arnie's stayed strong. They agreed that together they would choose a lover for Arnie—someone who was already a friend of theirs and would not threaten the solidarity of Ray and Arnie's relationship. Arnie could enjoy sex with the friend, as long as all three agreed to these rules:

1. The friend had to meet with both men to discuss expectations and rules. If Ray did not feel comfortable after this discussion, the next step would not take place.

2. Sex with the friend could be only on the day of the week that Arnie was away from home for business anyway, so Ray would not be deprived of Arnie's company.

3. Sex with the friend could not take place in their house or even in the same town where they lived—only in a hotel out of town.

4. The arrangement could be cancelled at any time that Ray changed his mind.

These rules let Ray know that he came first in their relationship, and respect for his feelings was paramount.

If you and your partner were to make a nonmonogamy agreement, what would it look like?

Open, honest communication is a must, and we could not manage our play relationships without it. We've learned that there can be a tricky balance between letting a play partner know how much we've enjoyed our sexual encounter and saying something that makes one or the other of us feel threatened. The two guidelines that function here are being sensitive to each other's feelings and trusting the other to let us know when something we've said to or about a play partner starts to border on threatening or hurtful.

READERS TALK ABOUT THREESOMES

- *It seems that over the past ten years or so threesomes have become a rite of passage for many couples, almost like some kind of trust test for many. Threesomes are fun at any age, as are foursomes and moresomes, but it does take trust, common sense, and openness.*

- *No one should enter into a threesome just to please a partner. I've encountered a few older couples where it was apparent that one partner was simply engaging in order to please the other, and it rarely works out for anyone.*

- *I was very nervous about having that first real encounter with a woman. I wanted it to go well, I wanted to be with someone who knew what she was doing, and I wanted to feel attracted to the woman. Neither of us was convinced we could guarantee that kind of experience our first time out as swingers. We decided to "hire it done." We started following courtesans online and found women who we both felt were attractive and whose profiles said they would work with couples. This was an expensive option, but it met the criteria of safe (complete with condoms and dental dams, plus they are tested frequently), appealing, skilled, and incredible fun for the three of us.*

- *If you have a threesome with your new lover and if it doesn't work out, that is kinda okay. If you have been in an established relationship for five or ten or more years, then you both are entering a whole new ball game. The risks are higher. Don't take it lightly.*

- *What matters is open communication among all who are involved in the encounter, so if someone starts to feel left out, they feel free to say so. In any case everyone is looking out to be inclusive and create enjoyment for all involved.*

POLYAMORY

Polyamory is a modern word created by people who were involved in nonmonogamous romantic relationships where all the people involved knew and consented to the inter-laced partnerships.

—Loving More, www.lovemore.com

Tristan Taormino defines polyamory as "the desire for or the practice of maintaining multiple significant, intimate relationships simultaneously." It's not just about sex—there's an emotional connection also. As with other forms of ethical nonmonogamy, all partners know about and accept all other partners. Sometimes they're all close friends or consider themselves family.

Sometimes people come to polyamory (from Greek πολύ *[poly]*, meaning "many" or "several," and Latin *amor*, "love") because they have discovered that loving one person just doesn't work for them—it leaves them feeling unfulfilled, and often they leave a relationship because it can't be *everything* for them. They blame the relationship for being inadequate, and they move on to another person, usually with the same results.

Finally they realize or decide that one relationship does not have to be everything—they are capable of loving more than one person, and they are most fulfilled when they can express that fully.

I got so frustrated not being able to have a traditional relationship that would last even five years, including my marriage. It's painful to have to keep starting over. I want my relationships to last much longer. I've tried monogamy every way I could, and it didn't work for me. So about five years ago I started looking around and asking, "What else is possible?" I want relationships, not just sex. I've found ethical polyamory to fulfill my needs and wants.

Sometimes a polyamorous relationship emerges out of need: one person is less desirous or physically incapable of the sex that the partner desires, or one partner may be bisexual and wants a sexual connection with a gender other than the primary partner's. Sometimes the primary relationship is perfectly loving and satisfying except for That One Thing. Doing without satisfying sex can make a person feel incomplete, restless, and immensely sad. Opening up the relationship to allow for a new lover doesn't have to take away from the primary relationship—it can add to it instead. As many polyamorists say, the more love you give away, the more love you have to give.

An old boyfriend of mine told me that he and his committed partner were polyamorous. With her approval, he and I became sexual friends. I had struggled for several years with wanting to become sexual again after my husband died, and this seemed like a perfect solution. In fact, our dates have been wonderful, very satisfying.

A couple may shift from monogamy to polyamory when one of them becomes deeply attracted to another person. Rather than leave the original partner to pursue this attraction, squash down the attraction, or cheat, the couple decides to invite this new person to become part of their lives. This doesn't mean a *ménage a trois* (unless the couple wants that)—it just means that the three work out an arrangement allowing for the expansion of sexual and emotional boundaries.

Again, you need communication, rules, and respect. What does your primary partner need to feel loved, valued, and secure if you bring another person into your life? What do you need if he or she does the same? Most poly relationships give the primary partner veto power over a new lover. How will scheduling work? Be sure that safer sex is a part of your agreement.

Have a plan in case someone breaks the rules, because that can happen. How will you deal with it? If you don't have this part of the agreement, as awkward and unpleasant as it sounds, the person who breaks a rule may try to hide it out of fear and shame. That can put all of you at additional risk.

I'm a woman, age fifty-one, in my first poly relationship, and I love it. My girlfriend and I—both bi—have been together for seven-and-a-half years. She was poly before I met her. Our initial agreement centered on safe sex. With women we used dental dams and gloves. With men it was condoms for both oral and intercourse. However I had unprotected sex with a man I had been dating for six months, clearly breaking our agreement. I didn't tell my girlfriend right away. When I did, she was understandably angry. The three of us sat together and talked. It was a difficult point, but we worked through it. I have not broken another agreement.

When polyamory works, it can be ideal. When it doesn't work, it can be awful. "Poly-agony," a friend of mine called it. Honest communication is the key: with your partner, with your new lover, and with others who are already living this way and can give you advice.

I am a fifty-eight-year-old woman, married for forty-one years. About ten years ago, our relationship hit a snag. We pulled ourselves back together, and I decided to do some things that I wanted. I had been a devoted wife and mother for many years, but I had always wanted more sexually. During that time we met a single man who I was instantly physically attracted to. He became a friend to my husband and a lover to me.

The three of us have been together for ten years now. He is part of our family, and my grandchildren do not know a time that he was not around. Although we don't talk about our relationship to others, I believe most of our friends and family know that I have two "husbands." Over the years my husband has had medical issues that make sex more difficult, but we still have sex occasionally. I have a wonderful, fulfilling sex life with my lover.

SWINGING

Let's say that you're looking for a freer lifestyle, with multiple sex partners and little emotional investment in these relationships. That's what swinging is—sex with other people as an accepted part of *the lifestyle*, as it's called. Sex is often viewed as recreational—no-strings fun.

Swingers have communities, parties, clubs, conventions, websites, resorts, you name it. Swinging can encompass many different styles, from couples who only have sex in view of each other or only *swap* with another couple, to singles or couples enjoying many partners, to anything goes.

To play with another couple, we both have to feel enough of a spark or attraction to think it's going to work. Once in a while one of us will have a much greater positive reaction, while the other might be more neutral or even somewhat negative. Either one of us has veto power.

Go to a swing party, and you'll find rules: safer sex only, no means no, tell the host if anyone is out of line, and so on. If you want to have sex with someone who approaches you, go for it. If you don't, just decline politely. Often unpartnered men are not allowed at heterosexual private swing parties, but solo women are. Be sure you know and understand the rules at each event—and the rules that you and your partner have agreed on.

Our major rule is that we play together. This doesn't always mean in the same room, though that's our preference, but we're at the same event together and never far away. Part of our enjoyment in this lifestyle is seeing the pleasure our partner experiences, so we don't want to be left out. We're in love with each other, and we are each other's favorite sexual partner.

Although some swingers have been in the lifestyle throughout their adult lives, many couples and singles lived decades in monogamous relationships and now want to experience more sexual partners. They may say, "We have talked about this, fantasized about getting together with another couple, and now we are looking for an experienced couple to show us the lifestyle. We want to spice up our lives."

What excites me about swinging:
- *The visuals of group sex—arousing to watch and know I am being watched.*
- *Arousal and sex itself, watched or not.*
- *Wrapping bodies together for a night, without the stress of sniffing out and weighing the emotional needs and wants of a more committed relationship.*
- *Meeting people who are comfortable, often eager, to share their bodies for mutual sexual pleasure.*
- *Attending events where all of the above is encouraged.*
- *Having confidence that I have satisfied another person's sexual interests, not just my own.*

WHEN YOUR PARTNER WANTS YOU TO SWING

My new lover is a swinger. He's into threesomes, couples, naked resorts, and everything else. I was not brought up that way, but I am thinking about it. I have put in many hours reading about the swingers' lifestyle, and I finally feel that if I decide to participate, I am doing so based on my decisions and not being pushed into it by someone else. My guy is totally upfront about it and tells me it does not have anything to do with love. We arrive together as a couple and leave together as a couple, and there is no playing outside of each other's view.

Often one partner introduces the other to swinging rather than both of them coming to it simultaneously. If you're trying swinging on for size because your partner wants it, be very sure whether you're just going along to please him or her, or whether it's really something that excites you. If you don't want to do it, trying it anyway is not likely to change your mind.

Getting involved in nonmonogamous sex to save a troubled marriage is a road to disaster. Been there—it ended in divorce. Seeking to add excitement and adventure to a stable, happy relationship can lead to incredible benefits. Most couples we've talked with report that apart from the adventure of being sexy and having sex with others, their own sexual relationship has expanded in depth, frequency, repertoire, and excitement.

You don't have to dive in and go from monogamy to orgies and gang bangs—there are plenty of little steps you can take. You might start with an *off-premise* club, which meets in a hotel banquet room or other public place. There you'll meet other swingers, but nothing sexual happens right there, so there's no pressure. You have to take your private party off-premises (hence the name) if you want to do more than talk, flirt, dance, and make connections for later.

Swingers who want to do more than meet each other may go to an *on-premise* club or private party where sex is permitted. Even there, you don't have to jump in completely if you want to take small steps.

> One rule is pretty universal: no means no. If anyone doesn't want to do something, it doesn't happen. That's one of the things that make clubs, resorts, and conventions so safe and so much fun. Both of us can be sexy and flirty with the confidence that it's not going to lead anywhere we don't want to go. Most venues will permanently ban members who violate this basic rule.

Some couples agree to *soft swinging*, which means that when it comes to intercourse, they only do that with each other. The other limits on what they will and won't do vary: perhaps you agree to watch others without participating, or maybe certain kinds of sexual activity are okay with other people and certain kinds are not. A soft-swinging agreement is a good idea for the first time at a private swing party or on-premise club where people are free to have sex. You can always go in with the agreement that you'll just watch, or you can just have sex with each other in view of others, if you're comfortable with this. You decide.

> Condoms? Always. If we lose a few dates because someone doesn't want to use them, too bad. Even though our profile says condoms, there are couples who try to talk us out of it once we get together. We've held to our guns, and so far no one's walked out.

The most important part is to plan out ahead what you are and aren't willing to do, and keep negotiating this as it changes. Don't worry about losing the excitement of spontaneity—you'll have plenty of spontaneous decisions within your agreed framework.

Many swingers recommend Swingers Board (www. swingersboard.com) as a resource for learning more about swinging and finding like-minded individuals and clubs.

> Over-fifties (or over-sixties, or even seventies) have no need to worry about being perceived as too old. It's easy to find other swingers in those age ranges (even given that a lot of people tend to fudge on their real age when they put their profile together), and many lifestyle events and clubs have a wide age range. In our late sixties, we've never been the oldest people at a club or event. And no one has to look perfect. For the most part, there's great acceptance of enjoying whatever body a person is endowed with, although we do find most older swingers work hard to take care of their bodies, as do we.

A LITTLE KINKY?

At sixty-five, I'm mostly a vanilla guy, but my wife and I have recently gotten into some power exchange and mild kink: light spanking, light flogging, nipple clamps. We are both shocked how it is helping, giving us something to talk about, and providing spark. Give me edge and ways to get there. Give me some badass. Give me some power play toys. Give me a little Dark Eros even. And this from a 98 percent vanilla, traditionalist guy.

Maybe you need more physical stimulation than you're getting from your usual sexual habits, as pleasant and familiar as they might be. Or maybe it's the variety you crave, a new experience, a break in the routine, a thrill, a sense of danger, an adrenalin rush.

I am becoming kinky. I love that it adds a dimension to my sexual expression. I am fascinated by BDSM, role-playing, bondage, female domination. When I fantasize while masturbating I might take an image of a female dominating a male by tying him up and pegging him and use that as a starting point to a stronger fantasy that enhances my pleasure.

Exploring something a little kinky doesn't mean that you're throwing yourself over to the dark side (unless you want to)— and you don't even have to call it "kink" unless that appeals to you. The point is just to explore the intensified sensation and emotional high of taking a fantasy to the next level. If it doesn't feel right, end the scene with your safeword—a word you've agreed will halt the action immediately. If you see it through and then wish you hadn't, don't repeat it. If you find it tickles your fancy in ways that your fancy wants to be tickled, you can explore further.

> *I eventually met the man I stayed with for over seven years. He was turned on by me and he made my body sing. He was interested in types of sex I was unfamiliar with, such as light S&M, light bondage, and various sex toys. He found videos I had not known of, and introduced me to fetishes I'd known little about. I had wonderful orgasms with him as we tried various things. He had physical limitations but we never felt impaired by them.*

If your own curiosity or a partner is suggesting activities you've never tried, educate yourself first. Read one or more of the kink books I've recommended in the Resources section. Check out NewToKink.com, a paid subscription video site that helps beginners learn about BDSM, fetishes, and other kink topics. These videos offer graphic instruction and demonstration; they're not just talking heads.

If you have a good, woman-friendly sexuality store in your area, see if they offer workshops. Whether you're interested in an overview of kink or information about a particular practice or fetish, you may be able to find a workshop locally.

My partner's libido has jumped significantly in the past few years. This has led us to try new things in our sexual play. Our play used to be very vanilla. Now we engage in light bondage, discipline, and some other light BDSM activities. As a result, I can honestly say that our play is far more varied, intense, interesting, and pleasurable for both of us. My partner's jump in libido and increased areas of interest in sexual play have caused mine to increase as well.

INTRODUCING YOUR PARTNER TO YOUR KINKY SIDE

I broke up with my lover because I need the BDSM lifestyle badly, and she is basically vanilla. We're both grieving over our split, and she says she'll consider doing what I need if it will make it possible for us to be together again. Is it possible for a person who has no real interest in BDSM to adapt to it?

Yes, it's possible for a vanilla partner to shift into kinky sex, especially if you're both committed to making the relationship work, and your partner is open to a kinky turn-on.

Tell and show your lover what turns you on. Whisper your fantasy, or share erotica or porn featuring your activity of choice before actually doing a scene together. Solicit your lover's kinky fantasies about you, or suggest some scenes to see what gets a response.

Once your partner is ready and willing, start with small

steps rather than proceeding full-out. One of four reactions will follow:

1. Your partner loves it. Problem solved.

2. Your partner doesn't love it, doesn't hate it, and is willing to do it for you. Problem solved.

3. Your partner doesn't like it and finds it a turn-off. Problem needs negotiation; see if you can get a pass to indulge your kink elsewhere, then come home to your lover.

4. Your partner hates it and thinks you're a perv. Okay, now you know the relationship can't work.

If all goes well, be sure to do what your partner likes best more than half the time—don't make it always about you and your preferences.

TEN WAYS TO START HAVING KINKY SEX
by Kali Williams

1. Decide on a safeword that either of you can use to put a halt on the kinky play if you need to.

2. Give up control and be your partner's sex slave for the night.

3. Take control of your partner and use sexy, sensual, and kinky commands to direct the action.

4. If you usually keep quiet during sex, then let those sounds out! Usually loud? Try keeping quiet.

5. Use a silk tie to gently tie your partner's hands to the bed.

6. Role-play a classic power dynamic, such as doctor/patient, boss/employee.

7. In a safe public location, have a make-out session. Know that people might be watching, but you just don't care!

8. Lie together naked in the dark and whisper kinky fantasies into each other's ears in between kisses.

9. Go to a bar or restaurant and pick up your partner, pretending to be strangers. Get a hotel room to make it feel more scandalous.

10. Use nipple clips as a sexy, kinky addition to your bedroom play. But keep it light until you're both comfortable with more intense sensations.

—Kali Williams, aka Princess Kali,
a lifestyle Dominatrix and BDSM educator;
she runs three video websites: NewToKink.com,
Passionate U, and Kink Academy.

WISHING FOR A PERFECT WORLD

In my view, whatever consenting adults agree to do is fine with me. If it isn't sexy to me, *I* don't need to do it—but if you like it, you do it.

It just doesn't seem any more complicated than that.

If we could all just enjoy what we enjoy without moralizing about what other people enjoy, what a wonderful world it would be. It seems clear to me that the answer to "I think XYZ sex is disgusting!" is "Then don't do XYZ sex." How does it harm you or your relationship if others have a different behavior or point of view? It doesn't.

Unfortunately, our society marginalizes and condemns people who prefer sex in a way that's not mainstream. If you like it rough, or you enjoy swing parties or anonymous sex, or you get turned on by wearing a ball gag, you have to worry about being found out. Your sex practice of choice may be perfectly legal, but you may risk losing your job, your faith community, and sometimes the love of your family.

I'd like to go "Whoosh!" with my magic wand (or with my Magic Wand, though it doesn't go "whoosh") and change the world so that no one cares what you do in the bedroom, or dungeon, or wherever, as long as it's with other consenting adults.

The best I can do is encourage you to talk out loud—safely, maybe anonymously—about what turns you on and how it makes you feel. This will begin to change society's view by bringing it out in the open in a nonsensationalistic way.

You may help others who feel the way you do but don't dare pursue their desires because they've been told that they—the desires and the person desiring them—are weird, creepy, and immoral. They don't know where to turn.

I recall seeing an afternoon television show that interviewed a young trans man who knew from childhood that he was in the wrong body—a girl's body. He spoke eloquently about his experience and about being educated and inspired by an earlier television program when someone else had come forward to talk about the same thing. And yet, before this program started, the host said, "Warning: the contents of this show may not be suitable for children." Duh, yes, it was! That was the point, it seemed to me.

Even at our age, we need to know that we're all right. We may feel *different*, but that doesn't mean we have to condemn ourselves to not going after what is right for us.

It's essential to be honest with ourselves and our lovers about the kind of sex we need in our life. At our age, we realize that life is too short for bad sex, and sometimes we've got to follow our urges and fantasies. Often we're emerging from series of unfulfilling relationships, and that makes sexy, silver-haired folks like us say, "If not now, when?"

7

WHEN INTIMACY ENDS

I am eighty-one and haven't had sex for twenty years and now am almost obsessed with desire. I ordered vibrators for the first time. My husband had prostate surgery, and we don't have any sexual partnering. I can't talk to anyone about this for fear it will be seen as lunacy on my part.

If you're in a sexless relationship, look at what the lack of sex means to you. We can get orgasms on our own. Often what we miss the most is intimacy and connection, that feeling of bonding with another human being. Although this book is about sex, it isn't *just* about sex. (Even sex isn't ever *just* about sex.)

As an eight-year prostate cancer survivor with a wife with no interest in sex, I have turned to solo activities. During these times I fantasize about sex with my wife. I miss the closeness and resulting intimacy, afterglow, and being held by my loving wife.

We can still strive for that intimacy and connection even if what we used to think of as *sex*, however we used to define it, isn't in the picture. There may be health reasons, or the relationship changed for myriad other reasons. If the love is still strong and you are committed to staying with your partner, a companionate relationship may fulfill you. *Companionate* means you love each other, can't imagine being without each other, thrive within the relationship—but it doesn't happen to be sexual. You can express your sexuality in other ways—through masturbation, through a creative outlet, or, if your partner agrees, with another or others.

All this takes conversation and being willing to expose your vulnerability by expressing what you really want and need. The more complicated the issues, the more reason to involve a counselor, who has the skills and experience to guide you.

Some couples feel intimate, bonded, and perfectly content in a relationship that no longer includes sex. But more often, I hear from people whose sexual expression was shut down by health problems, relationship conflicts, or a partner's unwillingness or inability to be sexual with them.

I'm sixty-two, and my wife lost all interest in sex about fifteen years ago at menopause. She feels that this is natural and normal, and you don't try to fix normal. In my social circle this seems to be the common opinion. I don't know any men over fifty-five who are still having sex with their wives.

SEXLESS AND SUFFERING

My wife and I have been married for thirty-five years. I have never gotten as much sex as I would like, and for the past eight years it has been zero. My wife refuses to talk about it. I want physical contact and passion. I want to be crazy in love with a woman I can't take my hands off. I do not want an endless monologue of insignificant chatter that requires nothing more than an occasional "uh-huh" from me. Is happiness worth the cost of losing my daughters, home, friends, and half my stuff?

* * *

I have tried everything to get my husband of thirty-three years to talk to his doctor, go to counseling, anything to figure out his complete lack of desire. He gets very angry when I try to talk to him about it. He makes me feel like a freak, dirty, and not normal. I love my husband, but if I had known things would get this bad—well, I don't know what I would have done. I haven't seen a counselor by myself, because I fear that I'll be told to move out. My husband is a very kind man, but I am suffering. Everybody's got their cross in life to bear. I figure this is mine.

I often get emails and blog comments like the two above. One spouse is longing for sex, and the other doesn't want it anymore and thinks that's normal and fine from now on. The partner who still desires sex feels left behind, sometimes anguished and bitter.

How do you bring sex back into a relationship? Obviously, you have to communicate. It's important to know why your relationship has become sexless, and your partner (or you) may be reluctant to reveal the truth about that.

Of course we fear the worst: our partner doesn't find us sexy, doesn't love us, is having an affair, or wants out of the relationship. One or more of these may be true. Or it may be a health problem, physical discomfort, or diminished sexual function that's getting in the way, with the emotional repercussions of these problems. It may be anger in the relationship. Or it's a combination of any of these.

Getting a counselor involved to negotiate the tricky path to disclosure can be the key. Especially if the real issues have been under wraps for a while, don't expect that one good conversation will make it all better again. That's not a reason to give up—it's a reason to seek out a counselor or sex therapist who has the skills and experience to help you.

Which do you choose: the rest of your life with this partner without sex? Or taking a risk and doing the work to go after the possibility of more satisfaction and a closer relationship? If you do nothing, nothing will change.

My husband and I have been married for fifteen years and have basically been in a sexless marriage for the last seven years. What contributed to the lack of passion? So many things, including his chronic illness and ED. My desire and passion still burn strong at fifty, and it is killing me to think that my vitality is being wasted. I know the options, but I am paralyzed by the possible consequences of leaving the marriage. I know I cannot continue to live this way for much longer without being touched and experiencing the joy of physical connection with a person who is equally as passionate, spiritual, and creative as I am.

A MESSAGE FROM A PHONE SEX OPERATOR

Many of my callers are lovely older men who would really rather be sharing their fantasies with their wives. Very few of them would ever consider an affair, and they are even hesitant to call someone like me. I find this incredibly sad. When I ask them about it, many tell me that they've been open about their desires and that their wives don't feel comfortable with their bodies or their sexuality. Some of the women aren't interested in anything beyond traditional intercourse with the lights out, and often desire for that fades, so they end up shutting out their partners.

A MESSAGE FROM A PHONE SEX OPERATOR

CONT.

Many of these men would be happy with some shared sensuality, like just hugging or holding hands or giving their wives a massage, or even just talking, perhaps while masturbating. These men tell me that they love their wives' bodies, not in spite of but because of the changes that their bodies have gone through. Some will say, "Her body is so powerful— and the changes remind me of how beautiful and strong she is, and our history together."

Some of the men crave prostate stimulation, and they claim their wives would never consider the use of a sex toy, even if she didn't need to be involved with it, like a butt plug. I don't believe anyone should have to consent to sex they don't find enjoyable, but I do think we can learn a lot by being open to our partners.

I wish there was some way that I could reach out to the partners of my callers and tell them what amazing, loyal, giving, and loving husbands they have, and how they could do some very small things to reinstate closeness with these men.

CAN WE FIX IT?

I have never lost my desire to have sex, and I think about it often. I also often think about seeking a divorce, but that appears so selfish and disloyal to someone I have been with so long. To divorce for sexual desire, is that crazy? Honestly if I could have a sexual surrogate, I would. I know convention and society do not approve of such thoughts or actions. It is certainly no fun to be unilaterally relegated to celibacy!

If you and your partner are a monogamous couple, yet one of you wants sex and the other doesn't want it and doesn't want to work on it, the relationship is in trouble. When the sexual intimacy of a bonded couple shuts down and the decision is nonconsensual, many fears, needs, and regrets surface, such as these:

- Loss of intimacy

- Loss of trust

- Fear of abandonment

- Confusion

- Emotional pain

- Sexual frustration

- Avoidance of touching and affection

- Avoidance of communication

- Blaming oneself

- Blaming the partner

- Sadness

- Despair, depression

- Resentment

- Questioning whether to stay in the relationship

- Getting needs met outside of the relationship

- Suspicion

- Loneliness

- Lack of self-worth

- Estrangement

- Magical thinking: it will be all right tomorrow

Any and all of these lead the relationship to the brink of dissolution. Even if the couple stays together, there's no harmony, no connection, and one or both of you stay unhappy.

The first solution is to work with a counselor or sex therapist to find out what the real issues are that are disrupting the relationship, repair them if possible, and figure out whether you'd be happier apart or together. This might not be quick or comfortable, but the growth and understanding can't be underestimated. Definitely do this. If your partner won't go, go on your own.

Once you're satisfied that you understand the issues and have some tools for resolving them, you may decide to stay together—or not. If you do, you may agree to work on becoming sexually connected again. Or you may agree to stay together without sex and relax your monogamy agreement, so that the partner who still wants to enjoy sex can do so.

The other solution may be to dissolve the relationship to let both partners find happiness separately. It will hurt horribly, but down the road, you may realize that it gave you the best chance for happiness in the future.

> *I met my current husband when we were in our fifties. The experimental sex during our dating was very unsatisfactory. I had explained to him that I was very sensual and enjoyed sex as often as possible. He did not believe in sex before marriage, but after the "I dos" it would be fine. It wasn't fine. After only a year into marriage, and after trying several drugs for ED that did not work, he gave up trying.*
>
> *Oral sex had been the only way I could climax. Now, he won't kiss me or touch me, or even flirt. He thinks that all that leads up to sex, and he feels like a failure with sex. I have tried to explain the intimate things I needed. We love each other and respect each other. But I continue to climb the walls with sexual frustration.*
>
> *I do occasionally use a vibrator, but not in my husband's presence as he stated he is not comfortable with that. I feel stuck sexually and wonder how I will live the rest of my life without sex. I have contemplated an affair. I remain conflicted and frustrated.*

WHEN YOU CAN'T FIX IT

We never saw this coming. My wife had multiple surgeries that ended sex abruptly. Her last surgery left her paralyzed from the waist down. I became a primary caregiver, and this has destroyed my own health. Sex is just a thing of the past. I feel like all I am good for is fighting battles and meeting needs. I have suffered great depression and resentment because of the hand life has dealt me. I love her just as I promised her I would forty years ago, but I live in depression and despair, with little to offset the aftermath of this nightmare.

No, we never see this coming. But as psychotherapist Larry LeShan, PhD, says, "You come to what all human beings face sooner or later. Everybody faces this when they get old enough."[18] LeShan, who has had much experience with people and families in extreme physical distress, recommends getting professional help, both to cope with the depression and loneliness and to see how you can create a life with your partner that nurtures both of you.

A good therapist will help you, support you, give you coping strategies for the suffering that both of you are experiencing, and help you go forward in a more positive way.

NEGOTIATING A CHANGE FROM MONOGAMY

Some couples agree that in case one person no longer desires or is capable of sexually fulfilling the other, sex outside the marriage is permitted. Other couples have no such agreement, although one person wishes for it, and the other wishes that the whole subject of sex would go away.

Let's say that you want to stay in a sexless relationship because in other ways, it's a good one. When cheating seems to be the best option, I encourage you first to try to negotiate a compromise. Try expressing something like this in your own way: "You say you're done with sex. I'm not! I want to stay with you, but I am not willing to give up my sexuality. Let's see a therapist together to explore ways that we can bring sex back into our life together." If your partner says no and just repeats that she or he is done with sex, you might add this, if it's the way you feel:

"If you are not interested in working this out together, the only way I see that we can stay together is if I get my needs met elsewhere, discreetly and safely, with no upheaval to our relationship. I promise not to fling this in your face, not to embarrass you, not to tell you anything that you don't ask me—and to be honest with you if you do ask me.

"Would you please think about whether you can agree to that? When you're ready, let's talk about what boundaries you need me to respect so that you feel loved and secure going forward."

Realize that this is the beginning of a whole new conversation, not the ending. Your partner may say, "Do what you need to do, but I don't want to know about it," as some do; if so, planning and discretion are essential. If your partner wants to know, carefully discuss what should or should not be revealed. Be sure you understand each other. Surprises here are relationship killers. (Please read chapter 6, Stretching Boundaries, and don't skip the part about setting up rules and boundaries. Then read *Opening Up: A Guide to Creating and Sustaining Open Relationships* by Tristan Taormino.)

> *My wife's severe medical conditions ended the intimate side of our marriage many years ago. I have not been able to make love or even romantically hold my wife for roughly the last twenty years. I have found outside sources—a local massage parlor, and a couple of times I had sex with someone I met on Craigslist. But to have actually made love to a woman or really enjoyed it, I have to say no. I have these urges now and then, and yes, I give in to them, but I would much rather have my wife back. Since that's not possible, then someone close in age, who either lost her husband, or is tending to him at home and in a similar situation, wanting intimacy but not wanting to give up her husband.*

WHEN IS IT OKAY TO CHEAT?

I can think of about a dozen women who kept their marriage but stepped out with me to have their sexual needs fulfilled. One woman said she and her husband had not had sex in eight years, and she missed it. I've also met ladies online who did leave their sexless marriage then went online to meet a man to solve that drought situation. They tell me the husbands had lost any desire for sex. No clue whether that is a physical thing or something from the relationship dynamics. It seems all too common.

If your sexual needs are not being met, and you can't get your partner to work on changing that, and your partner refuses to give you a pass to go outside the relationship for sex and insists that you honor your monogamy agreement, you feel stuck. If it's a bad relationship for these and other reasons, get counseling on your own to help you decide whether leaving would be better than staying. A clean, honest break is usually better than living a life of deception and fear that you'll get caught. And you probably *will* get caught.

I endured a sexless marriage for ten years or so, then stepped out but kept the marriage. She found out, we sepa-rated, reconciled with her determined to be more sexual— and was. But she couldn't live with my betrayal, and we divorced after twenty years.

If you want to stay in the relationship because it's good for other reasons, though, you may find yourself deciding that cheating is a better solution than sexless misery. Readers: don't come down on me for this viewpoint—I'm not condoning infidelity if you have an agreement of exclusivity, but I know from your emails that it sometimes comes to that. Some of my readers have told me that going outside the relationship for unmet sexual needs lets them stay with a partner whom they love very much.

Let me pass the buck to Dan Savage, whose skin is thicker than mine if you get angry at the idea that it's ever okay to cheat:

> *The rules for cheating spouses—the circumstances under which a spouse has a right to cheat (or isn't entirely in the wrong to cheat)—are fairly limited. Cheating is permissible when it amounts to the least worst option, i.e., when someone who made a monogamous commitment isn't getting any at home...and the sex on the side makes it possible for the cheater to stay married and stay sane. An exception can be made for a married person with a kink that his or her spouse can't/won't accommodate, so long as the kink can be satisfied safely and discreetly. Someone who meets the criteria and cheats is merely a cheater (with cause); someone who doesn't and cheats anyway is a cheating piece of shit (CPOS).*
>
> —Dan Savage, in his column at www.slog.thestranger.com [19]

SEX WITHOUT INTIMACY

There is no communication—he wants it and expects it with no frills. No warning, no tenderness, no talk, no way. For me, it has been horrendously painful—mentally and physically. He says he loves me, that he wants sex—but I need tenderness, time, and touch. Without those, attempts at sex cause pain. When one person needs a change, the other's dismissal is one mass of pain and profound loss.

Most of this chapter has been about relationships without sex, but sometimes it goes the other way: there is plenty of sex—maybe good sex, maybe bad sex—but the rest of the relationship is a shell of what you want.

Our long marriage was not a happy one for me as he was manic-depressive, rarely took any meds, and emotionally abused me. But he enjoyed having sex, and we had it almost daily, sometimes several times a day. Most of the time, I just did it to keep the peace. On good days he was a good lover and helped satisfy me. Most of the time, though, I just wanted the session to be over.

The bottom line is what I frequently say: if not now, when? If the relationship isn't loving and nurturing, if there's no emotional connection, if you're being abused or neglected, you deserve better. A counselor can help you retrieve your self-esteem and the courage to leave your relationship, if this would be better for you.

A THERAPIST'S ADVICE: WHEN NOTHING SEEMS TO WORK

By David M. Pittle, PhD, MDiv

If one person's needs are being ignored in the sexual realm, it's likely that they're not being met in most other parts of the relationship as well. Both people need to be meaningfully open to change to meet the other's needs if there's to be any hope for a loving relationship.

When the relationship is unfulfilling and the other person won't work on it, your choices are to continue living in an unsatisfactory way or to bring the problem to a head. Be aware that this may lead you to a single life—which may happen anyway, if your partner is also dissatisfied.

Take these steps first:

1. Inventory your needs which are not being met. Accept that your partner is not targeting you to make you miserable. Your partner probably does not understand your needs—he or she may get the words, but not the emotions. Begin with the expectation that he or she would be glad to fulfill your needs once fully understood. This allows you to begin engaging from a position of alignment, not opposition. You're aiming to engage your partner in a new learning process.

2. Confront your partner with honesty and without rancor or anger, and expect the same in return. The surest way to sabotage the process is to allow either person to treat the other with a semblance of contempt, or to assign blame.

3. Recognize when you are digging yourself into a hole. Then stop digging. It sounds so simple, but it isn't. Quite often, you've each dug yourself into a hole of vituperation, anger, hurt, and sadness by now, and it will be difficult to get out of the hole.

4. Negotiate changes. It is almost always the man who has the most difficulty acknowledging the justice of the woman's point of view, her needs.

Counseling is almost an imperative at each stage of this process. First, it is difficult, if not impossible, for either person to truly hear the other and negotiate changes without help from a professional. Second, whether this results in an improved relationship or a decision to end the relationship, either or both of you will need help restructuring your lives.

—David M. Pittle, PhD, MDiv
is a therapist in San Rafael, CA, who has been helping people with sexual and other issues for over thirty years.

I didn't realize how unhappy I was until my husband dropped the bomb on me. I had asked a question about our close-ness as a couple, and the answer, after a long, uncomfort-able pause, was, "I don't love you anymore." Don't ever do it the way my husband did, which was to begin an affair at work and keep it and his feelings hidden until I started to realize something was amiss, and then deny the affair while pretending to work on the relationship at counseling.

* * *

At this point my ex is dating the woman who broke up our marriage and family. My grown children are having one hell of a time adjusting to that, while my ex seems bliss-fully unaware of their pain. If he had waited to date until after everything was final, there would be much less of a problem. So finish what you started—properly, legally—and try to understand how the relationship met its demise. Do the homework before moving on to a new relationship.

SHOULD I STAY OR SHOULD I GO?

How many of these are true?

- I feel lonelier when I'm with my partner than when I'm alone.

- We keep rehashing the same issues and nothing ever changes.

- I feel like I'm wasting my life.

- I've known for years that our marriage was a mistake.

- I'm happy only when my partner isn't with me.

- My partner is emotionally abusive—tries to make me feel worthless.

- My partner is verbally abusive—insults me and demeans me.

- My partner is physically abusive—hits me, injures me.

- My friends and family have advised me to leave my partner.

- My partner isolates me from my friends and family.

- I get a sick feeling in my gut when my partner approaches me.

- I am afraid of my partner.

- I am staying with my partner only because I'm afraid to go.

- I am staying with my partner only because I don't have the means to support myself.

- My partner engages in self-destructive behavior.

- My partner engages in behavior that's destructive to our relationship.

- My partner is addicted to drugs or alcohol and won't get help.

- My partner's pornography habit is out of control.

- My partner lies to me.

- I keep catching my partner in deceptions.

- My partner engages in behaviors that are causing us financial ruin.

- My partner insists that he or she will change but keeps repeating destructive patterns.

- I want to hurt my partner.

- I engage in behavior that's destructive to our relationship.

- I deceive my partner.

- Sex with my partner is demeaning.

- Sex with my partner is nonconsensual.

- I dread sex with my partner.

- I feel worse after sex with my partner than if we don't have sex at all.

- Sex with my partner is nonexistent.

- My partner doesn't love me anymore.

- My partner is in love with someone else.

- We've been in therapy, but nothing changed.

- I'm in love with someone else.

- I don't love my partner enough to work on this relationship anymore.

- I don't love my partner anymore.

If you find yourself agreeing to items in this list—or if your eyes fill with tears just reading it—consider moving out of the relationship. If there's still a connection between you, be sure you've exhausted all attempts to fix it first, especially therapy. But if you know that the love is gone, the bonding is over, and a future with this person fills you with dread or despair, then the best option for you is to get out.

After twenty-eight years of marriage, I moved out this past week. At sixty-six, I finally admitted to myself how unhappy I'd been for years. Unfortunately, inertia had kept me in place and, perhaps, fear of the unknown, loneliness, and financial problems. But because I'd had a recurrence of breast cancer, I realized that however many years I have left to live are very precious to me. I didn't want to waste any more time feeling trapped in a bad situation.

If there is abuse, violence, or fear in your relationship, consult a domestic abuse hotline or your local police to learn your options and get immediate help. Do not stay in an abusive relationship, hoping it will get better. It will get worse instead.

Many people, particularly women, cling to a bad relationship out of fear of the unknown. Please don't let that be you. Your self-esteem may be so damaged that you don't think you deserve better, or can ever find better. Getting therapy on your own will help you rebuild your feelings of self-worth and create a vision of a new life that allows the joy to enter.

It's also true that many times, what we see as problems in the relationship are actually problems within us. Until we fix them, we'll take those problems with us out on our own and into the next relationship. That's even more reason to work with a therapist.

I'm thirty-five years into a marriage. My wife was always orgasmic. But by menopause, she was totally without libido and had multiple medical problems. Masturbation is all there is for me if I want to stay in the marriage.

But now, after sixty, I'm educating myself about all things related to older women: vaginal dryness, hormone therapy (not an option for us), and sex therapy. Communication, it seems, was where I dropped the ball. I didn't want to bother her due to her numerous miseries. Big mistake! Now, we're talking about seeing a sex therapist and doing the intimacy exercises that are not sexual, but that bring intimacy back between us. I feel we can find common ground and achieve some level of sexual fulfillment together.

I've joined a gym, exercise at home, too, and walk two miles a day. I have a huge amount of energy. Before, I was too tired and depressed to even think I could find intimacy. All of us should focus on getting ourselves into our best physical condition when dealing with stressful aspects like this. More self-respect equals a better chance of success.

YOU AND
YOUR DOCTOR

About half of all sexually active men and women aged fifty-seven to eighty-five in the United States report at least one bothersome sexual problem; one third report at least two. Yet doctors rarely address sexual concerns in older adults, particularly in women.[20]

And—

A total of 38 percent of men and 22 percent of women reported having discussed sex with a physician since the age of fifty years.[21]

Getting older isn't in itself the problem—it's the array of medical conditions and treatments that wallop our sexuality. Chronic pain, movement limitations, medications, surgeries, reduced blood flow, fatigue—all these and more can leave our sexuality behind, physically and emotionally.

In my ideal world, we'd say to our doctor, "This [insert medical issue] is causing [insert sexual limitation symptom]. Let's fix it, because my sexuality is a vital part of my quality of life."

In reality, though, when we need medical help for sexual problems at our age, we encounter an array of obstacles. The first and most obvious is that the doctor doesn't ask how we're doing sexually and we don't bring up the subject. We're too embarrassed, or we don't think a doctor can help us, or our medical appointments are too rushed to let us edge our way gingerly into a sexual question. If the doctor doesn't bring up sexuality, the topic usually stays under the covers.

A survey of 1,154 gynecologists revealed that only 40 percent ask their women patients whether they are experiencing sexual problems and only 28.5 percent routinely ask about their sexual pleasure[22]—and that's across all ages. I'd make an educated guess that the numbers are much lower when the patient is our age. Even more cringe-worthy: "A quarter of ob/gyns reported they had expressed disapproval of patients' sexual practices."[23] Oh, great. How will that encourage us to bring up the subject? But bring it up, we must. As sex therapist Marty Klein, PhD, says, "Let the docs deal with their discomfort. They're getting paid, and it'll benefit their personal lives."[24]

If you're a doctor reading this book and wondering how to bring up the subject of sex with your older patients, here's a question guaranteed to get results: "How has sex changed for you lately?"

A doctor who is considerably younger may not view us as sexual beings and is likely to assume that we don't have a sex life, or care about it. The doctor won't think to ask us about sex, concentrating on helping us treat our ailments. It's up to us to start the conversation.

We can overcome our own reluctance by preparing ahead what we want to say. Writing down our questions is a good strategy. Then we need to assert ourselves. When another issue is the reason for the appointment, a good plan is to say at the beginning, "I have something else I want to discuss with you. Let's leave time for that." Now you can't back out.

We must commit to bringing up our sexual issues assertively and unapologetically. Only this way can we help ourselves, help our doctors know what we need (and want!), and—ultimately—help our generation and those that follow.

Even then we may run into what seems to be a dead end: our doctor may not know how to help us with a sexual issue. Again, it's in our court. Please practice this statement:

If you can't help me, please refer me to someone who can.

When I first began to experience ED, I assumed it was a psychological etiology and did all the "right things" that I would recommend to a client—I am a sex therapist after all. When that didn't help, in a flash of awareness, I realized that it was the new medications I was taking for blood pressure and Type II diabetes that were causing the problem.

For a while, just not taking the meds on the day I expected intercourse helped. But eventually it wasn't enough. So I visited a urologist. He just wrote a script for Levitra and assured me that would suffice. The Levitra didn't work, so he next prescribed Edex, the penile injection. That did help, but it is expensive and the shelf-life is short.

That exhausted his knowledge. He didn't know about vacuum therapy. He was shocked when I asked him about penile implants: "I'll have to find out more about that and get back to you." He knew nothing about psychological issues.

He had no idea that "older" people still had sex. In fact, he was surprised that I even wanted sex. I've had similar experiences now with a second urologist. But equally shocking, several of my women clients have reported similar lack of knowledge in their gynecologists.

I'm a doctor's daughter and a doctor's sister, and doctors have literally saved my life. I believe that most doctors are doing their best to help their patients heal what ails them and enjoy the best quality of life. They're well educated, they are constantly updating their learning as the world of medicine changes, and they care about their patients.

However, the lack of sexuality education in medical training is appalling—and little or none of it specifically addresses sex and aging.

That's where the problem starts, but we can make sure that the story doesn't end there. We need to talk out loud about our sexual needs and problems that might have a medical solution, and not go away defeated. We can't let embarrassment stop us from describing vaginal pain or erectile problems, even if our doctor looks like he's barely shaving.

We also have to take responsibility for reporting to our doctors when we're having trouble with function or libido, because sexual problems can be the first warning sign of a serious underlying illness that can and needs to be treated—for example: diabetes, heart disease, an infection, urogenital tract conditions, and cancer.[25] Other health conditions that cause sexual problems are high blood pressure, underactive or overactive thyroid, lung disease, depression, kidney disease, chronic alcoholism, multiple sclerosis, atherosclerosis, and more.[26]

The point is this: **If there's any change in your libido, arousal, or sexual functioning, please consult your doctor.**

WHEN MEDS ARE THE CULPRIT

Medications themselves may cause sexual problems. Most of us are taking medications regularly these days—people over sixty are likely to be on three different meds.[27] These are among the drugs that can have sexual side effects: [28]

Cholesterol-lowering drugs: Statins and fibrates prescribed to treat high cholesterol can also affect the production of sex hormones such as testosterone and estrogen, resulting in reduced arousal, erectile dysfunction, and difficulty achieving orgasm.

Blood pressure medications: Many blood pressure drugs can have sexual side effects. Diuretics can affect the flow of blood to the genitals and cause erectile dysfunction, female arousal problems, and orgasm difficulties. Beta blockers can affect testosterone levels and the nerve impulses associated with arousal.

Antidepressants: Antidepressants can cause decreased libido in any gender, erectile dysfunction and difficulties ejaculating in male bodies, and difficulties in arousal and orgasm for female bodies.

Antihistamines: Drugs used to treat allergies, including over the counter drugs, can cause vaginal dryness and erectile dysfunction.

Tranquilizers: Drugs used to treat anxiety can reduce libido and cause erectile dysfunction and female arousal difficulties.

Antifungals: Drugs used to treat fungal infections can cause erectile dysfunction.

Anti-ulcer drugs: Drugs used to treat acid reflux, heartburn, and ulcers can cause low libido and erectile dysfunction.

Heart medications: ACE inhibitors, nitrates, beta blockers, and calcium-channel blockers can affect erectile function, arousal, and libido. (For more, see chapter 11, Heart, Brain, Joints, and Sex.)

Never just stop the medication that is causing the unwanted sexual side effect. You can worsen the original medical condition that warranted this medication. "Do not stop taking any prescribed medicine without your doctor's advice," advises pharmacist Paul Roberts. "If you suspect your medication is interfering with your sex life, it's time to have a conversation with your doctor. Often lowering the dose may be possible, and the side effects will lessen. More likely is your provider can change you to something else that won't have that side effect. Rarely do you just have to live with it."

Ask your doctor or pharmacist about the best time to take your medications so that they affect sexual response or sexual function less. "Sometimes timing can make all the difference in preventing side effects from interfering with your sex life or daily life," says Roberts.

Level with your doctor about the sexual side effects and

that you value your sex life. Be clear and determined, and not confrontational. Assume that your doctor is willing and able to assist you and just needs to understand what the problem is and how important it is to you.

HERBS FOR SEXUAL ENHANCEMENT
by Paul Roberts, RPh, MS, Certified Geriatric Pharmacist and nutritionist

Some herbs are reputed to enhance sexual libido and function. Do they work? Herbs for sexual function are rarely used alone—they're found with several others in combination. Therefore it's difficult to determine which individual ones work, and adequate studies for safety are generally lacking. Fortunately herbs have generally mild effects and a good safety record overall, compared to prescription medications.

Be sure to tell your doctor what herbs you're taking or considering taking, because they may interact with another medication you're taking or aggravate a condition you have. **Avoid these if you have hormone dependent cancers or other hormone-linked medical conditions**.

These herbs are commonly used for sexual function:

Tribulus (Tribulus terrestris) "Puncture Vine"

Uses: to treat impotence and infertility. Tribulus is widely used in combination with other herbs for sexual dysfunction in men.

Contraindications: Do not use if you are diabetic (it may lower blood glucose levels), take lithium, or have benign prostate enlargement or prostate cancer. Tribulus may interact with some heart and blood pressure medicines, such as beta-blockers, calcium channel blockers, digoxin, and diuretics. Avoid this herb for sexual dysfunction in women, as it's likely to aggravate the condition.

Conclusion: Although there is little scientific evidence that it works, Tribulus is possibly effective for men and may be worth a trial for up to 8 weeks if you do not have any of the contraindications.

Korean ginseng (Panax ginseng)

Uses: to improve erectile dysfunction, libido, sexual arousal in women, and orgasmic function.

Contraindications: Avoid if you are taking blood thinners or have autoimmune disease. Avoid if you have schizophrenia unless prescribed by your doctor.

Cautions: Use only under medical supervision if you are taking antidepressants, antipsychotics or are diabetic. It may cause insomnia and increase the effect of caffeine.

Conclusion: Adverse effects rarely reported in doses of 500 mg to 2,000 mg for four weeks to six months. Found to significantly improve sexual function over four to twelve weeks. Libido, orgasmic function, and sexual satisfaction have been shown improved over eight weeks. Ginseng can be considered for improving ED in men and enhancing sexual arousal in women if you do not have any of the contraindications or cautions.

Maca (Lepedium meyenii)

Uses: for impotence, as an aphrodisiac, and to relieve stress. Maca root in dried, processed form has been consumed by Peruvians regularly for several thousand years.

Cautions: Although traditionally used to establish female hormonal balance, no studies have been done in women.

Conclusion: Maca is possibly effective for increasing libido and increasing sperm amount at 1.5 to 3 grams daily of the dried powdered root. More studies are needed to verify other uses. Likely safe (in the dried form) for short term, up to three to four months. Due to widespread use and safety, in spite of lack of studies, combinations with Maca may be worth a trial in healthy individuals.

Chrysin "Passion Flower"

Uses: for impotence and increasing testosterone. It is purported to inhibit the conversion of testosterone into estrogen, however studies that show this are lacking.

Contraindications: Avoid with prescription aromatase inhibitors (Femara®, Arimidex®, Aromasin®) because it may increase the drug's effect. May interfere with anticoagulant, platelet treatments or cause low blood pressure. Avoid if you are immu-nosuppressed or immunocompromised.

Cautions: May increase levels of some drugs cleared by the liver enzyme "Cyp1A2" including caffeine. Ask your pharmacist or doctor if this could affect any of your prescriptions.

Conclusion: Avoid this herb until more is known.

Wild Yam (Dioscorea villosa)

Uses: to increase energy and libido in women.

Cautions: Claims that Wild Yam is a natural progesterone or has progesterone effects are not supported by studies.

Conclusion: No reports were found of adverse effects when used in appropriate doses for short term. However, Wild Yam is not converted to hormones in the body as is commonly believed, only in the laboratory. Avoid this product.

Damiana (Turera diffusa)

Uses: to prevent and treat sexual dysfunction and as an aphrodisiac.

Cautions: The research studied Damiana in combination with other ingredients, however studies of the herb alone are lacking.

Conclusion: May be safe in appropriate doses for short term, but possibly avoid this herb until more is known.

[For a longer version, see www.NakedAtOurAge. com, with "herbs" in the search box.]

IS HRT FOR YOU?

You *and* your medical provider need to decide together whether hormone replacement therapy is the right option for you, and, if so, in what form. So many factors go into this decision that I can't possibly give you a simple answer. You need to decide in the context of your symptoms, your medical conditions and risk factors, concerns based on your family history, and more. What hormones are you lacking, and to what degree? How is this affecting you? What are the pros and cons in *your* situation?

HRT for Women

Hormone replacement therapy for women may be estrogen only or a combination of estrogen and progestin. Often started at perimenopause to alleviate symptoms of hot flashes and vaginal dryness, HRT can remain helpful after menopause to combat bone loss and vaginal thinning and dryness.

However, research studies starting with the Women's Health Initiative in 2002 have called into question the benefits versus the risks from HRT. Combined estrogen and progestin and estrogen-only therapy may increase risk of stroke, deep vein thrombosis, gallbladder disease, and urinary incontinence. It does not protect against heart disease as once thought. Estrogen-only therapy increases the risk of endometrial cancer. Combined estrogen and progestin increases the risk of breast cancer. [29]

In a 2013 update, researchers reaffirmed that hormone therapy can be beneficial in short-term use to manage menopausal symptoms, but "there are no reliable data on the risks or benefits of long-term hormone therapy use for the prevention of chronic diseases."[30] At the time of this writing, researchers continue to investigate the risks and benefits, and whether the risks relate to duration, age at which the therapy was started, how it was given, and other factors.

Meanwhile, your doctor will work with you to determine whether the benefits of HRT outweigh the risks in your particular case, and if so, what form should you take? Hormone therapy can be *systemic* (released into the bloodstream and used throughout the body) or *local*, such as the vaginal ring that releases small doses of estrogen directly into the vaginal tissues to increase lubrication, thickness, and elasticity,[31] or a dab of testosterone rubbed onto the clitoris.[32]

Older women have a very high incidence of urinary tract infections. While it's often related to sexual intercourse, it happens to many older women who are not having sex, too. I went through utter hell for five years until my primary care doctor, in concert with a new urologist, urged me to try an aggressive application schedule of Estrace vaginal cream every other day. This changed things markedly, improving comfort level and bringing more blood and natural lubrication to the area.

If you prefer to use plant products or bioidentical hormones, please consult your doctor—don't just proceed on your own. These can also carry risks and may have additional safety issues.[33] Whatever you decide to do, take the lowest dose that helps and for the shortest time necessary, and get checked out every six months.[34]

HRT for Men

Men experience lowered testosterone with aging and with some medical conditions and treatments. Low testosterone can lead to erectile dysfunction and a lower sex drive. If your doctor determines that testosterone replacement therapy is right for you, there are many options: injections, patch, gel, tablets, subcutaneous implant, and more. Caution: Have a thorough prostate cancer screening first. Men with prostate cancer or breast cancer should not take testosterone.[35]

About ten years ago, I was living with a lovely lady and I became a couch potato. She encouraged me to see her doc. We did labs and my testosterone levels were nil. I started with hormone replacement shots and not only had more libido, I also felt better day-to-day. I love the testosterone shots every month. They make life so mellow, and the libido is back. Now they make a big thing of low testosterone on TV, but back then there was nothing.

I READ IT ON THE INTERNET

The Internet is helpful for background information, but never for the final decision. Researching online is helpful only if you have the skills and background to do all of these:

- Evaluate the information and the credibility of the source.

- Weed out unsubstantiated claims.

- Realize that someone's anecdotal evidence is just one person's experience, and will not match yours.

- Recognize when a site is just trying to sell you something.

- Spot frauds, uninformed opinions, and well-intentioned but wacky resources.

You know that saying, "take it with a grain of salt"? You need to take most of what you read on the Internet with a full saltshaker of skepticism. Don't make medical decisions based solely on what you read online.

CHOOSING A LGBT-FRIENDLY HEALTH PROFESSIONAL

In *The Whole Lesbian Sex Book: A Passionate Guide for All of Us*, author Felice Newman recommends that you consider these questions when choosing a healthcare professional:

- Do you get a gut sense that this practitioner will treat you respectfully—regardless of your gender identity or sexual choices?

- Do you feel comfortable talking to this practitioner? Do you feel listened to?

- Does this practitioner have other lesbian, gay, bisexual, or transsexual patients or clients? Who's recommending this individual?

- Does this practitioner support you in prioritizing sexual satisfaction in your sex life?

If you're looking for a new health professional, Newman recommends checking the listings at www.glma.org/, the website of GLMA: Health Professionals Advancing LGBT Equality (previously known as the Gay & Lesbian Medical Association), the largest and oldest association of lesbian, gay, bisexual, and transgender healthcare professionals.

BREAKING UP WITH YOUR DOCTOR

What if our doctor's attitude is demeaning and getting in the way of us getting the right treatment? Especially when we're seeking help for a sexual concern, when we might be embarrassed to begin with, the wrong reaction from our doc can mean the difference between getting the help we need—and not.

It's time to get a new physician if your doctor does any of these consistently:

- Blames any complaint on your age rather than trying to resolve the issue.

- Never brings up sexuality and seems surprised if you do.

- Flinches or looks away when you bring up a sexual concern.

- Prescribes medication without fully diagnosing the cause of the problem.

- Tells you, "You just have to live with it."

Remember these magic words:

If you can't help me, please refer me to someone who can.

HOW COUNSELING CAN HELP

When sex goes awry, it affects your sense of who you are as a person and, if you're partnered, as a couple. Partnered, single and dating, or solo: you'll need communication tools and strategies to remain sensual—especially when not everything is working.

Even when your problems are medical and in no way "just in your head," counseling can be a useful adjunct to medical treatment. If your medical condition is limiting you outside the bedroom as well as inside, a counselor can help you cope with the limitations. You can work toward a new sense of yourself.

For these and many other reasons, please give yourself the chance to find out how a therapist or counselor can give you a new way of seeing your life moving forward, whatever challenges you've been given.

WHEN SEX
IS PAINFUL

*At age fifty-three, after being very ill and finally in recovery
from the illness, sex is very painful and I am devastated.
I used to thoroughly enjoy vaginal sex and had fantastic
vaginal orgasms, now I have pain. I feel old and shriveled
up and feel like my sexuality is gone.*

If you're experiencing pain with sex or avoiding sex because of
pain, you need a medical diagnosis. That's sometimes tough,
because most doctors don't know enough about sexual pain to
diagnose it. If your doctor advises you, "Just use more lubricant," or assumes it's all in your head, or prescribes a medication that might or might not be right for your problem, ask
for a pelvic/sexual pain specialist who knows how to assess

what kind of pain you're having and its cause. This assessment needs to include the pelvic floor muscles and nerves—and that takes a specialist.

Sexual pain is complicated. It can be caused by a number of medical issues, and each one is treated differently. Until you and your doctor understand why you're having pain, you can't treat it effectively.

SEX SHOULDN'T HURT [36]
By Melanie Davis, PhD

Pain is the body's way of asking you to put on the brakes and ask questions. Some causes of sexual pain can be easily remedied: Do you need more lubrication? A different position? A slower pace? Others require sex therapy or medical assessment and treatment. If pain occurs regularly, get a pelvic exam to get a medical opinion on possible causes. If the pain is chronic, you may need to redefine sex so it features physical sensations you still find pleasurable.

If it's been a long time since you had sex, you may have jumped into intercourse before your body was ready. Try more pre-penetrative sex play to allow yourself and your partner to get very physically aroused. Also, your vagina may be out of shape due to lack of attention. The muscles, tissues, and blood vessels in your vagina need exercise, and without it, the muscles get weak and inflexible, and lubrication, which may already be decreased due to menopause, flows even less.

Schedule a pelvic exam and speak openly about what you were doing when you felt pain. Some reasons for female sexual pain requiring medical attention include muscles that clamp shut involuntarily, yeast infections, skin conditions, and sexually transmitted infections. Internal conditions like endometriosis (scar tissue), fibroids (benign tumors), and cysts can cause pain with penetration.

If there is no medical condition needing treatment, try some self-pleasuring and long warm-up time to get your body ready for sex. It may help to let your partner watch you masturbate to learn how to touch you without causing pain.

—Melanie Davis, PhD, AASECT Certified Sexuality Educator and consultant, co-president of the Sexuality and Aging Consortium at Widener University.

WHERE, WHEN, HOW DOES IT HURT?

Prepare to tell your health professional: [37]

- What kind of pain is it? Burning, shooting, throbbing, tearing, itching, stabbing, stinging, cramping, numbness, tightness?

- Where do you feel it? Certain parts of the vulva? Clitoris? Vaginal opening? Deep in the vagina? Bladder? Pelvis? Abdomen?

- When does it hurt? All the time? When wearing underwear? Just when touched? During intercourse/penetration?

To prepare for your appointment, I recommend filling out the questionnaire in chapter 5 of *Healing Painful Sex: A Woman's Guide to Confronting, Diagnosing, and Treating Sexual Pain*[38] by Deborah Coady, MD, a gynecologist and pelvic/vulvar pain specialist, and Nancy Fish, MSW, MPH. This questionnaire helps you pin down the answers to the topics above. There is also a list of fourteen descriptions of symptoms for you to match with yours.

Your clinician will do a physical examination. Part of that will be finding out exactly where the pain is using the *Q-tip test:* gently touching different parts of the vulva and vaginal opening with a moistened cotton swab. When you feel pain, you'll tell the clinician the severity of the pain on a scale of one to ten. This doesn't sound pleasant, but the clinician will be slow and gentle, and it's important for a good diagnosis.[39]

Your exam may include cultures and blood tests, because pain may be caused by an infection or skin disorder. Assessing levels of estrogen, progesterone, and testosterone may also be helpful. [40]

POSSIBLE REASONS FOR VULVAR/VAGINAL PAIN[41]

Vaginal atrophy: the lining of the vagina gets thinner and lubrication diminishes due to lower estrogen levels after menopause. The vagina narrows, shortens, and becomes less elastic. This results in dryness, irritation, and vulnerability to vaginal infection (atrophic vaginitis) and urinary tract infections.

High-tone pelvic-floor dysfunction: the pelvic-floor muscles that support the vagina, bladder, and rectum become tense and cannot relax and stretch enough to allow penetration.

Vaginismus: involuntary tightening of the outer third of the vagina when penetration is attempted, making intercourse difficult or impossible.

Vulvodynia: burning, stinging, raw pain, which may be diffuse or localized to the vulva and vagina. The National Vulvodynia Association offers free, helpful online patient education, "Everything You Need to Know about Vulvodynia" at www.learnpatient.nva.org.

Provoked vestibulodynia/vulvar vestibulitis: a type of vulvo-dynia characterized by burning pain at the vaginal entrance with touching, penetrative sex, or pressure, even from tight clothing.

Interstitial cystitis: inflammation of the bladder's lining, which causes urinary urgency, frequency, and pain.

Dyspareunia: any pain associated with intercourse.

Bacterial vaginosis: a form of vaginal infection characterized by a thin odorous discharge due to an out-of-balance shift in the vaginal ecosystem.

Pelvic pain (can affect women or men): Many possible causes include adhesions, scarring, interstitial cystitis, and endome-triosis.

This is just a partial list of conditions that can cause sexual pain. Treatments differ depending on the diagnosis and the cause, so there's no way I can offer a magic solution here. Your pursuit of relief may take you through a frustrating journey from doctor to doctor—one Harvard study found that 60 percent of women who sought treatment for vulvar pain saw three or more doctors, many of whom could not provide a diagnosis.[42] I must point out that the women in this study were age eighteen to sixty-four—can you imagine the results if they all had been over fifty?

Your best bet is to get an appointment with a sexual pain

specialist, who will likely also refer you to a pelvic floor physical therapist.

PELVIC FLOOR THERAPY

"Too often I have had patients with pelvic floor dysfunction come to my office and say they have been to ten different doctors and healthcare providers and their symptoms have not improved, or have worsened," says Amy Stein, MPT, author of *Heal Pelvic Pain*. "Their medical professionals do not assess—or know how to assess—the pelvic floor muscles and nerves."

Consult a pelvic floor physical therapist who has specialized post-graduate training in diagnosing and treating pelvic pain (not a regular PT who has minimal training in this specialty). Among other assessments, pelvic floor therapists do an internal pelvic evaluation, assessing the three muscular layers, how well they both tighten and release, and where pain is felt.[43] Your PFPT will use a variety of techniques to treat your problem and rehabilitate your pelvic floor muscles and will also teach you a regimen to follow at home.

AVOID THESE IRRITANTS [44]

Many common products and activities irritate the vulva and vagina. If you have vulvar irritation or pain, The National Vulvodynia Association, www.nva.org, suggests that you:

- Wear all-white cotton underwear and loose-fitting pants or skirts.

- Avoid pantyhose.

- Remove wet bathing suits and exercise clothing promptly.

- Use dermatologically-approved detergent such as Purex or Clear.

- Double-rinse underwear and other clothing that touches the vulva.

- Do not use fabric softener on undergarments.

- Use soft, white, unscented toilet paper.

- Avoid getting shampoo on the vulvar area.

- Do not use bubble bath, feminine hygiene products, or perfumed creams or soaps.

- Wash the vulva with cool to lukewarm water only.

- Urinate before the bladder is full and rinse the vulva with water afterward.

- Use a water-based lubricant for sex that does not contain propylene glycol.

- Avoid bicycle riding and other exercises that put direct pressure on the vulva or create friction in the vulvar area.

- Avoid highly chlorinated pools and hot tubs.

WHEN YOUR PARTNER HAS PAIN

I am a seventy-four-year-old man with a strong sex drive. My wife can no longer have intercourse due to pain when I penetrate. I have always wanted to give pleasure, not pain, so it does not work for either of us. I give her oral sex at least weekly and she has wonderful orgasms that not only satisfy her but turn me on too.

It takes me much longer to reach orgasm now than it took when I was younger, so she is not able to get me off either manually or with oral sex. She tries to reciprocate but it does not work, as it takes me too long and I don't get aroused enough. As a result I masturbate two or three times a week while reading erotica or watching porn. We are monogamous and care deeply for one another. I sometimes feel a bit guilty about my sexual habits but seem to need them to control my strong sex drive. I have had a very active sex life since puberty.

I have not tried using sex toys and maybe it is time to try that. My wife has consulted a specialist but had no good results from the effort. She is working on other health priorities currently so I do not expect a change there.

A sexual problem at our age is rarely just *one* problem. I am grateful to the reader above for illustrating that point. She has too much pain for intercourse. She can have orgasms through oral sex, but because of his age-related, slow arousal and lessened sensation, he can't have orgasms when she tries to reciprocate.

Reader, there's absolutely no need for you to feel guilt or embarrassment if masturbation with porn or erotica is the best way for you to reach orgasm. Instead of seeing your strong sex drive as a problem that should be controlled, I'd like you to celebrate that drive and your orgasms—which are strongly beneficial to your health.

You're not doing anything wrong. In fact, you're honoring your intimacy with your wife with the ways you're working through your challenges and keeping your sex life intact. And yes, a good sex toy, such as a vibrating sleeve or the Pulse—which works even when you're not hard!—will hasten your orgasms. Your wife might enjoy watching you use your sex toy and maybe stimulating you while you use it—she clearly wants to give you pleasure.

HEALING YOUR RELATIONSHIP

A very valuable guideline is to define sexuality as mutual pleasure rather than intercourse. Too many couples get into the pattern of "intercourse or nothing." Defining sex as intercourse is an extremely risky, self-defeating approach because ultimately you will have ignored the all-important mind-body element of sexuality.

—Michael E. Metz and Barry W. McCarthy
in *Enduring Desire: Your Guide to Lifelong Intimacy*

When one of you has sexual pain, it affects your whole relationship, both in and out of bed. The National Vulvodynia Association suggests that you look at these issues:[45]

1. How satisfied were both of you with your sexual relationship before the sexual pain developed? Were there conflicts that you still need to resolve? How has sexual pain changed your sex life? How do these changes make you and your partner feel?

2. Teach your partner which areas of your body, sexual activities, and positions are painful and which are enjoyable. Ask which body parts are especially pleasurable to your partner, too.

3. Plan ahead for how you will deal with pain flares. If you agree on a plan for those times, such as cuddling only, you'll avoid feelings of rejection and prevent misunderstandings.

4. Which nonsexual gestures of intimacy make each of you feel loved? Communicate this to each other, and make a point of doing at least one of these each day.

5. Redefine sex and intimacy to mean any sexual activity that gives you and your partner pleasure without pain, whether or not it includes penetrative sex. Be open-minded about new sexual practices that you may find exciting.

6. For help redefining your sexual relationship and dealing with all the other issues, see a sex therapist or couples counselor with experience dealing with sexual intimacy issues related to chronic pain.

I am left with an awful feeling of inadequacy in the bedroom. It feels as if my sexuality just dropped off the map. My husband tries to be sympathetic. He tells me his performance is not what it used to be either, but I know he still can perform and does still enjoy sex. This has changed our whole relationship and how we relate to each other. We have become roommates instead of intimate partners.

IF YOU HAVEN'T HAD SEX FOR A LONG TIME

At fifty-six, I'd been without a partner for eleven years. I'd assumed that I'd be alone for the rest of my life. Out of the blue, I met an amazing man a month ago. We have fallen madly, deeply in love. Physical contact is so exciting and joyful, but I've discovered that vaginal penetration is very painful. Use it or lose it, I guess. My new partner and I are open and creative about sex and talking about sexuality. We've both been through long marriages destroyed by years of silence around sexual dysfunction. We won't let that happen here: we have a connection so rare that is it worth almost any effort. I'll be consulting a vulvo/vaginal pain specialist ASAP.

You read in chapter 4, Sex with Yourself and Toys, the importance of keeping yourself sexually healthy through unpartnered times with regular self-pleasuring, including penetration. If you let sex go at our age, it's harder to get it back once you're in a relationship. It's important "maintenance" to keep the blood flow going to our genitals and keep the pelvic-floor muscles in good working order—whether or not we're having partnered sex or planning to again.

After menopause, if we don't have regular penetrative sex (whether with penis, sex toy, dilator/wand, or fingers), the muscles at the vaginal opening can lose their ability to fully relax (known as high-tone pelvic-floor dysfunction), and they stay in a clamped position where penetration is painful or impossible.

If your goal is to accommodate a penis, Ellen Barnard, co-owner of A Woman's Touch, suggests these steps for teaching your pelvic-floor muscles how to relax:[46]

1. Get fully aroused first.

2. Using plenty of lubricant, insert a slim penetrative sex toy that is slender enough not to cause pain.

3. Take several deep belly breaths, concentrating on feeling your vaginal opening relax with each long exhalation.

4. If there's no pain, start to gently insert a finger alongside the toy as you breathe deeply. You can substitute a tapered toy for the toy-plus-finger.

5. Once you feel the opening relax, slip your finger or tapered toy in a little more.

I'm a post-op transwoman. I had been having problems dilating, and the Gyno from Hell (now my ex-doctor) suggested instead of the dilator, I should try the real thing. Oh sure, I thought, I'll just call Dial-a-Stud.

Turns out I went to dinner with a guy I knew, and we went back to his place. He was seventy-one. I don't know if he took a blue pill, but he was ready. He was of the mindset that girls should go down on guys but not the other way around. Before I knew it, he was on top of me trying to gain entrance. He didn't even put on a condom.

(I know—my bad, and it will not happen again.)

The sex was painful and he could not get all the way in. I stopped him and saw I was bleeding. He ran for a towel so I wouldn't get his bed bloody. He then went out to the living room and let me take care of myself.

The next day I called my regular doctor (not Gyno from Hell). She saw me and said that I had a condition called vaginal stenosis. A request was put in for an outside specialist, and I am waiting to hear about that.

MEN HURT, TOO

The most annoying side effect of my prostatectomy is that I have pain whenever I orgasm. It's a deep aching pain— primarily on my left side and below the base of the penis. I've discussed this problem with urologists and urology nurses, and most either scratch their heads or shrug their shoulders. One urology nurse laughed at me. The pain is more pronounced after intercourse versus masturbation. This has put a serious crimp in any sexual activity and enjoyment.

When a man experiences sexual pain, he often doesn't report it. When he does, his problem may not be taken seriously or it may be misdiagnosed. For these reasons, it's hard to estimate how common male sexual pain is, although a 2008 study of over four thousand men in Australia suggested that 5 percent of men suffer from pain associated with sexual intercourse.[47]

Other studies have found that men with prostate cancer who have a radical prostatectomy may experience painful orgasm,[48] although doctors do not warn patients about this and are often not knowledgeable about it.

Men may experience genital or pelvic pain in the penis, perineum, anus, urethra, testicles, lower abdomen, or tailbone. There are many possible causes of male sexual pain, including abnormalities of the pelvic (pudendal) nerves,[49] yeast or urethritis, prostatitis, bladder infection, sexually transmitted infections, skin conditions, side effects of surgery, nerve damage, adhesions, scarring, and Peyronie's disease [50] —and that's not a complete list. As with female sexual pain, only an accurate diagnosis can ensure effective treatment, so it's important to get evaluated by a specialist.

Fortunately, the man who wrote me in the quote above kept persisting in his quest for relief, and he found it. Here's his update:

I've discovered that pelvic floor therapy works for men. I've seen my pain with orgasm diminish by 50 percent after three sessions. It's also helping with my occasional stress incontinence. Because of my prostatectomy and earlier surgeries, my abdomen was full of adhesions and scar tissue.

I found a pelvic floor physical therapist with specialized training. The exam was both external (abdomen, groin, upper thighs) and internal (rectal and internal pelvic floor assessment). She also used biofeedback to assess my ability to relax the pelvic floor and ultrasound therapy.

The therapy sessions and home exercises have helped

to start breaking down some of these adhesions and scar tissue. It's a shame that urologists don't consider or prescribe this therapy more often for men, especially prostate cancer survivors. I also wish I had known about the benefits—physiological and sexual—of prostate massage and practiced it before my cancer diagnosis.

FROM HERE?

This chapter is just the first stepping stone for getting information and treatment for sexual pain. Fortunately, several books and websites are available now to help you, and many of these contain referrals to finding a specialist who can help you.

Once you have a diagnosis and a practitioner, there are helpful, reliable websites that can add to your knowledge. See also the books and websites in our Recommended Resources in the back of the book.

One superb resource for women is the Vaginal Renewal™ program from A Woman's Touch (www.a-womans-touch.com/documents/VR%20booklet.pdf). This comprehensive, easy-to-understand, self-help program was created to help menopausal and postmenopausal women who were experiencing discomfort or pain during penetration. I recommend it enthusiastically.

CANCER, CANCER TREATMENT, AND SEX

After the physical and emotional upheaval of cancer treatment, sex may be the farthest thing from your mind. The emotional and physical turmoil and the challenges of everyday living may have taken all your focus. Then at some point, you'll want to live your life as fully as possible. Part of that is affirming that after the chemotherapy, radiation, and/or surgery that you've endured, your body can be your partner in pleasure again.

How do you bring satisfying sex back into your life after cancer treatment?

1. Educate yourself about the sexual side effects of your treatment. Ask your healthcare profes-

sionals plenty of questions about what you can expect.

2. Educate yourself about what you can do to ensure the best outcome, including sexual rehabilitation that you can do now to make it possible to be sexually active later. (Don't wait until your desire returns to start this.)

3. Read some of the books and websites on cancer and sexuality in the Recommended Resources section to understand the physical effects of treatment and how they affect sexual function. They were written by sex educators who have made sharing information about cancer and sexuality their life's work, and they will answer the questions from #1 and #2 that your own doctor may not be able to answer.

4. Make use of classes and support groups offered by the patient advocacy organization for your type of cancer.

5. Read online resources, but be wary—the Internet is also full of crazy advice, so get solid recommendations about websites that are credible.

6. Grieve the losses, and then embrace the new possibilities. Expand your idea about what sex is and how you can receive (and give) pleasure now.

7. Commit to moving forward as a sensual, sexual person.

STAY IN TOUCH

You can receive pleasure from a lover's touch or your own, despite the effects of cancer and cancer treatment. Most cancer treatments, other than those that affect the spinal cord or some parts of the brain, do not damage the nerves or muscles and still leave the sense of touch and the possibility of orgasm intact, according to the American Cancer Society.[51] The sensations may be different, though—you'll need to explore what feels good now, and what doesn't. If the ways you used to enjoy sex and reach orgasm don't work for you now, give yourself permission to grieve their loss. This allows you to let go of the past and be open to discovering different ways to stay sensual and sexual.

Explore which parts of your body and what kind of touch give you pleasure now. You may not have any sensation where you have scar tissue, but the rest of your body is still capable of enjoying pleasurable sensations. Reclaiming your sexuality can enrich your life and make your body a source of comfort and pleasure again.

Robert's six months of chemotherapy left him ill, fatigued, and depressed. He felt that his body, which he had to submit to needles and chemicals, was no longer his own. Deciding to make love with me as soon as possible let him repossess his body and his drive to live fully again. It wasn't a sex drive—it was a "live again" drive—and a love drive. You may need to reconnect with your body *before* you can feel sexual, however. There's no one right way.

If pain during sex interferes with pleasure and orgasm, explore ways to have pleasure without pain, and get help from healthcare professionals to resolve the pain. (See chapter 9, When Sex Is Painful). It's helpful to practice having orgasms on your own before returning to partnered sex, so you know what arouses you and what causes pain.

WHAT YOUR ONCOLOGY CARE PROVIDER WON'T TELL YOU ABOUT CANCER AND SEXUALITY

By Anne Katz, PhD, RN

Oncology care providers are notoriously silent on the topic of cancer and sexuality. Their primary aim is to cure you of the cancer with a secondary role of preventing a recurrence and managing treatment side effects. Sexual difficulties experienced by the cancer survivor are almost always a side effect of treatment, so it is strange that they are mostly silent on this topic. Here are some suggestions to help you get the help you need:

- Bring up the topic with your oncology care provider. While you may think it is their responsibility to ask, realize that they may be people with the same hang-ups about talking about sexuality as the rest of the population.

- Oncology care providers say that they are willing to talk about this, but they want the patient/survivor to raise the issue rather than appear to be invading your privacy.

- Sexual difficulties after cancer encompass a broad range from changes to body image to specific issues with erections, lubrication, orgasms, etc.

- Ask for help and don't stop asking (or requesting a referral to someone who will help) until you get the help you need. Don't assume that there is nothing that can be done.

- One of the biggest changes to couples' sex lives after cancer is the loss of spontaneity. Something that was once easy and routine often requires adaptation and change, which is difficult for most couples.

- Communication lies at the root of any solution—commit to talking honestly with your partner/spouse about this topic.

- Couples who successfully adapt to the *new normal* after cancer are flexible in their attitudes and behaviors and are able to imagine a different way of doing things.

- Cancer survivors who are single can still find a partner. Do not assume that a rigid erection or a moist vagina is an essential starting point. Potential partners are often looking for companionship and affection rather than penetrative intercourse.

- The brain remains the biggest sex organ—use it with creativity and curiosity and see where your imagination can take you.

- There is always hope—and moving from hope to action requires information, motivation, and effort.

—Anne Katz PhD, RN (www.DrAnneKatz.com) is an AASECT-certified sexuality counselor at CancerCare Manitoba, Winnipeg, MB, Canada and author of several books about sexuality and cancer.

TALK ABOUT IT

One of the hardest parts of staying sexual after cancer is talking about it honestly with your doctor and your partner. Often your doctor is waiting for you to ask, not wanting to be intrusive. Or he or she may not think beyond treating your cancer. It's up to you to speak up, ask questions, request more information. If your doctor can't help, request a referral to a health professional with experience and expertise in sexual function after cancer treatment.

Talking to your partner can be difficult also, but it's so important for intimacy and for the future of your relationship. Share what you're learning, thinking, feeling. Share your fears about being sexual again, or feeling desirable. Let your partner express his or her thoughts, questions, and fears.

Be honest if a sexual activity hurts or makes you anxious, or if a different kind of touch will feel better, or if you'd like your partner to take a more active role because you're feeling fatigued. Guide your partner's hand away from parts of your body that are sore or numb and toward the places that please you most. It will be a learning curve for both of you, and it can bring you even closer together.

COMMON SEXUAL SIDE EFFECTS FOR WOMEN

The Mayo Clinic reports that these are the most common side effects of cancer treatment reported by women: [52]

- Difficulty reaching climax

- Less energy for sexual activity

- Loss of desire for sex

- Pain during penetration

- Reduced size of the vagina caused by tightness of the pelvic floor or radiation scarring

- Vaginal dryness

VAGINAL RECUPERATION AFTER CANCER OR SURGERY

You may think that intercourse will not be possible for you following radiation or surgery, but it is possible to explore the ways that you can heal your vagina, if this is something you want to pursue. An excellent resource is "Vaginal Recuperation after Cancer or Surgery" from A Woman's Touch (www.sexualityresources.com), one of my favorite sexuality resource centers (and one I'm referencing many times in this chapter). In this guide, Myrtle Wilhite, MD, MS, explains the four steps to vaginal recuperation after genital cancer treatment:

1. Have the treatment necessary for your medical condition.

2. Soften the scar tissue left by radiation and surgery with vulvar and vaginal massage morning and night with a moisturizing lubricant such as Liquid Silk. Massage the whole outer area of the genitals with "press and release" circular strokes to bring new blood to the skin and push out old blood and fluid. If this comfortable, also massage the lubricant into the vaginal opening.

3. After about two weeks of #2, also insert a smooth vibrator (slim enough to be comfortable) coated with a moisturizing lubricant into your vagina. This will help break up the developing

scar tissue. Turn on the vibrator to a comfortable level and let it run for five to ten minutes. The goal is to bring blood to the area, exchange blood/lymph fluid, and increase your vaginal skin's flexibility so that you'll be able to adjust to penetration later if you want to.

4. Learn how to have orgasms again. "If you are able to bring yourself to orgasm, you have my prescription to bring yourself to orgasm *at least* once a week (for the rest of your life)," says Dr. Wilhite. "This is really preventive maintenance of your body."

(Please also read "The Vaginal Renewal Program" from A Woman's Touch, a superb resource for any woman who is experiencing dryness, atrophy, scarring, or discomfort during penetrative sex play, after cancer treatment.)

REDUCING GYNECOLOGICAL SCARRING

Radiation treatment for any gynecological cancer produces scarring that prevents the vagina from flexing and expanding. Regular use of a vibrating wand in the vagina increases blood flow and reduces scar tissue.[53] "Vibration directly to the scar tissue starts breaking up that scar tissue, allowing it to expand, become more comfortable, and allow penetrative sex if we want it," says Ellen Barnard of A Woman's Touch, who specializes in counseling women after cancer treatment. She recommends adding a good moisturizing lubricant to the wand surface and applying the wand directly against the scar tissue, pushing gently into the scar but not to the point of discomfort. A wand with a vibration that is throbby works better than buzzy. This method is effective even long after cancer treatment, although it will take much longer to see results.

PENILE REHABILITATION AFTER PROSTATE SURGERY

I was sixty and in a non-sex-positive relationship of many decades when I found out I had prostate cancer. Add to the mix of having a sexless marriage, herpes, and a strong libido, I was now facing ED from prostate surgery. My urologist saved my life but was embarrassed to discuss sexual function. All I got was a sample pack of Viagra and a prescription for more.

Prostate surgery results in some nerves being cut and others are unavoidably stretched, no matter how skillful the surgeon. "Stretched nerves become stunned, and although they are complete and in place, they cannot function until they recover," explains Myrtle Wilhite, MD, co-owner of A Woman's Touch, in the valuable resource, "Penile Rehabilitation after Prostate or Pelvic Surgery or Radiation."[54] This recovery may take up to three years for some men.

During the entire recovery time, it's essential to keep oxygen-rich blood flowing into the penis to prevent scarring and to enable the nerves to function once they recover. Dr. Wilhite recommends using these penile rehabilitation steps together to keep the blood flow going while the nerves can't do it, and help to maintain penis length and girth:[55]

1. A low nightly dose of PDE-5 inhibitor medication (Viagra or Levitra preferred) to help deliver oxygenated blood to the inside of your penis while you sleep.

2. Gentle stretching and massage of the penis. Stretching the penis activates the vessels that bring blood into the penis, and lubricated, gentle massage helps keep your penis comfortable with sexual touch. Gently stroke, squeeze, and stretch the length of your penis both toward and away from your body. (A hard erection isn't your goal—soft is fine.)

3. Use of a Vacuum Erection Device (VED) twice daily (see chapter 12, Sex without Erections) to gently draw oxygenated blood into the penis, then allow it to flow out again. You're not aiming for an erection, just using the vacuum pressure to stretch the penis internally and help with elasticity later on.

4. Pelvic Floor Muscle Exercises (see "Kegels for Men" in chapter 2, What's Happening to My Body?). The relaxation portion of these exercises is as important as the contraction portion.

(Please read the full description of the "Penile Rehabilitation" process from A Woman's Touch at https://sexualityresources. com/sites/default/files/documents/PR%20booklet%20 2013_0.pdf.)

> *I have a big issue about how insurance companies regard ED medicines, especially for prostate cancer patients. ED medicine is generally regarded a "lifestyle" medication and insurance will only cover three or four pills a month. This policy does not take into consideration the special and sometimes difficult circumstances of prostate cancer patients. Such medications are therapeutic for prostate cancer patients and regular use of ED medication is often a necessary part of a post-treatment recovery.*

WHEN "NERVE-SPARING" ISN'T

Sex counselor Anne Katz works exclusively with cancer patients. She warns men undergoing nerve-sparing prostate surgery that erections are not guaranteed. "Erectile nerves are found on the outside of the prostate, and although they're depicted clearly as bright yellow cords in diagrams, they're actually very difficult to see," she explains. "The nerves can't be seen with the naked eye. If cauterizing instruments are used anywhere near the nerves, they are damaged." Nerves may, however, recover from the pushing and pulling of the surgery, though it takes a long time. "The nerves go into shock and stop sending the message to blood vessels to relax and let blood into the spongy tissues of the penis."[56]

ONE MAN'S PROSTATE CANCER STORY

At forty-eight, I was diagnosed with prostate cancer. I had surgery using a 3D robotic laparoscopic technique. This technique was minimally invasive, allowing for a quicker healing time, and boasted better results for both incontinence and sexual function. I took about four months to regain urinary control, and I was essentially impotent for close to five years. For a couple of years after that, erections were sporadic and unreliable.

It took me much longer than I expected to begin recovering and feeling confident after prostate surgery eight years ago. It also took me a long time to deal with the side effects: the anger, frustration, and grief as a result of the prolonged impotence; the occasional stress incontinence during sex; and the pain that occurred with orgasm.

It also took me a long time to regain a feeling of passion—that magic of getting lost in each other and in sensual stimulation. But I remained a highly sexually focused person and I turned to other means of sexual expression—kissing, oral sex, caressing, anal play, and self-stimulation.

Thanks in part to a wonderful urology nurse, I'm now doing much better. I take a 5 mg Cialis every other day. My erections are more reliable now. I've started pelvic floor therapy with the objective of easing, if not eliminating, the pain with orgasm. Right now, despite no longer having the ability to ejaculate (how do women feel about seeing or feeling their lover ejaculate?), I'm feeling better about myself sexually than I have in a very long time. And I'm alive and cancer-free more than eight years after my diagnosis.

What I wish they had told me about prostate surgery and sex:

1. The length of your penis will be shortened.

2. ED medications, while therapeutic for prostate cancer patients, are not covered adequately by insurance.

3. There may be some pain associated with sex/ intercourse/orgasm.

4. Even with the best nerve-sparing techniques, some sexual sensations may not be as intense and your orgasms may be not as strong as they were before the surgery.

BREAST CANCER

Whether I'll pursue another relationship remains to be seen. I'm hesitant because of my mastectomy. I didn't have reconstruction at the time but am considering it now. It seems incomprehensible to me that any man would be attracted to a one-breasted woman. I'm very self-conscious about my disfigurement. The thought of trying to meet someone suitable and begin a relationship at this age is scary. However, since my marriage lacked both physical and emotional intimacy for many years, I'm longing for them now in a surprising way. I'm just not sure what to do or how to go about it.

Body image is a huge issue after a mastectomy. Women and their partners grieve the physical changes, the loss, the need to adapt to life in a different body. The initial emotional impact and the long-term adjustments can be difficult, even devastating.

A support group and/or a therapist can help you through this challenging process. For more, see "Sexuality and Relationships for Breast Cancer Survivors and their Partners," A Woman's Touch, www.a-womans-touch.com/sex_counselor.php?articleID=2941.

SINGLE AFTER CANCER

I am sixty-two, single, and once was a very sexually active woman. I've undergone treatment for breast cancer twice. After rounds of chemotherapy, surgeries, radiation, and continued estrogen blocking medications, sex with another became a thing of the past. My recovery required my full attention for years, but now I feel ready for new adventures—hopefully including sex. Sexual intercourse may not be possible for me—but I still enjoy having orgasms and I desire the wonder of touch.

However, I am so concerned about my limitations as a sexual partner that I am afraid to attempt to date again. I have no idea what men in my age group expect or desire in terms of performance from their partners. Would my current physical circumstance deter most men from being interested in exploring an intimate relationship with me?

We never lose our need for touch and affection. I am grateful to this reader for her message and all it conveys about hope and healing and moving forward. I understand why she is apprehensive, but I encourage her—and all of you, whatever your challenges or limitations—to go after whatever it takes to live life to the fullest.

Would single men be deterred by her inability to have intercourse? Many single men in our age group also fear performance expectations when erections are no longer possible or predictable. There are many who would welcome a sexual partner who did not expect intercourse, who would be happy exchanging touch, oral and manual stimulation, and fabulous orgasms.

These men may be cancer survivors themselves, wanting to return fully to life, including sex and intimacy, but they don't know how to navigate the dating world either—when to divulge the cancer, when to divulge the sexual issues.

If you're in this situation, find out if there's a local cancer survivors' singles group or try online dating: I did a search on "cancer survivors singles" and came up with several sites that promote themselves as dating sites for cancer survivors. There's even one—"2date4love"—that "enables people who cannot engage in sexual intercourse to meet and experience love, companionship, and intimacy."

Just because you have had cancer doesn't mean you need to limit yourself to dating companions who share a similar medical history, though. Just be up front about your cancer on a first or second date if it looks like there's potential for more. (If not, you don't need to mention it.)

Then if you progress to a few dates and there's chemistry, it's important to explain that yes, you are interested in sex, and discuss what sex is for you, whether it includes penetrative sex play or not. Be prepared: Men who desire intercourse will likely drop out of your entourage, and that's okay. With those who want to be with you after all the cards are on the table, you have the delightful journey of exploring all the ways you can be sexual without intercourse!

Even when a date doesn't progress to more, it's still worth getting to know new people, "practicing" dating, trying out how to tell a potential partner about your needs, desires, and challenges. If you take it all as part of the brave new world of dating experience, you don't need to feel regretful or shamed when a new relationship (or potential relationship) doesn't work out. Most of them will not work out—that's the nature of the game. (I go into this more in chapter 14, The New Rules of Dating.)

MORE

Reading one chapter is only the beginning of your journey to reclaim your sexuality after cancer treatment. Fortunately, several excellent books and web resources about cancer and sex will guide you step-by-step. See our Recommended Resources section. (A special thank you to Ellen Barnard of A Woman's Touch for her help with this chapter.)

HEART, BRAIN, JOINTS, AND SEX

Disease and treatment, more than age, affect one's ability to enjoy sex. People with arthritis and other movement disorders, for example, may have chronic pain or lose their ability to move well. People with diabetes, which can affect the circulatory system, may have reduced blood flow to sex organs, causing men to have difficulty achieving an erection or women an orgasm. Heart disease can be associated with fatigue and reduced physical strength. Dementia can have a number of effects, including loss of emotional connection with one's partner and the inability of the partner with dementia to consent to sex.

—"Can we talk about Sex? Seven Things Physicians Need to Know About Sex and the Older Adult" in *Minnesota Medicine*.[57]

How do we stay sexual when medical conditions alter us? What does *staying sexual* even mean now? Our new sexuality might mean more comfortable positions for partner sex, or maybe just sharing caresses, with or without orgasm. Whatever is happening in our body and mind, or our partner's, will need adjustment, but we never lose our need for touch. Life is hard enough without giving up that.

Whatever medical challenge you're facing, be open to expanding your definition of what sex is. Instead of insisting that "real" sex is over because it can't be the way it used to be, focus on what's possible now—and making that the best it can be, one step at a time. If you are partnered, explore ways to touch, kiss, please each other, and express physical and emotional intimacy without focusing on just one goal. If you are unpartnered, find the kinds of touching and sex toys that arouse and satisfy you.

GREAT SEX DESPITE CHRONIC ILLNESS[58]
By Michael Castleman

Your doctor announces that you have diabetes, lupus, heart disease, rheumatoid arthritis or some other condition. To enjoy the best sex possible despite your chronic condition, follow these six steps:

1. **Define Sex Differently**. Sex isn't just vaginal intercourse. If your definition of sex is more flexible, then bidding farewell to intercourse is passing up one dish at a huge buffet. There are many other ways to enjoy physical intimacy, fulfilling lovemaking, and orgasm. Focus not on your disabilities, but on your abilities. Where there's a will, there's a way.

2. **Find Information and Support**. Ask your doctor about the sexual implications of your condition and the sexual effects of your medications. Then ask your pharmacist. Next, search the Internet. Join the organization devoted to your condition. Find it by searching the Internet, or visit the American Self-Help Group Clearinghouse (www.mentalhelp.net/selfhelp). Ask the organization for information on coping sexually, and possibly for a referral to an expert. Join a support group related to your condition and ask members how they cope sexually.

3. **Stay as Healthy as Possible**. "How can I be healthy?" you ask, "I have this damn disease." Yes, you do. But you'll feel better, manage your condition more easily, and retain more sexual interest and ability if your lifestyle is as healthy as possible:

    • If you smoke, quit.
    • Don't drink more than two alcoholic drinks per day.

- Eat at least five servings of fruits and vegetables a day.

- Within your abilities, strive for regular moderate exercise, ideally, at least thirty minutes a day.

- Get at least seven hours of sleep a night.

4. **Look for New Opportunities.** Having a chronic condition means grieving the loss of things you can no longer do, among them, how you had sex. But if you stop there, you wind up depressed. Look for new opportunities for fun and personal growth—including new approaches to making love.

5. **Use Lubricants and Toys.** Diabetes and other conditions may decrease genital sensitivity. Lubricants and vibrators often help. (See chapter 4, Sex with Yourself and Toys.)

6. **Consider Sex Therapy.** Sex therapists are psychotherapists with advanced training in sex problems. They discuss your situation, suggest ways you can enjoy sex, and assign erotic "homework." Studies show that two-thirds of people who consult sex therapists report significant benefit. To find a sex therapist near you, visit the American Association of Sex Educators, Counselors, and Therapists (www.aasect.org).

—Journalist Michael Castleman
has covered sexuality since 1975.
He publishes www.GreatSexAfter40.com.

ARTHRITIS

Arthritis causes joint pain, stiffness, and flexibility problems. When it's difficult to find a comfortable position for arthritic hips, spine, or knees, it's even more difficult to abandon yourself to sexual feelings. Arthritic wrists and fingers make it difficult to please a partner or yourself manually. Oral sex can become—quite literally—a pain in the neck. These tips may help:

- Experiment with timing—when are you most comfortable during the day? Make that your sex time.

- Try taking a painkiller and a warm bath or shower an hour before sex.

- Do some gentle exercise before sex to loosen stiff joints. Move through the joint's full range of motion. Stretch and reach to make yourself as limber as possible.

- Experiment with different positions. Often people with arthritis in the hips, knees, or spine find lying on their sides most comfortable. Try the sex cushions described in the Sex Furniture section of chapter 2, What's Happening to My Body?

I have pretty bad osteoarthritis in one knee, so some positions are difficult. We do a side-lying position that works well to accommodate that. Some positions even help at times. If I am bent over a chair and my hamstrings are being stretched, it actually feels good!

- During sex, reach to caress your partner's whole body. That will pleasure your partner— and your joints!

- Use sex toys to compensate for what your fingers used to do. And be creative!

I'm a younger man, and I assumed that your advice for staying sexual while getting older would be useful for me someday in the future. I didn't anticipate having a partner who already had these issues. I was recently with a man in his midfifties who had arthritis in his knees and his fingers. This meant no kneeling for him on the floor while we played, so we did everything in bed. Not terribly unusual, except that I rarely have sex in a bed!

Then, as I moved his hands to my nipples to pinch them, we discovered another issue: the arthritis in his fingers makes it painful and actually impossible for him to squeeze at the strength or for the duration I like. He mentioned this and I made a mental note: next time, bring the wooden clothespins! They'd be perfect to use on me and would relieve him of that concern—and pain.

Once we figure out how to be comfortable, we may find that sex actually improves our arthritis, as sex therapist Marty Klein, PhD, explains:

> *Sex is terrific for people with arthritis. Sex involves gentle, range-of-motion exercise, which minimizes pain and inflammation. It also releases endorphins, the body's natural pain relievers. Sex strengthens the muscles around the joints, which helps support them. And it's mood-elevating, which likewise helps alleviate pain.*[59]

JOINT REPLACEMENT

Most people find that joint replacement surgery helps everything about their enjoyment of life, including sex. In one study of people with severe osteoarthritis, 90 percent reported improved overall sexual function after hip or knee replacement surgery.[60]

If your doctor doesn't bring up sex, bring it up yourself. Ask about safe sexual positions if he or she does not volunteer the information. Check out www.recoversex.com, which offers large, clear diagrams of recommended sexual positions after hip replacement and knee replacement. Although, unfortunately, they only illustrate male-female couples, most of the positions are translatable to other gender combinations.

Knee replacement: You can resume sex once you feel healed and comfortable, usually four to six weeks after surgery. At first, stick to positions where you are the passive receiver, and use pillows to support your knees. Avoid kneeling positions until you fully heal.[61] Face-to-face positions with you on the bottom or side-lying positions that allow you to drape your leg over your partner are recommended.[62]

> *My surgeon did not specifically address sex after my two knee replacements. The discomfort level was sufficient for a couple of weeks to preclude any sex but masturbation and fellatio. It was just too uncomfortable to get into any position to do anything else, even to pleasure a partner. My doctor wanted me back on my motorcycle in three months. I would rather have known that I could be sexual as soon as my pain level was down enough to be comfortable.*

Hip replacement: Your doctor will probably tell you to abstain from sex for six to eight weeks after surgery.[63] After that, avoid bending your new hip more than ninety degrees, crossing your leg past the center of your body, opening your hips widely, or turning your toes in.[64] Recommended positions include face-to-face, letting your partner be on top (without putting all of his or her weight on your new hip), or lying in spoon position.[65] Once you heal, you'll most likely find that hip replacement improves your sex life, because your hip pain is gone.

HEART DISEASE

Mentally I think I'm twenty, but physically I know I'm eighty-five. After two cardiac events, I haven't limited my sex at all. I've certainly changed my ways because of age and medications for heart, high blood pressure, and diabetes. These eliminate erections. For a long time I used hormonal injections directly into the penis. I got erections. One day, I decided, the hell with this, it isn't very romantic. The loss of erections doesn't change my libido. We have a lot of foreplay, a lot of oral sex, which I enjoy thoroughly. I have orgasms without erections or ejaculation. I don't feel any difference.

When your arteries have been narrowed by fatty deposits (called atherosclerosis), your genitals as well as your heart do not receive enough blood. The penis cannot engorge, neither can the clitoris or the vagina.[66] Erectile dysfunction and difficulty with arousal and orgasms in women can be signs of heart disease, and you need to get medical attention pronto.

After a heart attack, it's natural that you or your partner may be afraid that sex will cause another attack. Often people are so anxious about the risks that they don't dare resume sexual activity following a heart attack or heart surgery.

In 2013, the American Heart Association released guidelines advising healthcare professionals to counsel heart patients about sex, including assessment of when they're healthy enough to resume sex, recommendations for best positions and activities, and individualized counseling.[67] Your doctor may order an exercise stress test to determine if your heart is strong enough for sexual activity, or recommend a regimen of brisk walking to work up to it. Once you're cleared, sexual activity carries very little risk.

If your doctor doesn't offer all this information to you as a matter of course, please ask for it. Again, it's up to us to let our healthcare providers know that our sexuality matters.

Sex educator Cory Silverberg points out,

> When medical texts refer to "sex" it almost always means intercourse. Only recently has information for physicians and patients begun to acknowledge other kinds of sexual activities, and we don't yet have any empirical research on how activities like oral sex, anal sex, fantasy role-play, or BDSM may differ from intercourse in terms of heart health. There's no evidence that what you consider "kinky sex" is any riskier than what you call "normal" sex.[68]

If your doctor assumes that your goal is vanilla heterosexual intercourse and that's not what floats your boat, speak out. Your right to accurate and helpful medical information trumps any embarrassment that your doctor may feel because he or she is not prepared for your question.

> In 1991 at the age of forty-seven, I had a moderate heart attack. I was put on Cardizem, which did wonders cleaning out my arteries, but it prohibited me from getting fully aroused and maintaining an erection. After a year, my

cardiologist took me off the drug, and I bounced back. We changed our diet to a lower fat regimen and I began a regular exercise routine which included walking and lifting weights.

At fifty-four, my wife and I decided that our sex lives, which had been somewhat neglected since my heart attack, needed to be revitalized. We feared that if we didn't enliven that part of our lives soon we might indeed "lose it."

We invested in toys and sexy clothes and we began watching adult videos, both porn and instructional videos. We continued to eat heart-healthy and exercise routinely. And we were having sex once or twice a week.

Even after doing so many things right, at the age of sixty-two, I underwent a triple bypass for badly clogged arteries. Given my age and this life threatening event, we both thought that this might be the end of our sex lives. But we were both determined not to let that happen unless absolutely necessary.

Fortunately I did not have to take medicines that compromised desire or function. Within six weeks of surgery I had the go ahead from the doc to become active sexually again. The major warning was not to put any pressure on my chest and risk doing damage to his handiwork.

HEART DISEASE MEMDICATIONS

These medications used to treat heart disease can have sexual side effects. [69]

- ACE inhibitors, such as captopril (Capoten), enalapril (Vasotec), and ramipril (Altace), can cause low libido and erectile dysfunction.

- Nitrates for chest pain, such as isosorbide dinitrate (Isordil) and isosorbide mononitrate (Imdur, Ismo), can cause erectile dysfunction. Do not take Viagra, Levitra, or Cialis with nitrates because the interaction can cause a dangerous, potentially life-threatening drop in blood pressure which can cause kidney failure or stroke. [70]

- Beta blockers, such as penbutolol (Levatol), propranolol (Inderal), and timolol (Blocadren), can cause low libido, erectile dysfunction, female arousal problems, and difficulties reaching orgasm.

- Calcium-channel blockers, such as diltiazem (Cardizem), nifedipine (Procardia), and verapamil (Verelan), can cause erectile dysfunction.

HIGH BLOOD PRESSURE

Hypertension can contribute to sexual problems, and so can the drugs that control it. High blood pressure can cause lack of desire; erectile dysfunction and difficulty ejaculating in male bodies; and uncomfortable or painful penetration and difficulty having an orgasm in female bodies.[71]

These recommendations from the American Heart Association[72] will benefit your sex life as well as lower your blood pressure:

- Eat nutritious foods

- Shake the salt habit

- Get regular exercise

- Maintain a healthy weight

- Manage stress

- Avoid tobacco smoke

- Limit alcohol consumption

Since high blood pressure is a leading cause of stroke and can lead to heart disease, it is essential to take any medications that were prescribed, even if they have sexual side effects. Tell your doctor about these side effects and ask whether another medication might work as well to control your hypertension, with fewer side effects.

STROKE

A stroke, sometimes called a *brain attack*, happens when blood flow to a part of the brain stops.[73] Stroke survivors often report decreased desire and increased sexual problems due to the stroke, pain, medications, and, often, depression. Women may experience less vaginal lubrication and decreased ability to have an orgasm. Men may experience weak erections or no erections. The part of the brain where the stroke occurred affects the stroke survivor's sexual response, attitude, and behavior.[74]

The National Stroke Association recognizes the need for intimacy and sexuality and recommends honest communication with your partner and your doctor. Sometimes a change in medication can decrease the sexual problems, so tell your doctor what you're experiencing.

Experiment with positioning, pillows, and props so that the weaker side is protected. The partner with greatest ease of movement should be the top if intercourse is possible. You may find manual and oral sex to be easier physically, less stressful emotionally, and more satisfying.

You may fear having another stroke during sex, but this is very unlikely.[75] The increase in breathing and heart rate during sex is normal and not a cause for worry, and you use about as much energy as walking up a flight or two of stairs.[76] But don't try to tough it out if you're scared—anxiety is a libido killer. Admit your worries to your partner and also to your doctor. You may want to get counseling to deal with your feelings and fears and to help you and your partner work through the changes.

PREPARING TO LOVE SOMEONE WITH DEMENTIA: 10 WAYS
By Peggy Brick, MEd

1. Become an advocate for dementia research, education, care services, and progressive public policies. If you're lucky enough to live to be eighty-five, there's a 50 percent chance you will experience dementia.

2. Do your best to prevent or delay dementia by promoting brain health through regular exercise, a heart-healthy diet, social connections, and brain-stimulating activities.

3. Get an early diagnosis by a primary physician and then a psychoneurologist if you're concerned about a loved one's memory, so you can plan, make choices, and get support.

4. Understand the experience of dementia by reading books such as Richard Taylor's *From the Inside Out* and viewing films, such as those from Terra Nova Films, www.terranova ondemand.org.

5. Learn how to connect with a person with dementia by listening, touching, hugging, respecting, and loving the person who remains.

6. Recognize that dementia profoundly affects partner relationships. You may experience

decreased attraction after assuming care-taking duties. As the disease progresses, your partner may no longer recognize you.

7. Understand that sexual expression is important in a nursing home, and physical contact may be a beneficial and calming means of communication.

8. Ask whether a home you are considering has a sexuality policy that documents residents' sexual rights, adequate staff training, and abuse prevention strategies.

9. Be prepared to experience difficult and exhausting loss and grief as you interact with someone who is both there and not there.

10. Take care of yourself, which is challenging—but essential—when you love and care for someone with dementia.

—Peggy Brick, MEd, teaches "Alzheimer's: New Perspectives" at Osher Lifelong Learning Institute, University of Delaware, and is the founder of the Sexuality and Aging Consortium at Widener University.

(Read about the sexual rights of people with dementia in a long-term care facility in chapter 17, Sexy Aging Going Forward.)

IF YOU'RE A CAREGIVER TO YOUR LOVED ONE

The change from spouse or lover to caregiver is life-altering. If at all possible, hire someone to provide some of the daily care. If that's not financially feasible, find out if the local chapter of the advocacy group for your partner's disease can help you get low-cost or no-cost help.

Friends, family, and members of your faith community are often eager to help out, but they don't know what to offer. Help them know! If you can't imagine asking people for help, ask one friend to coordinate this for you. The more people help you out with caregiving, the more physical and emotional energy you'll have to interact with your loved one in a way that's nurturing to both of you—with smiles, hugs, and laughter.

It's essential that you make it a priority to take care of yourself, too. You need both time alone and time with friends. Keep yourself healthy, including physical and social activity. Get involved in a support group for other caregivers.

And since this is a book about sex, you know I'll also tell you to give yourself sexual pleasure! Keeping your sexuality alive is in your own hands, double entendre intended. Please reread chapter 4, Sex with Yourself and Toys.

OTHER CHRONIC CONDITIONS

Every medical condition you might face as you age deserves its own section here, but that would make this book impossibly long. Use this book as a jumping-off place to take questions to your doctor and explore the Internet for books, articles, and support forums about your medical challenge. See Recommended Resources.

Whatever is going on for you, please consult your doctor and let him or her know how important your sexuality is to you. I can't stress that enough. It's the only way we can communicate to our medical professionals that health isn't defined by absence of disease—it's having a vibrant quality of life.

12

SEX WITHOUT ERECTIONS

I've stopped chasing my twenty-year-old libido. Someone needs to tell us boomer men that it is okay to move to a new way of experiencing pleasure.

In your youth, erections used to spring to action automatically. Now they're less quick to rise, less rigid, and less dependable. It probably takes manual or oral stimulation to get hard, and any distraction or anxious moment can deflate you. All this is normal aging.

Does that mean you have erectile dysfunction? No.

Sex journalist Michael Castleman makes the useful distinction between "erection dissatisfaction"—which is what I just described and affects most older men—and "erectile dysfunction" (ED). If your erections are unreliable, but you can make them happen during masturbation, you have erection dissatisfaction. If you cannot raise even a semi-firm erection after extended masturbation (while sober and not impaired by drugs), that's ED.[77]

> I have ED issues. While that has been difficult for us both to deal with, it has helped us to, as our therapist puts it, "stop focusing on the penis." We have integrated toys, light bondage, spanking, dirty talk, things of that nature into our play that we may not have, had I not had to deal with this.

Sex can be so much more than erections and penetration. Erection dissatisfaction is a wonderful opportunity to enjoy a slower, more creative style of sex. If you're partnered with a woman, your needs and hers will be well-matched: you'll both enjoy more kissing, more touching, more arousal time, a less goal-oriented approach to sex, and more enjoyment of all the moments along the way. The goal doesn't have to be intercourse—there are plenty of ways to satisfy each other.

The changing male sexual response is not a reason to panic, but an opportunity to see sex differently, and enjoy it fully.

> Many men of my age still see themselves as having to "perform" with a penis, and some are unable to. Personally, I am comfortable when I experience some erection problems. It happens. As I continue to age, I expect there will be a lot more of that. But if it doesn't bother my lover, it won't bother me.

THE MOST IMPORTANT MESSAGES OF THIS CHAPTER

Before we go further with the drugs and devices that can help you with erectile function, and ways to have satisfying sex without an erection, please take these most important messages to heart:

1. **You can have orgasms without an erection.** Many men don't realize this—they think orgasms are over if they can't get hard. Not true.

2. **You can give orgasms to your partner just fine without an erection.** There are many ways to please a partner that don't require a hard penis.

The best oral sex I ever had was with an older gentleman who told me from the get-go he could not get erections, but he loved to please the ladies, and he sure had a talented tongue.

3. **You'll cause real hurt and misunderstanding by turning away from your partner.** Talk to your partner about what you're going through and what you need. Keep your intimacy and communication strong.

One of my biggest turn-ons is seeing, hearing, sensing my partner's pleasure. If I can enable, enhance, or assist in that pleasure that gives me such amazing satisfaction on all sorts of levels! My pleasure feeds off her pleasure.

ELUSIVE ERECTIONS

If you can get an erection, but you can't count on maintaining it, these nonpharmaceutical tips can help:

- Have sex on an empty stomach, not after a meal.

- If you're a smoker, quit. Smoking raises the risk of ED by 50 percent.[78]

- Lose weight if you're overweight. Obesity increases ED risk by 90 percent.[79]

- Limit alcohol. More than two drinks a day can inhibit erectile functioning.[80]

- Exercise regularly to increase blood flow.

- Show your partner how you like to be touched and stimulated. Assume that your partner wants to please you but may be unsure about what you'd like.

- Explore sex toys to give you extra stimulation. See chapter 4, Sex with Yourself and Toys, for plenty of ideas.

- Try a cock ring or penile band to keep from losing your erection. Choose one that's stretchy or has Velcro or snap fastenings so that you can remove it easily, and wear it for no more than twenty to thirty minutes. If it's uncomfortable, remove it immediately.

• Explore the many ways to have satisfying sex without the goal of penetration. Open your attitude to encompass many different styles of sex that do not require an erection.

A great way to make love is to get in sort of an X position so genitals are touching. Look each other in the eye. She reaches down and pleasures herself. He reaches down and pleasures himself. On his upstroke, the meat of the top of his hand impacts her vulva, so she feels his rhythm and it replicates missionary position. By pleasuring himself, he'll probably stay harder. After a while he can occasionally "slip it in" while she continues to pleasure herself—just a few strokes, then back out and thumping away at the vulva as he goes. He can also take an interlude to rub the head of his penis all over her vulva while she continues to pleasure herself. Very erotic.

SOME CAUSES OF ERECTILE DYSFUNCTION

- Atherosclerosis (hardening of the arteries)
- Vascular disease
- Diabetes
- Kidney disease
- Multiple sclerosis
- Alcoholism
- Injury to the nerves and vessels that supply the genitals
- Scarring of penile tissue
- Smoking
- Obesity
- Sedentary lifestyle (lack of exercise)
- Performance anxiety
- Stress

From "Sexuality in Midlife and Beyond,"
a Harvard Medical School Special Health Report[81]

NO ERECTIONS

If you are experiencing true erectile dysfunction, you don't get hard through extended masturbation, nor are you hard when you first awaken. Your first step: Get a medical diagnosis. ED itself is not a diagnosis—it's a symptom that something else is going on in your body that interferes with your ability to raise an erection, a physical condition that hampers blood flow, nerve functioning, or both.

ED may be the canary in the coal mine that signals heart disease, high blood pressure, diabetes, a disease of the nervous system such as multiple sclerosis or Parkinson's, or a number of other conditions. It may be a side effect of a medication you're taking that can be changed. **Get a medical work-up—** run tests until you find out what's going on. This is vitally important.

Make sure your doctor understands that your sexuality is important to you, whether you're partnered or not. Find out which treatments and coping strategies might be appropriate for your situation.

MEDICAL OPTIONS FOR ED
By David Pittle, PhD, MDiv

If you have ED and penetration is important to you and your partner, talk to your urologist about which of these methods might be right for you:

- Cialis, Viagra, or Levitra. If one of these doesn't work, try a different one. These are not effective for everyone, however, and you must consult your doctor about whether these are advisable for your medical condition.

- Alprostadil injections work for most men. The idea of an injection in the penis is unpleasant, but the actual injection is almost painless. It is a bit expensive for frequent use, and the medication needs to be stored below 25 degrees Celsius (77 Fahrenheit). Alprostadil must not be used more than three times a week.

- The vacuum device (penis pump) works better for masturbation than for intercourse. It may work to raise an erection that is hard enough for intercourse, but some couples find it distracting, and the erection may not be satisfactory.

- A penile implant is the best solution for erectile dysfunction coming from physical causes. There is normally little discomfort the next day, little to none after that, and full healing takes three to four weeks for most men. The older implants have lasted twenty to twenty-five years. The newer ones are even better and should last a lifetime. It is usually covered by insurance.

—David M. Pittle, PhD, MDiv
is a sex therapist in San Rafael, CA.

ARE ERECTION PILLS FOR YOU?

Viagra, Levitra, and Cialis (PDE-5 inhibitors) work by relaxing smooth muscles and widening the blood vessels, enabling the penis to fill with blood. They work to raise erections in about 70 percent of men who try them. They are less effective for men with diabetes or following prostate cancer surgery.[82]

Check with your doctor about whether PDE-5 inhibitors are advisable, given your medical condition. Never try it out by borrowing a pill from a friend or ordering via the Internet. These drugs are dangerous if you take nitrates or have unstable cardiovascular disease. They may be ill-advised if you have low blood pressure or take drugs for high blood pressure. Ask your doctor—don't try to figure it out on your own.

Realize that even when these pills improve your erectile function, they are not a magic solution. They don't supply libido or stimulation—you'll still need to have a sexy mood and direct physical stimulation. They also don't resolve your relationship problems.

An erection drug will not make you a better lover. Some women tell me that they actually enjoy sex less when a man uses these drugs because "it's all about the penis." With the thinning vaginal tissues and decreased lubrication that most women of our age experience, a drug-enhanced erection that lasts and lasts can be more painful than satisfying.

Have an honest, heart-to-heart conversation with your partner about this—don't just take the pill and assume that she'll love it. And if your partner does love it, don't let it substitute for all the other ways that you stimulate each other. It's just one part of sex.

Performance enhancing drugs can be awesome, but only if the man is willing to be a giving lover in other ways.

PENILE INJECTIONS

If the erection pills don't work for you or are not advisable, your doctor may recommend a drug that is injected directly into the side of the penis to stimulate blood flow. Injections are effective for about 80 percent of men. They work better than erection pills for men with diabetes and following prostate surgery.[83]

You may feel squeamish about sticking a needle into your penis, but your medical professional can teach you how to do it properly. Once they get used to it, many men use injections as their erection aid of choice. Your doctor will also make sure you have the right medicine and the correct dose.

Limitations: These medications are expensive, need

refrigeration, have a short shelf life, and aren't always covered by insurance. Very rarely, scarring develops that can result in curvature of the erect penis (Peyronie's Disease), usually due to incorrect injection procedure. If this starts to happen, see your doctor right away—the condition can be treated.[84]

> The most successful for me has been the penile injections. When I used the injections the first time, I was not so psychologically skillful and the poor woman was grossed out by the idea. But later partners found ways to be okay with it.

MUSE PELLETS[85]

MUSE stands for "medicated urethral system for erection." In this therapy, the pellet form of the same drug used in penile injections is inserted about in inch into the urethra with a disposable plastic applicator. Some men find it easier to use than injections, although it is effective in only about 30 percent of men and it may sting.

PENIS PUMPS

I bought a medical grade vacuum pump designed for the purpose. It comes with a bunch of varied size cock rings. The reduced pressure in the tube pulls blood into the penis. The cock ring then keeps the blood in the penis. One partner used to like to use the pump on me herself, with me on my back, then she would slide herself down on my penis.

The vacuum erection device (VED), also known as vacuum constriction device (VCD), is an airtight plastic cylinder with a pump. Insert your penis and pump out the air, which draws blood into the penis and gives you an erection. Then slide the constriction ring or band from the cylinder onto the base of your penis to maintain your erection by keeping the blood from escaping.[86] Sex therapist David Pittle adds this advice:

The medical grade vacuum penis pump is great, and it has proven safe for frequent use by most men, but avoid a prolonged session. You should check with your physician if you have any doubt. If you remove the cock ring every half hour, there is probably no serious danger going for a few cycles, but several applications in sequence can damage small capillaries, eventually causing some discomfort, even pain. The vacuum not only draws in blood, but also frequently some lymphatic fluid. Excessive use can raise blisters. This will cause more pain. My advice is to enjoy using your medical grade vacuum pump in moderation.

IMPLANTS[87]

A penile implant replaces the spongy tissue (corpora cavernosum) in the penis with a device that creates an erection. While implants make the shaft firm, the head of the penis remains soft.

There are two types of penile implants:

1. Semirigid rods make the penis firm enough for penetration, yet still flexible enough to bend down for concealment while clothed. The size and firmness remain constant, so the man is semi-erect all the time.

2. An inflatable penile prosthesis has a reservoir that holds salt water, two or three chambers, and a pump that moves the salt water from the reservoir to the chambers. When the man wants an erection, he presses the pump, which is in his scrotum or lower abdomen. Afterward, he presses a release valve.

I tried all three erection pills. Each provided success for a while and then became increasingly ineffective. I moved on to injections, which also failed. The most annoying characteristic with all of our attempts was that the drug would provide an initial erection, which would then fail once inserted for sex. We started to joke that the penis didn't like to work in the dark.

My urologist at the time said that was it, but we are a

very sexually active couple and did not consider abstinence acceptable. We did some research online about penile implants and interviewed a short list of doctors. I had the inflatable implant device, and six weeks later, we were able to have all the sex we wanted, no ED problems. I have all the sexual feelings that I had when I was thirty.

"OUTERCOURSE"

I have had ED since taking Zoloft for several years and spent time and money chasing erections so that I could have "normal" penile sex. Finally I went to a therapist and realized that I could now move beyond penis-centered sex. That has led us to try dildos, pegging, more oral, spanking, and vibrators. For the first time in my life I feel that I can be authentic and try whatever we want. We have gone to sex shops and asked formerly embarrassing questions about all kinds of things. The people are nice and don't think us odd at all.

You can bring your partner to orgasm with your hand, your mouth, or a well-placed sex toy. Your partner can give you glorious pleasure, including orgasm, without an erection. Explore alone and together how to give and receive pleasure. Teach your partner what to do to please you. Sex can be satisfying for both of you with exploration, creativity, communication.

The adjustment is mental as well as physical—changing your attitude that a hard penis is a requirement for sex. If you're partnered with a woman, you've learned by now that most women do not get orgasms from intercourse anyway, but from clitoral stimulation, which is most easily accomplished with fingers, tongue, and sex toys.

Let yourself be open to letting go of intercourse as the goal, and explore the pleasures of "outercourse."

If I had a regular partner who really wanted my penis in her vagina, I would go for a penile implant. But right now it is hardly worthwhile. Most of the women with whom I have been sexual in the last few years were much more responsive to everything from sensual massage to cunnilingus, and so on. Intercourse is, if anything, secondary—so I often do nothing about the ED. My partners aren't always convinced, but I do enjoy fellatio and being masturbated, even if I don't get hard.

SEXUAL PLEASURE FOR YOU, TOO

I would appreciate information on what couples can do to achieve a man's orgasm who has ED. I have currently been told that I will not be able to achieve erections without having an implant. I believe that the surgeon is incorrect and that there can be stimulation, fantasies, and erotica that will either create erections or enable orgasm. I have already achieved erections occasionally with pornography, but do not find it adequate.

Most men have the misconception that male orgasms require erections—they do not. Even if you have a partial erection—or no erection—you can reach orgasm with the right sexual stimulation. So instead of focusing on whether or not you're getting hard, center your attention on what kinds of touch and sex play feel good, arouse you, and bring you pleasure. Tune into the *sensations* instead of the *expectations*. As sex journalist Michael Castleman says, "In an erotic context filled with kissing, cuddling, fondling, massage, oral, and sex toys, a man with a semi-erect or even flaccid penis can enjoy orgasms as intense as any he ever experienced during intercourse."[88]

STRAP ON A DILDO

If your own penis isn't erect enough for penetration, but your partner loves penetration, experiment with using a dildo either manually or while wearing it in a harness specially made for this. The dildo—a penetrative sex toy, often phallic shaped—becomes a penis prosthesis. You wear it, and you and your partner enjoy vaginal or anal penetration. Some of these harnesses are designed to let you or your partner fondle your penis at the same time. They may look like actual harnesses, or they may be specially designed, snug underwear with an O-ring to hold the dildo.

Until recently, harnesses for strap-on sex were designed for women and transgender men, and now a few smart companies are designing them to fit male bodies, also. Check out the Deuce by SpareParts (www.myspare.com) and the briefs and boxers by RodeoH (www.rodeoh.com). Although you can buy online, I strongly suggest that you shop at your local, progressive sexuality shop, where the well-trained staff can explain how they're used, help you pick out a dildo to fit the harness and your partner's preference, and describe the qualities of different styles and brands.

I'd love to see more men with ED get comfortable with strap-on sex. In a narrative published in the *Journal of Sex & Marital Therapy*,[89] a man with complete ED after cancer treatment was initially suspicious of using a harness and dildo, but discovered:

> *It caught me by total surprise how natural intercourse felt with this strap-on device. I discovered that my hip movements with the dildo on were the same as during normal intercourse. Our body contact and embrace were full and natural, as well. The first time that we used the dildo, my partner reached down and held my penis in her hand. She had coated her hand with the same lubricant used to coat the dildo and stimulated my penis in synchrony with my pelvic movements. There was little sensory difference between this act and intercourse—my penis was not in her vagina but it did not know that. It was in a wet, warm place being firmly mechanically stimulated. My hindbrain took over, and I carried the act through to orgasm, to the sexual satisfaction of both my partner and myself.*

ADVICE TO A PARTNER

I'm seventy-two. My partner of a year's time has just confessed to me that he no longer has any desire for sex. Prostate cancer surgery has left him with erectile dysfunction. He acquired a pump, which didn't do the job, and he then slowly became distant. We tried what we knew to no avail—the erection wouldn't last. I'm perplexed. There is no more affection, cuddling, or intimacy left, just roll over and go to sleep. We love each other but now live as brother and sister. I want to work on our sexual problem. Where do I begin? He wants to give me my own sexual pleasure once in a while, but I don't want that. I want either mutual or not at all.

I say to this reader (and to you, if your experience is similar): I know you want mutual pleasure, but take the first step of welcoming him to arouse and satisfy you, as he has offered to do. This will bring you closer, help you both feel sexy again, and let him see that his challenges are not preventing him from pleasing you. It's a gift to him to let him give that gift to you.

Later, once he feels comfortable and empowered by pleasuring you, tell him you'd like to make him feel good, too. Ask him to lie back and accept your touch—no goals, no expectations. Then give him a massage if he welcomes it. If he's squirmy and uneasy, don't pressure him, just see if there are places you can touch or rub that he enjoys without feeling nervous—maybe just his feet or the tight muscles in his back. Many men are not used to accepting touch unless it's sexual, so don't take it as a rejection of you if he seems on guard.

Men can get aroused and reach orgasm without erections. If he's giving signs through his breathing or body language that he's getting turned on—or would welcome getting turned on—pleasure his penis with your mouth and hands. The aim is not to give him an erection (take that out of the game plan entirely). The aim is to give him pleasure.

Ask him to show you how he likes to be touched—he may need firmer stimulation than he used to. Silicone lubricant will let your hands glide and won't dry out quickly.

Once he's comfortable that you want to give him pleasure and he doesn't worry that you're judging him or expecting an erection, indulge his fantasies. Does he like to watch you give him oral sex? Does anal or prostate stimulation turn him on? What fantasies would he like to enact? Experiment.

It would be a good idea to see a sex therapist while you're working on a new way of relating to each other. You'll learn ways to explore pleasure without anxiety or pressure.

To all of you who recognize your own situation in this reader's story, I hope you'll explore all the ways you can give each other pleasure without any need for an erect penis. There are so many ways you can arouse and satisfy each other that keeps the intimacy and joy strong in your relationship, without the pressure of penis performance.

I researched everything I could find on the web ranging from surgical implants to surrogate partners and "boner pills." I found some things that worked and some disappointments at being an underachiever at PIV [penis-in-vagina] sex. I worked with a marvelous sex therapist and several partners to regain a sense of being a sexual man in his sixties. I learned how to provide multiple orgasms to my partners and how they could best bring me to a climax—and that if they didn't, it was okay.

One chapter about erectile dysfunction cannot be definitive when there are so many causes, treatments, and coping strategies. See our Recommended Resources for books on this topic. You'll find readers' stories and expert tips which complement the information here in *Naked at Our Age: Talking Out Loud about Senior Sex.*

I am eighty-one, she is a few years younger, and there is one word to describe our sex life: breathtaking! We usually have to quit when she can no longer catch her breath, all within my loving poem of "fingers and toes, tongue and nose, when it comes to orgasms, anything goes." Five years ago I had a prostatectomy because of cancer. I lost about 25 percent of my ability to gain an erection, but oh, we do find ways to please. The imagination is the biggest part of sexual relations.

13

SINGLE AFTER
ALL THESE YEARS

I am a fifty-nine-year-old lesbian, not in a relationship. I desperately miss making love and experiencing the erotic warmth and excitement of a woman's body making love to me. I am continuously amazed by my erotic feelings! Forty years ago, I figured I'd be long past this at my age!

If you're in a loving relationship now, treasure each other. At our age, we know with every birthday how likely it is that one of us will be left alone. Of course that's true at any age—no one has forever. Now, though, as we trudge back and forth from doctors' offices with ailments we couldn't even spell ten years ago, we can't fool ourselves as easily.

Even if we're healthy, we may come home one day and hear

our partner say that he or she wants to leave. Hearing those words is a blow to the gut. It's even worse when there are no words: a woman told me that her husband of thirty years didn't come home from work one day. She never heard from him again—only from his lawyer.

When we lose a partner due to death or breakup and find ourselves solo, the world that we knew is gone. We may retreat from intimacy, feeling too vulnerable to handle it—or we may rush into it. Our response to loss will be highly individual—like everything else we do and feel.

One woman friend of mine told me that after her divorce, she "wanted to fuck everything in sight." I think it's a usual thing, to seek reassurance of one's attractiveness and capacity to give and receive love. The first time I kissed a woman after the separation at age fifty, I started shaking all over, so fraught was the moment.

LATER-LIFE DIVORCE OR BREAKUP

The divorce rate among adults ages fifty and older doubled between 1990 and 2010.[90] The end of a marriage or significant relationship can feel like a welcome, life-giving release or a death blow to the heart. Or both. You may feel decimated by a divorce or breakup, or finally free to be yourself. As for sex, that may be arduous, tear-filled, and reluctant. Or it may come quickly with a zest for new experiences and new partners.

I was married for almost forty years to a man who didn't give a rip about what I felt—he had his orgasm and he was done. We're now divorced and I'm seeing a man who gives me multiple orgasms every time and takes about one or one-and-a-half hours to get the job done. I am getting what I deserved all of those years that I was married, and enjoying it very much.

It's tough to regain your confidence and feel sexy after a breakup when it wasn't your choice. Being dumped leaves big bruises and a gaping hole in your world. But many say that after taking time to grieve the loss, they emerge with a new sense of self and sexiness, as if the sap is rising again and a new bud is ready to flower. The hunger for sex may come back stronger than it had been for years, especially if the relationship was stagnant.

First marriage: the most miserable five years of my existence. Second marriage: finally began to learn about good sex but she only felt amorous when we were drinking, and when I quit drinking, my sex life ended. Third marriage: an essentially sexless marriage and one more divorce. Then at fifty-five, I met a woman online. We developed a bad case of the hots for one another. When we finally got together, the sex was incredible beyond description. We married and, somehow, it's lasted. I'm sixty-four, happily married, totally faithful, and the sex is better than ever.

According to a 2004 AARP study of 1,148 forty- to seventy-nine-year-olds who divorced in their forties, fifties, or sixties, many take a hiatus from sexuality after divorce:

> *After their divorce...[t]he majority (56 percent) report sexual touching or hugging in varying degrees of frequency (daily to once or twice a month), while 38 percent of the total claim not doing any of these at all. Many women, especially those who have not remarried (69 percent), do not touch or hug at all sexually. An even larger majority of women who have not remarried do not engage in sexual intercourse (77 percent saying not at all), in comparison with about half of men (49 percent) who have not remarried.*[91]

Those statistics surprise me, because most of my readers tell me quite the opposite—they're eager to experience sex again. They want to free themselves from the previous relationship, get their sexy selves revved up again, and create an intimate connection with a new person who is not their ex. Maybe the discrepancy is because the people who write to me are more likely to be sex-positive and sex-desirous?

> *At age fifty-nine, my husband of eighteen years dumped me. I emerged after a nine-month mourning period feeling horny as hell. I hadn't had any sexual desire throughout our marriage because I had spent all my sexual energy avoiding sex with my husband. Except for a brief crush on our carpenter, which I wouldn't have done anything about, I had never looked at a man sexually since my wild, single-girl days.*

Now I was long past menopause and supposedly long past my sexual prime. My body didn't know this, however. It started twitching every time an attractive man came into the room. All of a sudden I was evaluating every man I saw as a sexual partner. I was on fire all the time.

—Erica Manfred
in "The Wacky Iraqi, the Shaman Lover, and Me" in *Ageless Erotica*.

TAKING TIME TO HEAL

An astonishing number of women go directly from one relationship into another, even though they know that they should take a break between relationships, give themselves time to heal, and clear out some emotional baggage. In my clinical experience, 90 percent of the time, at least one person has already begun another emotional/sexual relationship before there is an actual physical separation from the first partner.

—Glenda Corwin
in *Sexual Intimacy for Women: A Guide for Same-Sex Couples*

It's tempting to dull the pain by rushing into a new relationship that assures us that we're desirable and worthy of love (or at least lust) and gives us that adrenalin rush that we crave. But how do you know who you are—independent of half the couple you used to be—if you don't take time to be alone? Give yourself the gift of self-knowledge and independence, without jumping right into being half of a couple again. Experience being whole on your own first.

I've had several significant loves in my life, and I've grown and learned life lessons from each of them. But I honestly would not be the person I am today without a lot of time alone, unpartnered, to contemplate what is important to me, what I have to give in the world as well as to a lover, and what I need to change *in myself* to be the person I want to be. I honestly feel that I would not have been ready for Robert, the most important and loving relationship of my life, if I hadn't had many relationships that ended, and time alone to learn from them.

Although the love of your life may be just a minute away from the end of your last relationship, more often I see people rush into the next relationship and repeat exactly the same problems that destroyed the relationship they just left!

I had relationships with several women in the years leading up to my marriage. After my divorce at fifty-one, I became serially infatuated with each of them, all over again. The trail of past relationships eventually led me back to examine some themes in my own erotic and romantic history. I realized that throughout my adult life I had been attracted to women who were emotionally or otherwise unavailable to me. Not for nothing had my married sex life been pallid and infrequent. Whether I am capable of greater love and erotic fulfillment than I was previously, I have yet to find out. I do feel a greater sense of freedom and openness to possibility than ever before, as well as a much stronger, clearer sense of what I want and what is right for me.

GRIEF

On August 2, 2013, the fifth anniversary of Robert's death, *The Huffington Post* published an intimate memoir essay that I wrote, titled "Sharing Body Heat." I described crawling into bed with Robert after he died to hold him and say goodbye. Sharing this openly and widely to HP's enormous readership was a risky thing to do, because *Huffington Post* readers often delight in posting crass comments. Still, I risked it because I wanted to reach people who were grieving or had grieved, and had their own memories to share.

And share they did: 500 comments (almost all of them warm and positive), thousands of new visitors to my website and blog, about a hundred personal emails. Grief feels like such a private experience, yet once we share it, we realize how much we have in common.

Publishing this piece was also a way for me to take a huge step toward moving on myself. I had stayed sexually active with my delightful and ever-growing assortment of sex toys and my weekly date with myself—hurray for the pleasures of solo sex! I confess that the few attempts at partner sex during those five years had left me physically satisfied but emotionally sad, reinforcing for me that Robert was indeed gone and would never make love to me again.

I tell you all this because I want to share how confusing it can be to try to emerge from grief and become intimate with a new partner. Some of my readers report that having sex is the easy part—emotional intimacy is more difficult.

Going public with "Sharing Body Heat" had a powerful

effect on my own grief process. It was an intense experience to read the comments and the emails, and realize how deeply I had touched people. Those connections made me feel truly ready to move forward—finally.

At exactly the same time, in the way the universe works sometimes, a lover from my past surfaced again and became a "friend with benefits"—and I was able to open to him without sadness, without the interference of memories.

If you're wondering what's normal: The word *normal* has little meaning in the grief journey—it's all normal. We all grieve differently, and we all have our own time tables for being ready for sex again. Some get sexual right away, others wait months or years, some never want a partner again.

My love for my husband was so great that I am having a very difficult time considering another man. My head knows moving on is best, but my heart puts up a very good fight. I do believe that at seventy-four, finding someone with whom I am compatible from a distance would be best. His and her homes with visitation rights, perks, and genuinely being there for one another sounds like a plan to me! Easy to say and difficult to find!

DATING A SURVIVOR OF LOSS

I fell in love my first year of dating with a widow, who still had her last husband's ashes in the closet five years out. Her friends pushed her to date. Neither of us was ready. Yet those three delightful months—full of poetry and tears— were very healing and dear and soul profiting for both of us. Especially the sex. One cannot underestimate the mystery of healing, honest, soul-deep sex.

When I started dating after losing Robert, I thought that I could only date a widower, because only someone who has gone through this awful journey could understand. I later expanded my options, but I still have a special place in my heart for widowers. Here's why:

- When they talk with animation and suddenly sink into silence and sadness, I understand.

- When they bring up anecdotes about their spouse, I get it.

- When they slip into present tense talking about their spouse, then correct themselves, I remember how often I've done that.

- When they talk vulnerably about their grief, I know I can do that, too.

- When they laugh and talk about their future changes they want to make in their lives, I know what it took to get to that point.

This is one of the things that I like about the widower I'm dating. We can talk about our spouses, acknowledge how lucky we were in having them, sometimes be sad about their loss—and still enjoy our time with each other.

Don't judge us if we think we're ready to date, then realize we're not. We don't grieve for a time, and then suddenly we're done. It's a spiral: we cycle in and out of grief. We can feel that we're ready to move forward, and then we're struck down by missing our beloved.

If you date a widow or widower, please don't worry that you're in competition with his or her perfect spouse. Don't expect us to take down all the photographs or hide the urn. (Though once you get to bedroom status, I think you're within your rights to ask that the wedding photo be turned away from the bed or in another room.)

Understand that there will always be that layer of memories and love, and accept that part of us. You're not in competition with our memories. They show that we know how to love.

We were both widowed when we met—he for seven years, I for five. Many things have conspired to make us feel fulfilled and bonded, one being the way we can speak freely, and with warmth, about our spouses. We view them not as impediments, but rather as inspiration. The happy marriages we experienced have helped us find joy in each other without having to compromise our private memories.

Self-aware widows and widowers understand that dating new people is part of the attempt to create what they call in grief parlance *the new normal*. So yes, part of us cries out to the deceased partner, "Just don't be dead anymore!" as I've found myself doing. But the other part knows that it's healthy and necessary to meet new people on their own terms, with a fresh and welcoming attitude, and not compare them with memories.

> *I'm a social worker in hospice care. Many of my coworkers are uncomfortable at best—and shocked at worst—when the surviving partner of someone in their seventies and eighties brings up the issue of missing sex with the deceased partner, or about sexual concerns with a new partner. I lead a caregiver support group, and I make it a point to bring up sexual issues related to grief and loss. I can see the look of relief in the eyes of the group when someone is finally willing to acknowledge this!*

READY TO DATE AGAIN?

> *I spent a year in deep grief, not knowing how I was ever going to be able to love again. I surprised myself by falling in love with someone new a year later. He had plenty of space in him to absorb my grief attacks. Like the time he arrived on my porch to go to an art museum by bus just as I melted down about all the times my husband and I took the bus for fun day trips. My new love listened to my story, held*

me, and normalized the whole experience. He said I clearly had space for him in my heart, so he didn't mind and even welcomed hearing about the life I had with my husband. It was incredibly healing to be witnessed and loved through the last of my grief process.

How can you tell when it's time to put away the chocolate, air out the blanket you've been huddling under, and get back out into a social scene that could lead to a new relationship? If you're like me, you'll try to emerge and run back into hiding a few times—until finally it works, and you feel like you've stepped into the sunshine after a long time in the darkness.

In *Getting Naked Again: Dating, Romance, Sex, and Love When You've Been Divorced, Widowed, Dumped, or Distracted*, psychologist Judith Sills, PhD, offers these tips for knowing when you're ready to date again:

- You are functioning again, no longer curled in bed weeping, sleepless, or stuporous.

- The physical symptoms of loss have subsided (heart pain, headaches, whatever your body did in response to your loss).

- You have moved past the despairing feeling of being utterly lost and without a future.

- You are past the guilt and self-blaming, and past blaming him or her.

- You have taken active steps to sweeten and improve your life.

- You got rid of something filled with memories that you had been hanging on to.

- If you were dumped, you are beyond the need to hear every obsessive detail about your ex and his or her new partner. You've lost interest in analyzing your ex's personality.

- You are able to look in the mirror, look through your closet, look around at your social world, and smile at some of what you see.

A hint to widows: If you're dating again and invite a man to your home, please rearrange things so that your home is not a shrine to your late husband. That really takes the steam out of the new guy.

TRANSITIONAL LOVERS

Although it's certainly possible to fall in love right away after loss of a spouse or long-term lover, that's usually the rebound effect and not likely to last. The first lover after a loss is usually transitional—a way to get your sea legs, to see yourself as a desirable lover, to shake off the low self-esteem that often follows a breakup, and to practice being in a relationship in a new way. "Sexual mentors, palate cleansers, and other transitional relationships" Judith Sills calls them in *Getting Naked Again.* Gail Sheehy calls them "Pilot Light Lovers." in *Sex and the Seasoned Woman: Pursuing the Passionate Life.*

Transitional lovers can be really good for you. They can

reignite your sexual fire and teach you a lot about yourself and your capacity for rising from the embers. Just be careful not to let the glow of a new relationship and the zest of new sex blind you to good sense. Enjoy the rush, but don't confuse good orgasms with falling in love. Don't share finances, move in, or get married quickly.

> *Imagine my surprise post-divorce when I realized I was feeling the need for a lover. It took me about a year to feel like I was myself, but once I cleared the mental cobwebs and found my Happy, I started seriously checking out all sorts of men with speculative thoughts running through my head. I felt sexy. I attracted men because they recognized my sexiness. I purchased my own condoms.*

FRIENDS WITH BENEFITS

Many of us are independent, with full lives, but partnered sex is lacking. We're not always fortunate enough to be in a love-filled, committed relationship. Does that mean we should not have sex until that happens again (if it does)? That's the choice of some of us, but not all of us.

Friends with benefits means a friendship that involves sex—it doesn't mean a hook-up devoid of emotion (not that there's anything wrong with that if it's what you want). We can feel close to someone, even intimate, in a FWB arrangement, without wishing that the relationship could be exclusive, primary, full-time, or live-in.

I'm not interested in an exclusive long-term relationship—I have been independent too long to want to compromise on things. But I wish I had a man in my closet whom I could take out when I needed an escort or was horny. I would definitely accept a "friend with benefits."

I have had friends with benefits a few times over my many decades of single adult life. We were real friends—we cared about each other, confided in each other, enjoyed learning about each other, and delighted in conversation in and out of bed. We enjoyed activities that weren't sexual as well as those that were. We just weren't in love and we were not expecting commitment or exclusivity.

When it was time for the sexual part of the relationship to end—usually because one of us fell in love with someone else and was ready for a committed relationship with that person—we ended it cleanly and honestly, and stayed platonic friends after that. We remain friends to this day. We slide in and out of each other's lives with ease, secure in the lasting friendship, with fond memories from our past.

I'm over fifty, longtime divorced, and a friend with benefits is really the only type of relationship that appeals to me. I have no wish to marry again, or move in with someone. I don't want to do a man's housecleaning or cooking or deal with budgets or family drama. A friend with benefits sounds great to me.

I get occasional emails from women asking whether a FWB or *sex buddy* relationship is possible at our age. The women who write me usually worry that they'll become too emotionally involved. I say that if you're worried about this, heed that fear, because it's likely a warning sign that you will respond this way.

FWB isn't right for all of us. I'm not pushing you to try it—rather, to know yourself, your emotional needs and habits, and determine for yourself whether it would work for you.

> *It's nice to have orgasms with another person. I've just found that intimacy with a "sex buddy" is somewhat lacking. It's kind of like "Diet Sex."*

Sex without commitment can work if we believe in it ethically and personally, and we're clear with ourselves and our partners about the boundaries. Are we friends first, lovers second? Are we playing at romance, or refusing to let the relationship become romantic? Are the reasons that we want to be friends with benefits but not actual "in-love" lovers clear and valid to both of us? Honesty is required in this kind of relationship.

I believe strongly that if there's a third person involved—you or your friend or lover has a primary partner—it needs to be okay with that partner, too. Don't sneak or lie—if it can't happen honestly, it shouldn't happen. I don't moralize much because I believe that anything two consenting adults do is no one's business but theirs. But if another partner is involved, that partner has to give consent, too—either to the specific sexual friendship or to the idea in general, if the partner doesn't want to know the details.

Of course older people can have friends with benefits, though I don't think the label is particularly helpful. Relationships span a spectrum, and can be constantly changing. My philosophy is that if you feel like having sex with someone, why not? We're certainly aware of the precautions you need to take to be safe. The only reason not to is if you are in, and value, a sexually exclusive relationship with someone else.

MEANTIME, DO IT YOURSELF

If you don't have a partner, keep having regular sex with yourself. Do this whether or not you feel like it. I'm serious. We do harm to our health—physical, sexual, and emotional—if we forego sexual stimulation and orgasm. At our age, putting sex aside (yes, masturbation counts as sex) promotes vaginal atrophy and dryness in female bodies, and makes it much more difficult to reach orgasm and/or accept penetration if you want to in the future. For male bodies, lack of arousal and orgasm decreases erectile ability and is bad for the prostate. When preventive treatment feels so good, why not do it?

If you're not in the mood—and if you're grieving, you may not be—put self-pleasuring on your to-do list, and just do it. Along with all the other benefits, you'll sleep better and your mood will lift. Trust me on this.

If you skipped chapter 4, Sex with Yourself and Toys, I

hope you'll return to it now. You'll learn some surprising benefits of solo sex. And you'll want to know why a sex toy may become your new best friend!

Solo sex keeps everything in working order—brain, body, blood flow, ability to orgasm. And then if life surprises you and sends you a new love, you'll be ready and able to enjoy each other fully. You never know what—or who—is around the corner!

> *Seven years after my beloved husband of thirty-seven years died, my daughter nudged me to look for someone to go with to dinner, museums, and concerts. I was eighty. I joined a dating service online and met a gentleman who was eighty-five. The most shocking thing to me was how my body responded to being near this senior citizen. I had been forced to turn off those desires many years before when my husband was ill. I was embarrassed at how my body was responding to him at my age. We married a year later. Here we are, six years later, still active. I feel blessed that I found another love in my final years to make sweet love to me and make me feel pretty. My passion was never higher than with this gentle little man.*

14

THE NEW RULES
OF DATING

I am seventy-eight and have been widowed for ten years. Going on the dating sites took courage and a sense of adventure. I met some liberating and interesting men. Two were over sixty and became wonderful lovers. I used to feel that sex was only right within marriage. Wrong—at this age and stage, no need. I still have much to offer. There is still fire in the furnace.

You're ready to connect for dating, sex, love, companionship—but dating at our age feels awkward and downright weird. What are the guidelines? How do we meet someone? How do we navigate the jungle of online dating and avoid the tigers, snakes, and jackals? Welcome to the club! Whether you're widowed, divorced, a breakup survivor, or a longtime single, figuring out how single seniors meet and mate—or try to—may seem like a deep mystery.

SOME FACTS

- Thirty million Americans age fifty-five and older are single.[92]

- Single women seeking single men: there are only seven men for every ten women age sixty-five or above.[93]

- Forty percent of women and 13 percent of men over sixty-five are widowed and single.[94]

- Thirteen percent of women and 12 percent of men over sixty-five are divorced, separated, or for another reason living without their living spouse.[95]

- Five percent of women and 4 percent of men over sixty-five are single and never married.[96]

Note: I'm frustrated that the federal agencies and academic publications seem to track only traditional, legal marriages, with no mention of LGBT long-term partners in states without marriage equality, or alternative relationships. I hope that this changes.

As much as I would like to share my life with a significant other, I love my life the way it is and I'd rather not be in a relationship, than be in a relationship with the wrong person.

SINGLE AT MY AGE?

It's tough to be single after fifty or sixty. As a straight woman, I've felt invisible. Men my age and older seem to want younger women, way younger. When I tried to make the point on a dating site message board about the splendid qualities and joie de vivre of women our age, questioning why men wanted to date women more than fifteen years younger, men scoffed and talked about the "scenery." Hey, there's nothing wrong with our scenery, guys.

Not all of us old guys are slugs out chasing young stuff. That eye candy is nice to look at, but I prefer a woman my age that I can relate to and have something in common with. I don't even mind the baggage they bring along. God knows I have baggage of my own. The important thing is how we've processed and worked through that baggage. Actually, all those trials and tribulations add depth and character to the soul and make us more interesting.

I give a dating workshop called "How the Heck Do We Date at This Age?" We all seem distressed at the craziness of trying to mix and mingle as older people. For many of our generation, the last time we were single was in our youth,

when everything was different—the times, the social struc-
ture, and yikes, *we* were different. Opportunities were everywhere; practically everyone we met in our social circles was
also single, and a good many were interested, thanks to our
youthful hormones.

Maybe finding love wasn't easy (when has that ever been
easy?) but dating and getting to take off our clothes together
didn't take too much ingenuity, if that's what we wanted.
Believe me, I'd never return to those times filled with restrictive
mores (remember sitting by the phone waiting?), unrealistic
expectations (a mate would complete your life and you'd skip
into the sunset together?), and the constant fear of discovery
and pregnancy. Sure, it was simpler—we all knew the rules.
We either followed them or broke them, but we knew them.
But now...?

MAKE YOUR OWN RULES

If there are new rules of dating, no one knows what they are. So let's make up our own. Here are some of mine—which ones resonate with you?

1. If I want to attend a social event, I go. I don't need a date or a posse of friends. I arrive when I want, leave when I want.

2. I approach people I'd like to know. I start conversations, ask questions, once in a while end up with an exchange of email addresses or phone numbers.

3. I use online dating and feel free to send the first message.

4. I tell the truth about my age. I know that eliminates some potential dates who want to meet younger women, but what's the point of getting someone to meet me when I'm not what he's looking for? Duh.

5. I don't prolong the pain if I can see that we're not a match. I say no politely but clearly.

HOW CAN YOU GET WHAT YOU WANT IF YOU DON'T KNOW?

I recommend making a list of the qualities you're seeking. If you don't know what you're looking for, you either won't find it, or you won't recognize it when you do find it. Try this:

1. Make a list of thirty qualities that you'd like to find in the next person you date. (This is not as big a job as it sounds—just don't censor yourself. If you don't come up with thirty, you can stop at twenty.)

2. Sort those qualities into three columns:

    -   *Essentials* are those qualities that are absolute must-haves to make you happy.

    -   *Would be really nice* adds those qualities that you could do without if everything else is great, but they would add even greater appeal.

    -   *As long as I'm asking* gives bonus points to some preferences that might be whimsical, but would add a delicious flavor.

ESSENTIALS, NON-NEGOTIABLE	WOULD BE REALLY NICE	AS LONG AS I'M ASKING

3. Let the first column be a mental checklist to avoid bothering to date people who are clearly wrong for you. Let your list guide you toward the potential partners who will be right for you.

I developed this system by accident. I was cleaning out my old collection of journals after I met Robert. I found one that I wrote in my late forties, pre-Internet days, bemoaning that I wasn't meeting the kind of man I was looking for. I had made a list, which got so big that I divided it into the columns I described. In reading over this list decades later, I discovered that Robert had every last one of those thirty qualities—even those in column three. (Read *Better Than I Ever Expected: Straight Talk about Sex After Sixty* for our whole love story.)

Now, dating again (or trying to), I've revised this list several times. Is it time for you to make yours?

ONLINE DATING VERSUS OTHER WAYS OF MEETING

I'm a proponent of getting out and doing the activities you enjoy. If you meet someone, you already have that interest in common. If you don't meet someone, you still have a good time. I met Robert when he walked into the line dance class I was teaching. Without our love of dance, we never would have met. He had no interest in online dating—in fact, he didn't think he was looking for love at all. Falling in love blindsided us.

My situation is rare, though. Unless you live in a big city or a retirement community, the chances of meeting compatible, age-appropriate singles is low. So where are all those compatible, age-appropriate singles? Most are taking their chances with online dating.

There are sites specifically for seniors, but you don't have to restrict yourself to those. All the major dating sites have plenty of people our age, and most hopeful singles list themselves on several sites. When you put in your age and the age range you seek, you'll see them. Lots of them. I recommend online dating for our age group because that is where the people are.

I am a fifty-six-year-old, divorced, plus-sized woman who finally got back into dating after many years of self-imposed celibacy. I am now in a committed relationship, headed toward marriage, with a fifty-five-year-old man I met online dating! I constantly surprise him with my self-confidence and willingness to explore and experiment in the sexual side of our relationship.

AVOID WRITING A BAD PROFILE

I've read so many bad profiles. Here are the problems:

1. **Generic rather than specific.** If it sounds like all the others, it won't get read. What's special about *you*? Put forth your best qualities and most important interests. Don't waste your time with words like "honest, caring," and so on. Everyone says that, whether they are or not. And skip "walks on the beach"—if all the singles who say that's their favorite thing actually did it, the beaches would be jam-packed, especially in moonlight.

2. **Blah blah blah rather than enlightening.** Don't just throw down words that don't get us any closer to knowing you. This is your job interview! Unless your photo shows you as a Robert Redford or Sophia Loren double, you need words that attract us as well. If you sound like

you don't care and you're just doing this as a lark, we won't care either.

3. **No special qualities.** Ask an honest pal who knows you well, "What are my best qualities? What do I offer? How do I come across?" You may be surprised that you have qualities that you didn't think to mention.

4. **Badly written.** If you're not confident about your writing skills, ask a friend to help you. Don't have the friend write it for you, and don't hire someone to crank it out for you—it needs to be *you*. Proofread carefully. If you let spelling, grammar, and punctuation errors through, you give the impression you're uneducated and you don't care.

5. **Negative.** You can finesse how you say what you don't want without seeming unfriendly, unapproachable, and angry. Spend time making your profile sound welcoming to the right people, rather than trying to scare off or stomp out the wrong ones. Again, a friend can give you valuable feedback.

6. **Easy to skip.** Remember that list you made of the qualities of the person you seek? Now imagine that this person is skimming profiles, one after another. How will the person you're looking for know that you're someone worthy

of reaching out to? Work at presenting yourself so that the person you seek will be drawn to you in return. (Just please never post a "10 Requirements to Date Me" list—that's a terrible turn-off. Subtlety reigns.)

I'm sixty-four and been single since age fifty-three. I learned the hard way that it's best to be candid about who I am. I'm better off—and so are the men that I meet—if I'm a WYSIWYG (what you see is what you get) woman. There won't be getting-to-know-you surprises.

ADVICE ABOUT PROFILE PHOTOS

1. Use a current image that emphasizes your best attributes as your default photo. This should be a recently taken close-up of your face wearing a friendly smile. Do. Not. Wear. Sunglasses. I can't tell you how many profiles I skip over because the man is wearing sunglasses. I need to see your eyes. I also skip those that look unfriendly, so smile!

2. Make your default photo just you—no buddies on a fishing trip, no grandchildren, no pets, no arms around another person who might be your ex, and absolutely no edited photo with the person at your side cropped out. We can tell!

3. Have someone else take your photo. Our

phones make it easy to take "selfies"—photos of ourselves, which are easy to spot. We never look good in them, and we're usually scowling because we can't see the little screen without our reading glasses. You don't need to go to a photography studio—just ask a friend.

4. Include secondary photos that show you in some activity that you enjoy: hiking, playing music, creating art. Older photos are fine here, too—it's fun to see the long, bushy hair and patch-work jeans that you wore in 1970—but label them with the year, and make those secondary photos, not your main one.

5. Include a secondary, recent photo that shows your build as well as your face. Yep.

QUESTIONS YOU ASK ABOUT DATING

Is it okay to lie about my age? If I don't, no one will date me.

No. What's the point? If dating prospects don't want to date a person of your age, that's their loss. Starting with a lie compromises your honesty and authenticity. It will come out eventually, and then how will your date know when to believe you? Let's all agree to tell the truth, and create the world we want to live in, where aging isn't a bad word.

Why do women show photos of their pets and grandchildren on their profiles? I don't want to date their pets or grandchildren.

This is the most common complaint that I hear about women's profiles. One man told me, "It gives the message that there isn't room for me in her life." Women: take note!

Why do men wear sunglasses in their profile photos? It looks like they're shifty and hiding.

Either they're shifty and hiding, or they don't know that this bothers us. Men: take note!

Is there a nice way to ask women to send a full-body photo? Not nude or revealing, just showing their body type.

No, if she has chosen to post only head-shots, you can't ask for a full-body photo without sounding creepy. (If it's important that she be a certain body type, are you that body type, too? Do your photos show it?)

Why do men think that fifty pounds overweight is average build?

I wish I knew.

(From a man seeking women:) *I posted my profile and got so many responses that I can't possibly answer them all. What to do?*

If you're getting many responses from people who don't fit what you're seeking, make your profile more specific about what you're seeking. If that's not the problem, it's probably the odds. There are many more women looking for men than vice versa. Try to answer those who write to you, even if you just send a quick, "You sound like a wonderful person, but I don't see us as a match."

(From a woman seeking men:) *I posted my profile—why didn't I get any responses?*

See the previous question. Since men are in disproportionately in demand, many feel that they can just sit back and answer responses, rather than put out the effort to read through dozens or hundreds of profiles and make the first move. Go ahead and approach men who interest you—don't wait for them to find you.

When I'm ready to have sex with a new person, how do I know if he or she is "safe"?

You don't. Use barrier protection with everyone, every time. (Please read chapter 16, Safer Sex: Always.)

At sixty-five, I've been divorced for a few years now. Finding women my own age with whom I have a good mental connection has, surprisingly, been very elusive. I can't tell you how many times I hear, "My cat (dog, horse, or other companion animal) is my best friend," and "My life centers around my grandchildren." I ask, "What are you passionate about beyond pets and family?" I seldom get any substantive reply.

REJECTION

Rejection will happen. You'll reject many; many will reject you. It's not a reflection of your personal worth, it's just part of the dating game. It's so easy to make contact via online dating, that you have to accept that the answer is often *no*.

If someone messages you and you're not interested, don't lie. Do be polite. Do answer, unless the initial message is inappropriate or creepy.

Make your *No, thank you* clear and polite—something like, "Thank you for writing, and I enjoyed reading your profile… [Insert something complimentary about the person's qualities and/or interests here.] However, I don't think we're a match. [No need to give reason.] Best wishes for finding what you seek."

JUST SAY NO

Do not, please, lead someone on by email or phone, and then use responses like these to weasel out when your potential date presses you to meet in person:

- *I'm going out of town on business and will get in touch when I get back.* [You have no plan to get in touch again, ever.]

- *An old girlfriend/boyfriend has come back into the picture and we're going to give it another chance.* [There's no old girlfriend/boyfriend in the picture.]

- *My dog ate my homework.* [Wait—that's a different list. Sorry. But you get the idea—a lie isn't a solution, and it's hurtful and insulting to all who recognize that it's a lie.]

FIRST DATE

I'm quicker than many to suggest a meeting early in the message/email/phone call progression rather than dragging it out. You can exchange information before meeting and get an idea of who the person is, but you can't tell how you'll interact or whether the chemistry will be there. That takes an in-person meeting: a first date.

If you think of a first date as your way to learn about another person *and* about yourself without risking anything, it can be fun. Go for coffee or a walk, talk, see what you both enjoy discussing and doing, see how comfortable you feel together. Easy, breezy.

It's when you think of dating as interviewing a potential soul mate that it becomes fraught with anxiety, unpleasantness, and emotional danger. Tell yourself this: **"I'm not auditioning someone for the rest of my life. I'm only auditioning for a second date."** Seeing it that way may help you relax.

First dates aren't scary to me. I'm interested in learning what we do and don't have in common, and which of the divergences matter a lot. Plus, the writer in me loves hearing people's stories, and first dates are a great way to learn a huge amount in an hour, because it's expected that we share our stories. Here's what a first date is for me:

1. I get to know another human being whom I would not have met any other way. I listen a lot, ask questions, and try to learn about the other person.

2. I get to practice dating. How do I want to present myself? How much do I want to share?

3. I get to practice conversational skills. How can I do my part to create a satisfying give-and-take in our conversation?

4. I learn about myself as well as the other person. If I don't want further contact, why not? How can I use this experience to refine what I'm looking for, and how I'm looking for it?

Be yourself, be truthful, tell your date about yourself—and ask pertinent questions to encourage your date to do the same. Take the opportunity to show your date who you are and what matters to you.

Don't try to guess what your date wants to hear and enact that persona. We're too old to play the I'll-try-to-appear-to-be-who-you-want-me-to-be game. If someone would reject you knowing your political views, or number of divorces, or chronological age, get that over with early. Why waste everyone's time when it's clearly not going to work out?

Avoid talking in a nonstop monologue. Many of us chatter away out of nervousness and discomfort. You can't learn anything if you won't stop talking. I've had dates (first dates only) with men who talked on and on without ever asking me a question about myself. It made me feel that they didn't really care who I was. Your job isn't to avoid silences—it's to learn enough about the person in front of you to decide if you want a second date.

I've been known to interrupt a long monologue, try to wind it down with some compassionate statement, and then ask, "Is there anything you want to know about me?" That usually kickstarts a dialogue, but sometimes it just gets more painful. Sometimes you can't save a date.

I am fifty-three, and have found three romantic relationships and numerous casual female friends through online dating sites. The most important word is patience. For every one of my romantic relationships, I met twenty to thirty other women for coffee. Was I disappointed or frustrated that most of these meetings did not set off a ping of potential romantic spark? Not in the least! We had pleasant, stimulating conversations. They were almost all interesting women who could be nice friends (and several of them now are).

Don't waste too much time texting, chatting, or emailing before meeting face-to-face. I have found that you easily create inaccurate, overly idealized versions of that person if you spend too much time corresponding before meeting. Meet as many people as you have time for an hour at a local coffee shop to chat, get to know each other, and see if anything clicks. Do not expect chemistry in 95 percent of the meetings, just good conversation.

I am now madly in love with a woman I met six months ago on OkCupid. Our coffee meet set my romantic ping on overdrive, and it ended with a kiss that could flatten several small villages. Be persistent, and eventually the chemistry will be there. Enjoy the quest as much as the treasure at the end!

STAYING SAFE

You'll read some of this advice in any dating book, article, blog, or site. I'd be remiss if I left it out, though, in case you think it doesn't relate to our age group:

- Beware of strangers from afar who insist they're in love with you and want to visit you, but need a temporary loan. Disreputable people approach lonely seniors, seduce them with flowery language, fake photos, and assertions of love—and have a well-honed plan to rip them off. Any request for money is a red flag, whatever reason they claim. This is a crass and horrid business.

- Always have a few emails and phone calls before agreeing to meet in person. I recommend a video call such as Skype or FaceTime. The visual quality may not be stellar, but it's better than nothing, and you get to interact. There's a lot you can tell from people's speaking style, the energy they put out, and your dialogue with them.

- Know the real identity of the person before you agree to meet. This may seem obvious, but don't skip this step. Anyone can appear to be anyone online. (Have you ever watched the television program *Catfish*?) If a potential date won't give you a full name (which you can

Google), a personal email address, and a phone number, be wary.

- Meet in a public place: a coffee shop, park, or event that you'd both enjoy. Have a definite beginning and ending time so that you don't have to worry how to end the date. I like to schedule first dates in a park where I love to walk—if the date goes sour, at least I got an hour of exercise.

- Avoid expensive first dates—no one should have to invest heavily in a first meeting. Assume you'll be sharing the cost. Women: Throw out that old rule that the man always pays. If he says, "I want to treat you," that's fine, but don't assume that's the way the world works these days.

- If your date seems interested in your finances, close down the conversation.

- If your date seems creepy, gets too close, or makes you nervous, trust your instincts and end the date early. As much as I promote honesty, I'll give you a pass if you need to say simply, "I don't feel well. I need to leave." That's close enough to the truth.

- If you know at the end of the date that you'd like to see the person again, it's fine to say something like, "I've really enjoyed this. I'd like to know you better." But if the response isn't as enthusiastic, don't press. "Let's email and decide whether to meet again" is respectful and gives your date an out who isn't as eager to repeat the meeting. You're both juggling other first dates and potential dates—never assume that you're the only person in this stranger's life—and your date might need some time to decide which people to follow up on.

DISCLOSING

Being older, you likely have medical issues. How much do you reveal, and how soon? See if you're getting along and seem interested in seeing each other again first. If you can tell this will be the only date, you don't need to go deep. But if you like the person and you're enthusiastic about a second date, be honest about important issues that might impact the other person's choice of whether to go out with you again.

Don't dump endless details of your last health exam or therapy session, but do disclose up front what you fear will scare off a date—it's better to know now. If there's a health issue that would impact someone in a relationship with you, it's best to reveal it.

Charlie Nox is a sex blogger and dating coach who is a cancer survivor. She gave a talk about dating with cancer at a conference I attended. "Don't put cancer in your online profile —you'll get 'cancer spam,'" she advises. "Do tell on the first date." Be aware that the other person will be uncomfortable and not know how to respond at first. Let your own speaking style show the attitude you want to hear back. ("Yeah, cancer is a shit sandwich," Nox says to dates.)

If your health issue is sexual—erectile difficulties, vaginal pain—a first date is probably too soon, unless you sense a strong attraction and feel that you're likely to get naked quickly, or you're both at ease talking about sexuality. Otherwise, a good rule of timing is to keep sexual revelations until after the first passionate kiss or roaming hands. (You'll need to take a break and talk about safer sex anyway, right?)

Practice ahead of time so you know how much or how little you want to reveal, and what conversational style you want to use when disclosing your situation. Encourage your date to ask questions, and be prepared to answer them straightforwardly, without embarrassment. If your medical condition makes your date run for the hills, that person would not be right for you anyway.

IS THERE CHEMISTRY?

What determines whether there's chemistry for us as seniors? During childbearing years it serves a reproductive purpose— our biology is matching us with some people and not with others for the good of the species. But if we're not looking for a mate to propagate the species but for other reasons entirely, why isn't it easier to find that elusive chemistry?

I think it's all about electricity and whether that person completes your circuit or interferes with your pulses and all you get is static. That's how it feels to me when I'm near or touching someone. Either it feels natural and is a positive charge, or it's the opposite.

There are a lot of people out there, and there's no reason to settle if imagining our date naked doesn't turn us on. We're not driven by our hormones these days, but we still want the person who ends up in our bed to make us feel delighted to be there.

That said, we all find different types attractive, and chemistry can grow as friendship and common interests develop. We may find ourselves attracted to someone because he or she is funny or smart or committed to the same causes we are, or fun on the dance floor, or easy to confide in.

If the attraction isn't there, how important is that? Is sex and companionship with *anyone* better than with no one? That depends. Some enjoy a liaison for its own sake. Others are holding out for love and commitment. Most of us are somewhere in the middle, or it may depend on mood, circumstance, and how long it's been since our last partner. Like everything else, it's an individual choice.

The advice, then, must be to meet in person, give someone a chance, but if there's nothing there, admit it, be kind about it, and move on. Some version of this works for me: "I've enjoyed meeting you, but I don't feel the chemistry, I'm sorry. I don't see us as a match."

And if the chemistry is there and all goes well, how soon can you turn your date into a sexual encounter? Again, you make your own rules. Please read chapter 16, Safer Sex: Always, all the way through, and then read it again before going out on a date that you think might become sexual. Take responsibility for carrying condoms, dental dams, whatever you might need—don't leave it in the other person's hands. Be sure you've had the Condom Conversation long before any panting (or unpanting) begins. You are responsible for your own sexual health. Please don't take chances.

> *I have had several sexual encounters each with two different women. I am amazed how free each woman was, how willing and desirous of romance, and how orgasmic they were. It may be that these were exceptional women, but I am thinking that they have reached an age and experience that permits them to be free. They do not hold back. They do not let modesty get in the way. As a man, I must say that it is really inspiring. When we were younger, the man did all the work. Now the women do and want to.*

BAD DATES ARE USEFUL

I love this quote from sex columnist Dan Savage: "Every relationship fails—until one doesn't." It puts things in perspective. Most of your dates won't result in anything—that's just the way it is.

That doesn't mean that the process isn't working—actually, it *is* working. You're learning more about what you want, and what you don't, and how to screen for those. You're practicing dating—honing your skills of getting to know someone, finessing how much to divulge and when and how, experimenting with how to present yourself.

These are valuable skills, and your education is costing no more than the price of a cup of coffee and an hour out of your week. Each lackluster or bad date brings you one person closer to the relationship that won't fail. That's no waste of time!

And if your date is truly awful, then you have a good story to share with your friends. (Tell me, too.)

Ninety percent of the game was and is knowing who you are, what you want, and liking yourself. Honestly putting your heart out there is key, fine tuning as you go. Be kind. Be bold. The clock is ticking. Get busy!

15

SEX WITH
A NEW PARTNER

Your body trembles with wild lust and anticipation. Fantasy ignites your mind. You can't breathe. You shudder from the thrill of new, unfamiliar hands on your body. You tear off each other's clothes—ripping, shredding them, you don't care—unable to wait another minute. You never imagined it could be like this. You can barely control your orgasm.

Oh, wait. That's a romance novel, or a porn flick, or a best-seller about a college-aged girl and a kinky billionaire. It's not exactly real life. Especially *our* real life!

ENJOY THOSE LUSTY BRAIN CHEMICALS

Part of it is certainly true. The brain turns on powerful lust and attraction signals and we feel breathless, giddy, tingly, maybe a little crazy when we're embarking on a new sexual relationship. The mind and the body are excited by what poly-amorists call New Relationship Energy (NRE)—that over-whelming emotional and sexual craving for our new lover. We're amazed at the power of our emotions and how young and alive our bodies feel.

Anthropologist Helen Fisher, author of several books about lust and love, is known for exploring the brain chemicals at work during different stages of a relationship. Attraction, she hypothesizes, is associated in the brain with high levels of the neurotransmitters dopamine and norepinephrine and with low levels of serotonin. These combine to give us, as she puts it, "increased energy and the focusing of attention on a preferred mating partner. In humans, attraction is also asso-ciated with feelings of exhilaration, intrusive thinking about the beloved, and the craving for emotional union." [97]

That's true at any age, including ours! Many of you have written me—and I've experienced this myself—that a new lover sends all concerns about our aging bodies flying out the window, leaving us excited, aroused, and eager. Getting sexual with a new person can be fabulous—the excitement of having sex after a time without, discovering and opening to a new person, the thrill of new lust.

At sixty-seven, I'd had no sexual partner other than a vibrator for three years. I was hesitant to be naked with this rapidly aging body and saggy skin. Finally I let go of the nervousness and embraced my sexual being. That mind switch may have been responsible for finally finding the right lover. Yesterday was our first time in bed, and I have never had such a wondrous sexual occasion. It lasted more than an hour easily, but I was not concerned with keeping time. I was in the flow of enjoying and participating in the moment. We laughed together over our bodies' evidence of age. We rejoiced in sharing our sexual freedom and knowledge.

FIRST TIME ANXIETY

The first time we had sex, it was very difficult for me. I froze every time he touched me. I would not let his hands touch certain parts of my body, and only took off enough clothes to accomplish what we needed to accomplish.

Sometimes getting sexual with a new lover isn't fabulous. We're nervous and anxious, and often our bodies seem to be saying, "Say, what?" instead of "Go, go!"

We may be self-conscious about our looks, or our ability. Sometimes it's all awkward fumbling, not knowing how to please this unfamiliar person, not knowing how to communicate about how we want to be pleased. The sights, sounds, and smells are all different. Maybe grief wells up—this is not the person who used to share our bed and our body.

Sometimes it's physical discomfort, or lack of stimulation, or fear that it won't work. We may find ourselves very aware that we're no longer driven by our hormones (which would have let us overlook all of this in the past). We may even wish we hadn't started.

Anxiety doesn't lead to good sex. The brain is our primary sex organ, transmitting physical sensations, desire, pleasure, and a sense of well-being. But anxiety short-circuits the pleasure and causes the "flight or fight" response—we're on guard, not relaxed; ready to bolt, not receive pleasure.

This is not only an emotional reaction. Anxiety also sends blood away from our genitals—exactly the opposite of what we need at our age! Penises deflate, vaginas get dry and tight. A worried mind kills pleasure.

Performance anxiety—it's not just for the young. As if we didn't have enough to deal with at our age, inhibitions, fears, body image, and feelings of inadequacy are rearing their ugly little heads in our bedrooms and interfering with our sensual enjoyment. Here are a few worries you might recognize, and solutions for minimizing their impact.

Women worry that decreased lubrication will make sex painful, and our partners may think we're not attracted to them because we don't have that tangible sign of arousal. This is an easy fix—make lubricant part of the love play, and explain to your partner that you just don't lubricate as much as you used to, but that has nothing to do with how aroused you are.

Likewise, communication is the best antidote to the embarrassment that comes with slow arousal and orgasm. Just explain that it's physical, and give yourself more time. Tell your partner what you need.

Men have a much more visible issue to deal with. It's natural for erections to be less hard and less reliable with age, and that causes men considerable anxiety, especially if they think that the only "real" sex is intercourse. "Erection is such a defining element of men's sexuality that when it falters, many men find it unnerving and they think: I can't do it anymore," says Michael Castleman, MA, who publishes www.Great SexAfter40.com. "Older sex for men is less about erection and more about learning how to enjoy lovemaking without intercourse," he advises. (Learn much more about this in chapter 12, Sex without Erections.)

Some tips for overcoming performance anxiety:

- Be present and appreciate what *is* going on, rather than getting upset about what is missing.

- If erections are unreliable or out of the picture, spend more time on sexually exciting and satisfying activities that don't require erections at all: stimulate each other with hands and mouth, use sex toys if you enjoy them, massage each other (not skipping intimate areas), and whisper racy words.

- Laughter is a great anxiety reliever. If you can joke and play, you'll overcome the first-time anxiety more easily.

- If you're nervous about sex, just cuddle and

kiss without goals. You'll feel closer and more relaxed by eliminating the pressure of what is supposed to happen. Concentrate on the pleasure and sensation that's happening right now.

• Choose intimacy over anxiety. Tell your partner what about him or her turns you on. We all love to hear that!

It's often a choice whether to let a sexual change be an ever-worsening problem or an opportunity for new, sexy discoveries. Which path do you choose?

Getting naked the first time with a woman is like sacred cherry popping time for me. It happens only once. It's a ceremony.

HE'LL SEE ME NAKED!

I am fifty-six and I'm contemplating my first physical relationship in over fifteen years. I have a few more wrinkles, have put on a few more pounds, and have a few more scars and grey hairs. The thought of a man seeing me naked, or even touching me, has me paralyzed with fear.

The most common worry I hear from women about sex with a new partner is that they don't see themselves as attractive enough. They're fearful that the new lover will be thinking,

"Huh! She sure looked better with clothes on," or "Oh, dear, I had no idea she'd look so old."

I dated a curvy, round poet woman with fifty to sixty extra pounds. Getting naked with her was always sacred. And she was always beautiful.

Men are nervous about getting naked with a new person, too. They often worry about performance more than appearance, but they can also be self-conscious about their bodies. Gay men, especially, who date and mate in a culture that prizes youth, may be fearful of showing their bodies to a new partner.

Of course we're afraid of showing our bodies, especially to younger, hotter men. But since we're men with male libidos and sex drives, those tend to compensate for our fears of "The Big Reveal." It's just a further exaggeration of our body image issues that every gay man carries.

Whatever your gender or orientation, if this new partner wants to get sexually involved with us, he or she obviously finds us sexy and desirable. We defeat ourselves by worrying about this.

I believe all women are beautiful at any age if they believe it and allow it to exude and radiate from their inner being.

We—women, especially—make the discomfort worse by commenting on it. There's nothing sexy about saying, upon or before disrobing, "I'm planning on getting to the gym more," or, worse, "Let's keep the room dark." Please—your partner wants to enjoy the glorious sight of your naked body.

I learned that demure pre-coital attempts to conceal my aging body are counter-productive. From now on, bath-robes are out, light bulbs are in. To a sexually confident older man with the emotional maturity to want an age-appropriate partner and not a sex kitten forty years his junior, a mature woman's nakedness is stimulating, moti-vating, and arousing.

It's not a contradiction to recommend regular exercise and healthy eating so that we're the best shape we can be in. We'll look better and feel better physically and emotion-ally, including feeling sexier because we like our own bodies. But whether or not we're in shape on a first date, we need to accept our bodies with appreciation and confidence. Now *that's* sexy.

I love looking at a positive, alive older woman. I admire stretch marks, wrinkles, a little cellulite. They are the story of your life, the rite of passage, and not something to be ashamed of. More men should accept the beauty of the experienced woman. They should also look in the mirror at themselves and see that they have also changed. We all change and it should be celebrated.

DO I OR DON'T I?

Contrast this:

I do a lot of online dating and have met a lot of wonderful women. Despite the protest on the Internet profiles, a common first date includes making love at the lady's initiative. Most often I'm the boy toy and they want to use my body for their own pleasure. I think it's wonderful.

With this:

This whole thing about being sexual with just anyone, even multiple times, and quite freely, just confounds me! I have always felt that sexual relationships only belonged within a committed relationship where there is love and honesty!

Both are comments from single seniors in the dating scene. (No, they're not dating each other, whew.) Our views about sex are as widely divergent as our views about politics, religion, fashion, or anything else.

Some of us are eager for sex, the sooner the better, the more partners the merrier. Others believe that sex is only right in the context of a committed relationship or marriage. Between those two viewpoints is a range of attitudes about when and with whom it's okay to have sex. It's fine to have whatever experiences you want and whatever boundaries you choose. Just make your views clear to a date or a potential partner.

What if you're not sure? You find your date attractive, fun to be with, and you'd love to bring partnered sex back into your life. But you're not getting the "all systems go" signals from your brain and body that you'd like. You don't want to get into something that you'll want to get out of, and don't want to regret it afterward.

Tip: If you find yourself planning your exit strategy before you've even entered the sexual realm with this person, it's best to wait.

It may seem like everything has to go faster at our age, because we don't know how much time—especially healthy time—we have. But we can still take a few dates or a few months before making these decisions if we want to. Someone who isn't willing to wait will leave. Either decision is appropriate. Don't judge others—just be true to yourself, and spend your time with others who share your view, whatever that is.

ONE STEP AT A TIME?

So there we were on our fourth nonsexual date, wondering whether to take the next step. We were both afraid to make a move, weren't sure whether we wanted to. Finally I said, "You know, it doesn't have to be all or nothing. We can just kiss for now, without any goal." He looked relieved, and after a few minutes of kissing, we had a nice dinner and I went home.

If you haven't been sexually active for a while, and you're feeling unsure of yourself—or of whether this is the right person to share your bed—it's fine to slow down the whole process of becoming sexual. Instead of hopping from a platonic date into a sex date, do it in stages. Remember how sexy kissing and petting were in our youth? They're sexy now, too. Give yourself time to get progressively closer.

> *It might go in slow motion. First there is the exploratory stage where you try to figure each other out a bit, which may be more verbal then action. Let's face it, the new partner has no idea where your penis has been or if you have STDs so there are concerns for both of you. I found that when you get into that bed, let the lady lead and explore. If you move too quickly, it may turn her off. It is about getting to know each other better for gaining trust. Her life experience and yours will play a big part in gaining that trust.*

It isn't always the women who want to slow things down. Guys—you can let go of that old way of thinking that you must push for sex because that's what men do. You're not as driven by hormones as you used to be, and that's a good thing when you're getting to know someone new. You can take your time, make sure there's an emotional connection if that's what you desire, and let the physical part happen slowly. (That also lets you delay the awkward safer sex negotiations until you're communicating easily.) If you and a new partner are not compatible in sexual pacing or values, you'll learn that along the way.

I met a lady at a singles dance. I was at her house a few dates later, and we were cuddling on the couch. I told her how I was brought up and that I felt it was important to wait for sex, not get intimate quickly. She said that people don't think that way now. I told her I did.

TELL NEW OR POTENTIAL PARTNERS *BEFORE* YOU GET SEXUAL:

- True marital or relationship status
- Whether you're sexually or emotionally involved with another or others
- STD status
- Your safer sex policy
- Health issues that affect your sexuality
- Whatever they ask

COMMUNICATING YOUR CHALLENGES

In a sweet article in the *New York Times* called "My Body Changed. So Did Intimacy," the writer, Joyce Wadler, sixty-five, was about to get naked with a new man of sixty-six. He was fumbling through telling her that he had diabetes and needed to take pills a few hours before sex. She was fumbling through telling him that breast cancer had taken her breasts and she would reveal her new ones—with tattooed nipples. "We'd both had illnesses that could have killed us and left us scarred and that we had to talk about." The result: "trust... intimacy...real connection."[98]

This is a moving example of how to turn embarrassment and fear into self-confidence and a deeper bond. It takes trust, risk, commitment to the truth, and ultimately just blurting it out and diving into a new adventure.

I was in a near-fatal accident a year ago at age fifty-nine. I broke nineteen bones, had a brain stem injury, and the driver (who was the "love of my life") left me right after the accident. I wasn't supposed to make it, died six times on the operating table, and was never supposed to walk again.

After being unable to move for nine months, I gained weight and got stiff. My breasts, once my most beautiful feature, became swollen and saggy. Before the accident, I was in fantastic shape, working out every day. I have struggled to regain much of my physicality, and am finally walking. On good days, you can barely tell the severity of my catharsis, other than my scars and limp.

I assumed no one would ever find me desirable again. Then, miraculously, a boyfriend from thirty-five years ago contacted me and wanted to get together. I was terrified because the pics he sent showed him to be in perfect shape, making 250-mile bike treks. Then he told me that on one of his bike excursions, he was hit by a car and left for dead on the road. He has struggled to regain his physical prowess and to adjust to his new normal.

We met, and the sex and communion were so powerful and true. I have never had sex like that. I hadn't had a strong orgasm since before my accident, and it was such an eye opener to know I even still had it in me.

SEXUAL FLUIDITY

I started identifying that I was attracted to women in addition to men when my husband and I were watching adult videos as part of our foreplay.

Sometimes we're not just attracted to someone new—we're attracted to a different gender than in our past. Researcher Lisa Diamond described "sexual fluidity" in her ground-breaking book, *Sexual Fluidity: Understanding Women's Love and Desire*, as "situation-dependent flexibility in women's sexual responsiveness." In other words, a woman who considers herself heterosexual may, depending on the situation, a specific relationship, or a new life stage, find herself attracted to or in love with another woman. The reverse may happen with women who have identified as lesbians.

"Some women may be more likely to become aware of their capacity for fluidity later in life because often, at that point, marriage and childrearing don't take up the same amount of time, energy, and attention that they do earlier," Dr. Diamond told me. "Many women have told me that once the children were grown and out of the house, they finally had a chance to prioritize their own needs, interests, dreams, and desires. A growing interest in women—or often, one particular woman—blossomed in that context."

I left the convent because it began to become apparent to me, in a foggy sort of way, that I was attracted to women. I've had sexual experiences with a few males, never satisfactory, and many more sexual experiences with women, very few of which were unsatisfactory. In my opinion, sexuality exists on a continuum. There are those of us that are totally on one end of the spectrum from birth, and we may discover ourselves at different ages after many different experiences.

I remember having crushes on female babysitters from when I was three or four. As a young girl growing up, it wasn't about "below the waist," it was emotional: a longing from my heart, and a desire to be a part of that other female's heart. In my twenties, I was a closeted lesbian, terrified I'd be found out. Now, forty years later, I'm pretty open about my sexuality. Being a lesbian is physical, emotional, and spiritual.

COMING OUT CAN BE AGELESS
By Terri Clark

Though some of us in the LGBT community come out in high school or college, many more disclose and/or discover our sexual orientation later in life.

Q. How can someone who is gay live to age fifty, sixty, or beyond without coming out of the closet?

There's no "right" age for coming out. Our elders and baby boomers grew up in a time when homosexuality was a crime, a psychiatric disorder, and morally wrong. The LGBT civil rights movement is still rather young. Power, fear, shame, and violence were used to keep people in the closet. Many of us still face rejection by our family or community if we disclose our sexual orientation and/or gender identity.

Q. Does it really matter if you don't come out?

For many, yes. Living in the closet is stressful and can be emotionally taxing—especially with the fear that you may be outed by someone else and lose friends and family. Many seniors seize the opportunity to come out when a life change occurs, such as children leaving home or a spouse dying. They feel circumstances have aligned to give them permission to act on their true attractions. They have an "aha" moment, maybe in conjunction with meeting a particular person of the same gender, and it all comes into focus.

Q. Does homophobia affect LGBT seniors?

Aging LGBT folks often face a double whammy: society's ageism as well as homophobia/biphobia/transphobia. Nongay folks often reject LGBT seniors based on the assumption that heterosexuality is the norm, i.e., that the only morally and socially acceptable relationship is one between a biological man and a biological woman.

Thinking about coming out? Here are a few tips:

- *Educate Yourself*—You are not alone. People discover their sexual identity and come out at all ages for many different reasons.

- *Find Community*—Connecting with others and discovering the same struggles and joys creates a feeling of solidarity. Find out if there's a local LGBT community center.

- *Find Support*—Come out initially to people who you know will be supportive. The more positive reactions you get the better you'll feel, and will be better able to gain confidence in coming out.

—Terri Clark, MPH, CHES
is Prevention Coordinator at ActionAIDS in Philadelphia and Co-Chair for the Lesbian, Gay, Bisexual and
Transgender Elder Initiative (www.lgbtei.org), whose
mission is to advocate for services that are inclusive
and responsive to the needs of LGBT seniors.

(For more resources on LGBT issues in later life,
see Recommended Resources.)

THE FIRST TIME ALL OVER AGAIN

In March, I reconnected with an old girlfriend who was also just finishing a divorce. We have now made a very complete connection that includes the best sex of our lives. We had been lovers and in love decades ago, drifted apart, had separate lives, and now have discovered each other in deeper and broader ways, including tremendous sexual gratification.

Thanks to Facebook and social networking in general, it's easy to track people down from our past. I hear from people of our generation who have reunited with lovers from thirty, forty or more years ago. Sometimes the contact leads to nothing, but occasionally (and this is more frequent than you might expect!) it leads to a hot sexual encounter, even love.

In ways it's better than the first time, because we didn't really know who we were the first time around—or who we would become.

The first time we met up again we were feeling very unsure. He had found me online six months earlier, after losing track of each other for thirty years. It was a bit awkward when we finally met up. We went out to eat, then went back to his motel. It was the first time I had had sex with anyone in two years. We held each other and talked, then started kissing—and that was that. We were over the edge and he was eating my pussy and then we were fucking like crazy.

WHEN YOUR PARTNER ISN'T SEXUALLY GENEROUS

One man seemed to be caring, open, interesting, a good conversationalist, and fun to be with. When we finally graduated to having sex, he must have taken Viagra, because he proudly displayed a huge erection. We lay together naked after minimal kissing, which turned out to be his idea of foreplay. All he wanted to do was put his penis in me. Then he pumped and pumped. I tried touching, changing positions to enable fondling, gave suggestions for what would feel good to me.

Nope. The mission was to pump and pump and eventually climax. I was sore and tired and bored. Afterward, he glowed with success, seeming ready to do it all again. I asked for a time out. I said I needed to talk about it.

Nope. He was not open to discussion, taking offense that his fabulously long-lasting erection and performance were not to my liking. Then he sulked. I ended the relationship.

In chapter 5, Sex with a Longtime Partner, I discussed the term that Dan Savage popularized: "GGG," meaning "good, giving, and game." That means that a partner has sexual skills ("good"), is generous to a partner in bed ("giving"), and is open to new experiences that a partner might desire ("game"). GGG applies to new relationships as well.

Your aim during your sexual exploration with a new partner should be to find out what your partner needs or wants, and do your best to provide that, trusting that she or he will be doing the same for you. Communication is key—a partner who proceeds with what pleased a former partner will never know that you need something different unless you speak up. Likewise, asking, "What do you like?" will eliminate some of the guesswork on your part.

> *If you change your focus from yourself to "what can I do for you?" this will have a profound effect on your relationship. If you remember to put your partner first, you won't have to worry about a few extra pounds around the middle or the length of your Johnson.*

Sex columnist Walker Thornton, www.walkerthornton.com, lists these reasons that giving is as important as receiving:[99]

- You give because you care about this person and want to please him or her.

- You give because you know that your partner likes to give to you, as well. It becomes a mutually beneficial experience.

- You give because your partner turns you on so much that pleasing him or her sexually is arousing for you. Your pulse quickens at the thought of touching, tasting, and exploring your partner's body. You crave this.

But sometimes you get a dud in bed—someone who doesn't care about your pleasure, just wants his or her own, or has delusions of being God's gift to you, and you should be grateful for the crumbs. Ugh.

Can you salvage a bad first time? Maybe, if your partner really wants to please but doesn't know what you like or how you like it. Make it a teachable moment. No, if he or she doesn't care.

He was handsome and well-built, and I felt lucky to be in bed with him—until he just went for his orgasm without any attempt at helping me reach mine. Afterward he pulled out and started to get out of bed. "Don't you believe in 'affirmative action'?" I asked. "What do you mean?" he said, but he didn't listen to the answer. I never went out with him again, but I doubt he noticed.

Please don't assume that the lack of sexual generosity is a male trait exclusively. I also hear about women who are steadfast about what they will and won't do, despite a partner's request. For example, this email from a male reader:

I am sixty-six and single. I very much enjoy sex and love the female form. I'm dating a woman who loves cunnilingus but is opposed to fellatio. Unfortunately for me, this is a big part of my sexuality. I am clean, gentle, and not demanding. I focus on her pleasure and love satisfying her.

I tried to explain how important receiving oral sex is to me. I tried to do this without blowing it out of proportion. I feel that it is both the male's and the female's responsibility to provide as much pleasure as possible for their partner.

But for whatever reasons, she won't reciprocate. This is important enough that I may have to break off this relationship. I just can't see living my life in this one-sided manner.

My response: You absolutely have the right to sexual pleasure in your relationship, and doing without will sour the relationship. What did she say when you explained how important reciprocating oral sex is to you?

Suppose you ask her, "What exactly is it about fellatio that makes it distasteful to you? What can I do to make it more appealing?" Then the real issue might come out. If she's inexperienced and lacks technique, you (or a book like *The Ultimate Guide to Fellatio* by Violet Blue) can teach her. If she responds with, "It's yucky," or "It's not how I was brought up," I'm afraid the relationship may be doomed.

Some may disagree, but I don't think it's superficial or callous to call off a relationship if your partner is unwilling to please you with the kind of sex you like best. Life's too short for bad sex.

Over the years I had a few relationships that included satis-fying sex. I had a few other types, too, but moved past them. I was a very giving partner and talented lover. If my partner was not, and seemed unwilling to learn, then I bid him farewell.

WHEN THE SEX IS AWESOME

Maybe you don't need this caveat—but maybe you do: **Just because the sex is great and you have an amazing, partner-powered orgasm, it doesn't mean this is your soul mate for the rest of your life.** Realize that the bonding brain chemicals are at work, you're realizing how wonderful partnered sex feels, and your delight is peppered with a dash of gratitude to your new partner for such fabulous sex. Enjoy it!

But love doesn't happen in an instant. Enjoy the heck out of your new lover, but don't sign any checks or apply for a marriage license on the basis of the sexual high, okay?

16

SAFER SEX:
ALWAYS

I've been on a safer sex soapbox for years, and now that I'm dating again, I'm even more adamant about using barrier protection. I don't find that it lessens the erotic quality of a sexual interaction at all. In fact, I find the sound of the condom packet ripping open to be as erotic as a kiss. It means that sex will happen—not just in my fantasies, but here and now in this bed, with this partner.

I can't get pregnant, and I choose my partners carefully, so there's no need for protection.

When I hear a statement like the above—which is often—I sometimes ask how she chooses partners "carefully." Too often, I hear something like, "He says he's safe," or "I can just tell."

Right, how could someone who looks like a kindly grand-parent possibly have a STD? Thanks to the misconception that safer sex is unnecessary if we're no longer fertile and someone looks safe and says he or she has no STDs, sexually transmitted diseases are soaring among our age group.

Hearing "I got tested and I'm STD-free" is useless informa-tion if he or she is having unprotected sex with other people! If you and your partner are not sexually exclusive, test results from last month or even this morning won't give you any valuable information.

Being willing to go to bed with you without protection indicates that this new partner did that with other partners, and they did it with their other partners, and so on. Do you really want to have sex with all the people this person has had sex with? Imagine them all in bed with you, and just say no to unsafe sex and yes to barrier protection. It's the smart, safe, and sane thing to do.

Let's make this easy:

Use barrier protection every time unless and until you're in an ongoing, sexually exclusive relationship, and you were both tested for STDs, and retested three to six months* after your last unprotected sex with anyone else.

*Some sexually transmitted diseases are detectable much sooner, but HIV is not conclusive until after three months for most, and in rare cases, up to six months, using the common tests available, according to the Centers for Disease Control and Prevention.[100]

I think that eroticizing safer sex is an important step toward using it regularly. Buy a selection of condoms, gloves, dental dams—whatever you might need—and display them with the lubricants in a basket. Now the choice is not whether or not to use them—it's which one(s) to use.

SCARY STATISTICS

I'll be frank with you. I have dozens of scary statistics that should convince you that safer sex barriers are imperative for those of us in our age group who are sexually active outside a committed, exclusive relationship.

If I give you too few of these, you'll think that safer sex isn't really important. If I give you too many, your eyes will glaze over and you'll skip the whole chapter. But what if I omit just the statistic that would change your mind? It's a dilemma.

I'll give it my best shot:

- Cases of sexually transmitted diseases among fifty- to ninety-year-olds more than doubled between 2002 and 2012.[101]

- Fifty percent of males and 29 percent of females rarely or never use condoms and only 12 percent of men and 32 percent of women use protection regularly, according to a 2009 AARP survey of single, sexually active midlife and older people.[102]

- A 2010 study found that 91 percent of men

over fifty did not use a condom when they had sex with a date or casual acquaintance, and 70 percent didn't use a condom with someone they just met.[103]

- In a survey of single women ages fifty-eight to ninety-three, nearly 60 percent said they didn't use a condom the last time they had sex.[104]

- Cases of syphilis and chlamydia in adults aged forty-five to sixty-four nearly tripled between 2000 and 2010.[105]

- Among people over fifty who are HIV-infected, about 27 percent of heterosexual men, 37 percent of gay/bisexual men, and 35 percent of heterosexual women sometimes have anal or vaginal intercourse without using condoms.[106]

- An estimated 20 to 25 percent of HIV-positive individuals are not aware they are infected.[107]

- Older women are particularly at risk for blood-borne diseases like HIV or chlamydia because their thinning vaginal lining and lack of lubrication may lead to tearing during intercourse, permitting easy access to the bloodstream.[108]

If my partner is not monogamous with me, we don't do penetration. Instead of using barriers, we go to nonpenetrative sex, which is delightful in its own right. I have orgasms through finger play rather than penetration anyway. And, as for my partner—I give great hand jobs!

TALKING ABOUT SAFER SEX

You tell me that you *meant* to use barrier protection, but in the heat of the moment, you didn't. The best intentions can fall by the wayside unless you (a) prepare; (b) practice; and (c) plan ahead.

Prepare: Have everything you need for safer sex available and ready.

Practice: Try out what you want to say in front of the mirror. Look and sound assertive, not apologetic or giggly. Eliminate embarrassment. Have a couple of choice statements ready to plug into the conversation. For example,

- "I always use barriers with a new partner."

- "Do you prefer flavored dental dams or unflavored?"

- "Your condoms or mine?"

- "I bought this sampler kit—what would you like to try?"

Plan: Talk to your partner (or potential partner) *before* you get excited. Don't wait until the heat of passion to bring up the subject, because that's a recipe for disaster. Instead, have the safer sex discussion long before getting naked.

SIZE YOUR CONDOM

Did you know that condoms come in three different sizes? You want the size that feels snug but not constricting. Too loose, and it can slip off. Too tight, and wearing it is painful. Here's how to figure out your size, according to Lucky Bloke (www.thecondomreview.com), a website that reviews and sells condoms:

- Have an empty toilet paper roll ready.

- Give yourself an erection.

- Put your erection into the toilet paper roll.

- If there's extra room, choose a smaller, snugger, more tailored fit condom, best for 35 percent of men. If there's just enough room, use a medium, standard condom, best for 50 percent of men. If it's too tight, choose a larger, generous fit condom, best for 15 percent of men.

- Since few condoms are actually labeled by size, see www.thecondomreview.com/pages/find-your-condom-size for links to appropriate brands and styles for each size.

We are the ones responsible for our own health. If you can't talk about safer sex with someone, do you really want to invite that person inside your body?

> *I don't suddenly lose my safety awareness in the heat of the moment. Sometimes in the moment I wish I could have sex without barriers. Sometimes it's a strong desire. But instead of giving in to it, I mention how much I'd like to do it, even though I won't. It communicates how hot I think my partner is, even though safety comes first. If he finds that intolerable, then he can find someone else. I deserve someone who's willing to be safe with me.*

FEMALE CONDOMS

The new version of the female condom, called the FC2 (female condom, 2nd generation), is a vast improvement over the first product, which was like having sex in a shower curtain. The material is completely different now. It is soft and pliable, made of nitrile, like today's medical exam gloves.

The FC2 is a loose sheath with a large ring at one end, which stays outside the body, and a small ring at the other end, which helps with insertion and holds it in place. When using it vaginally, push the inner ring past the pubic bone, much like the diaphragm of decades past. The outer ring is large enough to cover much of the vulva and provide a barrier with the base of the penis, so there's no exchange of body fluids. It provides a protected tunnel with freedom of movement.

One big advantage for a woman is that she alone determines to use the female condom and can insert it at any time before sex—no need to wait for the heat of the moment or for a partner's erection or even agreement. This actually can make sex more spontaneous—no need to stop the action to fumble with a condom.

The female condom is a boon to safer sex with undependable erections, because the penis does not have to be hard. Since the woman inserts it on her own, it doesn't affect or require the man's erection. Men have said that the sensation is better than with a male condom. One partner should hold it in place by the outer ring especially during vigorous thrusting.

Although called a "female" condom, this can also be used for anal sex for any gender body. Sometimes called a "bottom condom," "internal condom," or "receptive condom," it's getting popular in the gay male community. I heard one man say that using the FC2 was a way "to feel bareback sensations while staying protected."

Before using it anally, you may want to remove the inner ring—or you may want to keep it for ease of insertion. Practice before you need it, so you know which you prefer. Push it in past the sphincter muscle. You can also use your partner's penis to push it in. About an inch of the condom should stay outside the body. Be careful during use to hold onto the outside ring to keep it from being pulled into the body by the sphincter muscles and to prevent the penis from entering to the side of the condom instead of inside it.

Yes, the FC2 does look funny emerging from the body, but give it a few tries to discover how comfortable and empowering it is. Use plenty of lubricant inside and outside the condom.

> We gave the new female condom a try. Wow, what an improvement! It's so much more pliable, soft, and quiet than the one six years ago. My partner says he gets way more sensation from it than with the male condom. That makes me happy. And I get a little clitoral stimulation as well, an unexpected plus. We're both completely sold on it.

Advantages of the FC2:

- It's very comfortable for both partners, and not constricting.

- It warms to the temperature of the vagina.

- It can be inserted long before needed.

- It can be left in after ejaculation, with no need to pull out immediately—more cuddling!

- It can be used with any kind of lubricant.

- Insertion is easy.

- Nitrile is very thin, conducting sensation better than latex.

- It's latex-free and can be used by those with latex sensitivity.

- Some women find that the outer ring stimulates the clitoris.

- Some men find that the inner ring stimulates the penis.

- It is under control of the wearer.

To remove the FC2, twist the outer ring three times so the contents can't spill, then pull it out, and dispose of it in the trash, not in the toilet.

Never use a male condom and a female condom at the same time. It's unnecessary, because either condom provides complete protection, plus the friction between the two condoms can lead to one or both of them tearing.

I am HIV+, healthy and undetectable. I will never get over the impact HIV has had on my sex life. My partner of more than twenty-one years is negative, so we have a "mixed marriage," and it has definitely impacted our ability to be intimate over the years.

The problem with being poz [HIV-positive] is that it always impacts sex with other partners, especially if the partner is negative. All the poz guys I know tend to sero-sort, meaning we play with other poz guys if we're poz and neg guys with neg guys. "Safer sex" often is tossed out the window if playing with other poz guys.

If it's a mixed pairing, though, negotiations are always complex. Mostly because every neg guy out there has a different definition of safer sex! What is off the table for one is fine with the next. Some guys want to wear a rubber suit if playing with a poz guy; others are fine with everything but receptive anal sex. Sometimes it's simply too much trouble to want to bother with. Then there's always the "mid-scene" act that's off the table but wasn't discussed until it comes up, so it can be very awkward, not to mention a buzz-kill, to hit that in the middle of things. I prefer to play with other poz guys because all that nonsense is gone with them.

LIVING WITH HIV AND ENJOYING SAFE, SEXY SEX
By Terri Clark

Many seniors who are living with HIV are concerned about how sexy they are to other people and how to protect themselves and their partner(s) while enjoying intimacy and sex. Here are some tips:

1. **Talk about your status**. For most HIV-positive folks, disclosing their status is one of the biggest challenges. HIV-positive seniors can enjoy satisfying relationships (with sex or not), and the key is to communicate open and honestly with partners. Plan ahead for the best time, the best place, and what you will say.

2. **Green Light, Yellow Light, Red Light**. Think about safer sex in terms of "Green Light": No-risk behaviors, such as masturbation, sexual fantasies, massage, holding hands,

showering together, using sex toys (using and changing condoms on sex toys if sharing them), hugging, and kissing. "Yellow Light": Low risk behaviors, like oral sex, vaginal and/or anal sex with condoms. "Red Light": High risk behaviors, such as vaginal and/or anal sex without a condom, withdrawal (pulling out). Reduce your risk by using condoms consistently and correctly.

3. **Lower your viral load**. HIV treatment works by reducing the level of HIV in the body (the viral load) to such an extent that a person's infectiousness is almost zero—sometimes called an undetectable viral load. This means that people living with HIV who are on treatment and taking meds as prescribed become less likely to transmit the virus. A lower viral load is important for your overall health and wellbeing, not just your sex life.

4. **Your most important sex organ is your brain**. It's not just what is below your waist and between your legs that counts. Remember that intimacy comes from communication, sharing and letting our partner(s) know we care. Sometimes the best turn on is a great conversation!

5. **You are not alone**. Approximately one quarter of the people living with HIV in 2005 were fifty or older, and studies project that by 2015 more than half of all people living with HIV in the US will be over fifty. There are terrific

resources available for support and information, such as POZ (www.POZ.com) and The
Body (www.thebody.com).

—Terri Clark, MPH, CHES is Prevention Coordinator
at ActionAIDS in Philadelphia and Co-Chair for the
Lesbian, Gay, Bisexual and Transgender Elder Initiative (www.lgbtei.org), whose mission is to advocate
for services that are inclusive and responsive to the
needs of LGBT seniors.

SAFE ORAL SEX

The risk of HIV transmission from an infected partner through oral sex is much less than the risk of HIV transmission from anal or vaginal sex. Measuring the exact risk of HIV transmission as a result of oral sex is very difficult.... [S]everal co-factors may increase the risk of HIV transmission through oral sex, including: oral ulcers, bleeding gums, genital sores, and the presence of other STDs. What is known is that HIV has been transmitted through fellatio, cunnilingus, and anilingus. In addition to HIV, other STDs can be transmitted through oral sex with an infected partner. Examples of these STDs include herpes, syphilis, gonorrhea, genital warts (HPV), intestinal parasites (amebiasis), and hepatitis A.

—Centers for Disease Control and Prevention[109]

Protecting yourself during oral sex with condoms and dental dams is the smart thing to do. Dental dams are squares of latex that are used to cover the vulva or anus during oral sex. Although they may seem weird and not very sexy at first use, you'll find that they transmit sensation and body heat well, and provide proven protection.

In cunnilingus, it may feel a little tricky at first for the giver to figure out exactly how to position the tongue with a dental dam hiding visual cues. In many women, the clitoris has a delightful habit of growing bigger and perkier when stimulated, making herself known by feel—but that's not true for all.

> With dental dams, the visual landmarks are missing, so it's harder to know when my tongue is at the right spot. I appreciate it when my lover says, "higher," "lower," "to the right," or "to the left." With her direction, I can relax and just enjoy her pleasure instead of being anxious that I'm doing it wrong.

You can get dental dams or the Sheer Glyde dams made especially for oral sex from a woman-friendly sexuality shop, or order online.

If you don't have dams, you can use Saran Wrap (avoid microwavable plastic wrap which does not offer enough protection). You can also create a dam from a condom:

1. Unroll the condom.

2. Use scissors to cut off the tip.

3. Cut lengthwise from the rim straight to the open tip.

4. Pull the condom into a rectangle.

For fellatio, use a nonlubricated condom—flavored or unflavored, your preference. If the man has trouble getting or maintaining an erection, a dental dam over a penis will work for fellatio on a soft penis.

For the pleasure of the person receiving oral sex, apply silicone, water-based, or hybrid lubricant on the vulva, penis, or anus first whether using dams, condoms, or Saran Wrap. Oil-based lube can degrade the latex.

My doctor (who was not shy!) and I talked about all this. I decided to a) date, kiss; b) if I really liked a new partner, get naked and stick to delightful outercourse intimacies: practice slow sex and share orgasms without penis in the vagina; c) still in love after three to six months? Get tested and wait for results; d) both negative? Then dump condoms and ring that P in the V bell for sure. Mix in poetry liberally. Stir, repeat.

SAFE TOY TIP

If you share insertible vaginal or anal sex toys with a new or nonexclusive partner, wrap the toy in a condom, and use a new condom when you swap. Whether you're using toys solo or with a partner, if you like to insert a toy both anally and vaginally, replacing the condom when changing body parts will prevent bacteria from the anus (even if well-scrubbed) from getting into the vagina and causing an infection. This is also true when a penis is going from anus to vagina—use a fresh condom before switching.

I'm a sixty-five-year-old female. After being celibate for twenty years (!), I met a lovely man online. Anticipating intimacy, I wanted to be able to demonstrate that I was STI free. I asked for blood tests for STI, HIV, HSV, HPV, and hepatitis. My doctor said that I didn't need a HSV (herpes) test unless I had an outbreak. I insisted on the test anyway.

I was stunned to discover that I have antibodies for both herpes simplex 1 and 2, even though I have never had a cold sore or genital herpes outbreak. Obviously, I have been carrying the virus for over twenty years.

I had "The Talk" with my friend. He took the news very well and did not panic. We discussed what it meant for our growing relationship, for sexual activity, and for his risk.

He agreed to get blood tests, although he had no partners other than his ex-wife for over twenty-five years.

It turned out that he also tested positive for herpes and never knew. What are the odds? Probably higher than we thought: we both had been sexually active in the seventies and eighties when easy and unprotected sex was the norm. We were young, horny, and stupid. We probably contracted herpes that far back. The bad news is that he has to tell his ex-wife.

SAFER SEX MYTHS AND TRAPS

Requiring barrier protection sends the message that I don't trust a new partner.

Actually, *not* requiring barrier protection sends the message that you're reckless and you don't care about your own or your partner's health.

If I keep a collection of condoms, a new partner will think I'm promiscuous.

That's an old idea from our sex-negative upbringing that we can let go of now. We're sexually active (or hoping to be), and we're responsible enough to be prepared in case sex happens. Don't leave it to chance that your partner might bring the condoms—take care of it yourself. If a partner thinks that naiveté trumps sexual responsibility, educate or dump that partner.

I try to use barrier protection, but I back down if my partner insists on not using it.

If you don't protect your sexual health, who will? Besides,

this new person is unlikely to be your final sex partner. If this one doesn't work out, and you're facing the Conversation with the next one, which one of these would you prefer to say?

- "Yes, I used barrier protection with my last partner. I always do."

Or

- "Actually, no, I didn't use barrier protection with my last partner."

My policy with new lovers is open communication about any limitations and sexual expectations. We answer these questions early on: "What are you into? What do you especially enjoy? What really turns you on? What do you need emotionally from this relationship? Where would you like things to go?" It's a continual process of discovery and growth.

Second is an offer to get tested as a sign of good faith. Third is the use of condoms for at least three months after test results if the decision of exclusivity is made. If there is an agreement of nonexclusivity, then condoms are always used and incorporated as an unashamed part of sex play.

The reason is multiple—for trust, for fun, for honesty, for safety, but primarily for caring. All of this must be clearly voiced as soon as the possibility of intimacy is considered.

17

SEXY AGING
GOING FORWARD

The nurse was frantic. She'd just seen two elderly people having sex in a room at the Hebrew Home at Riverdale, New York. She asked Daniel A. Reingold, then the home's executive vice president, what she should do.

"Tiptoe out and close the door so you don't disturb them," he told her.[110]

So begins "Sex in Geriatrics Sets Hebrew Home Apart in Elderly Care," an excellent article written by Bryan Gruley for Bloomberg.com. I am elated that we're starting to talk out loud about the issues of sex in long-term care facilities, despite the deafening clanging of the *ick factor* bell among people of all ages who—whether they themselves are sexual or not—do not want to think about old people still expressing themselves sexually.

But we need to think about it. If we're lucky enough to be active and independent now, we're smart enough to realize that we, too, will face these issues personally. What will you want for yourself? For your loved ones? How can you make sure that your wishes are respected? Take some time to think about these ideas and questions:

- When do we lose the right to sexual expression?

- Does our right to sexual expression end if/when we can no longer live independently? If so, why?

- Who determines whether we can still express ourselves sexually, and by what guidelines do they make that decision?

- If a staff member has a different personal belief about what's appropriate sexual behavior (or nonbehavior), do her/his values override our own?

- Do elders with dementia have the right to sexual expression? Who decides that, and on what basis?

- If family members are uncomfortable with us having a sexual relationship, should their wishes supersede ours?

As uncomfortable as this might seem, I suggest you write down your personal policy about your right to sexual expression in your later years, and share it with your loved ones. Just because you might be unable to voice your wishes when the time comes doesn't mean you no longer have those wishes.

> *Another item on the list for aging couples to talk about, and perhaps write down: If I'm suffering from dementia and living separately from my hubby, I hope he does heal his grief with the companionship—including sex—with another woman. But we have to talk about all this before one of us can't.*

"Many staff and family feel that the elderly should not be sexually active. My feeling is, whatever you were doing at thirty is okay to be doing at eighty, as long as it doesn't harm you or anyone else," says Jeannine Clark, MSN, who was a geriatric nurse practitioner for thirty years and now works as a geriatric consultant on topics including sexual attitudes, practices, and policy in long-term care facilities. Does this include older adults with dementia? "Absolutely," says Clark, "as long as they're not exploiting anyone, it is consensual, they have the capacity or competence to make that decision, and they're not causing any harm."[111]

Personally, I want the right to decide when and how I want to be touched sexually—whether by my own hand, a partner I've chosen, or a sex toy that they'd better not pry out of my arthritic hands—for the rest of my life. You?

If I end up living in a facility, I imagine I won't submit

to rules easily, unless they are as progressive as the Hebrew Home. I'll want only those rules that make sense to me, and they will include these sex-positive directives:

- Make sure I have an outlet and batteries to keep my sex toys in working order.

- Do not interfere with any warm connection I may be enjoying with any companion I choose, in any way I choose to express that connection.

- If I'm involved with a sexual partner, make sure I have easy access to safer sex protection.

- When I close the door—whether I'm alone or with another person—give me privacy.

- If I'm still capable of sharing information about senior sexuality with residents and or staff, provide me with opportunities to do that.

THE HEBREW HOME: SHINING EXAMPLE

The Hebrew Home at Riverdale...recognizes and respects the importance of emotional and physical intimacy in the lives of older adults. Such close human interactions are viewed as a normal and natural aspect of life.... This policy recognizes and supports the older adult's right to engage in sexual activity, so long as there is consent among those involved.... In assessing sexual activity in the context of this policy, professionals and caregiver staff...should set aside personal biases and judgment to maintain objectivity in upholding the sexual rights and choices of all older adults in the Home's care.[112]

—"Policies and Procedures Concerning Sexual Expression
at the Hebrew Home at Riverdale"

The Hebrew Home at Riverdale (www.hebrewhome.org) stands for the sex-positive attitude we want in senior residential care. Hebrew Home has a progressive policy about sex among the residents, including that residents "have the right to seek out and engage in sexual expression," including "words, gestures, movements or activities that appear motivated by the desire for sexual gratification."[113] They have a policy for determining sexual consent, even when a resident has dementia.[114]

"For all living under our roof, the Hebrew Home at Riverdale believes that there is still life to be lived, pleasures to be had, and sexuality to be celebrated, not curtailed," explains Robin Dessel, LMSW, the director of memory care and a sexual rights educator at the Hebrew Home. "Sexual expression should be sanctioned and rightly belongs in residential healthcare settings. Sexual rights should not be subject to change based upon age, place of residence, sexual preference, or the decision making of others.... After all, life in a health-care setting is more than bedpans and call bells."[115]

The Hebrew Home's sexual rights policy is progressive and unusual now—and it was even more progressive and startling when they first adopted it in 1995! (They revised it in 2001 and again in 2013.)

I've never visited the Hebrew Home, but I'd like to.

I've amended my Advance Directive for Health Care to say, "Dear Wife: If I don't remember your name, please get a boyfriend and don't tell the priest! Just do it. I love you. Take care of yourself. —Your Husband."

CHOOSING A SEX-POSITIVE ELDER HOME

By Gayle Appel Doll, PhD

Until recently, I would bet my bottom dollar that nursing and retirement home developers have never considered building or planning for resident sexuality at all. In fact, a colleague and I are surveying contractors who build senior housing to see if it has ever been mentioned. The answer we are finding is still no.

So is it possible to find housing that can be considered a sex-positive environment? Probably, and it will continue to get easier in the future.

For now, the savvy senior housing shopper will look for a home that publicly announces its sexuality policy. If you see it posted on its website or displayed prominently in resident application materials, you know that this home takes the sexual needs of residents seriously. True sexuality policies will use phrases like "sexual expression" and "sexuality as a basic human need."

A policy that explicitly addresses sexual expression is important. Some homes may state that they have a policy, but they may be citing just the residents' right to privacy—which doesn't suggest that the home has given sexuality any serious thought.

If a home does not have a sexuality policy, and very few of them do, look for a home that espouses a person-centered philosophy. Staff and administrators are trained to see the residents as whole persons with varying needs, rather than the medical diagnoses that brought them to the home. While these homes may not have a stated sexuality policy, if they are truly person-centered, they are more likely to understand how to meet sexuality needs because of this philosophy.

Most important: Do not rely on what is said in writing. Go see for yourself.

Probably the most important aspect of sexual openness and opportunity is privacy. Semi-private rooms are everything but private. If residents live in these spaces, are there opportunities for privacy like conjugal visitation rooms, private living areas, or planned nights in a hotel?

In our work we've found that it takes very little to get staff members to begin thinking more openly about sexuality. It only takes one resident asking for privacy for sex, or one family member asking about a resident sexuality policy, to begin the process of making a home more sex-positive.

—Gayle Appel Doll, PhD, is Director of the Center on Aging at Kansas State University and author of *Sexuality & Long-Term Care: Understanding and Supporting the Needs of Older Adults.*

SPECIAL ISSUES FOR LGBT ELDERS

Gen Silent is a powerful documentary film about the prejudice, hostility, and fears that lesbian, gay, bisexual, and transgender people face toward the end of their lives or the lives of their loved ones. A transgender woman had lost her entire family when she transitioned. Now she feared medical providers and caregivers who "don't want to touch my body." The film shows the dismay and stress of gay and lesbian couples who cannot find a long-term care facility that will treat them with acceptance and respect—and permit them to room together as a couple. Learn more about *Gen Silent* on the filmmaker Stu Maddux's website at www.stumaddux.com/.

We need to see the personal stories, and we also need to know the scope of the problem. These statistics are from *Gen Silent*'s website:[116]

- There are almost thirty-eight million LGBT Americans over sixty-five, or 12.6 percent of the population. This will nearly double by 2030.

- Four out of five LGBT elders say that they don't trust the healthcare system.

- Fifty percent of nursing home workers said their fellow workers would be intolerant of LGBT people.

- The Joint Commission, which regulates assisted living and nursing care facilities, issued regulations against anti-LGBT bias in 2006. However, these regulations have never been enforced, and LGBT culturally competent care is almost nonexistent in mainstream assisted living and nursing care.

• LGBT advocates have developed cultural competency programs that improve service to LGBT elders, but there is no funding or mandate by state and federal aging agencies to train caregivers.

• In 2000, the federal government noted in its Healthy People 2010 campaign that LGBT people face specific and magnified health vulnerabilities. Despite identifying these risks, Healthy People 2010 failed to research or track LGBT elders in this landmark health program.

• According to the National Transgender Discrimination Survey: Report on Health and Healthcare,[117] 19 percent of the respondents of all ages were refused care because of their transgender or gender nonconforming status, 28 percent were subject to harassment in medical settings, and 2 percent were victims of violence in doctors' offices. Fifty percent of the sample reported that their providers lacked the knowledge to treat them.

WHAT TO DO FROM HERE

Whatever your age, medical situation, or relationship status now, I hope you can look forward with a commitment to being the best you can be—and keeping a gleam in your eye.

- Stay in the best shape possible physically, through good nutrition and exercise. Whatever your limitations, find what can move, and move it regularly. Exercise affects not only sexuality, but also quality of life.

- Stay in the best shape possible intellectually, learning something new every day. Read, listen to audiobooks and discussions, learn a new subject, and listen to different points of view.

- Stay in the best shape possible emotionally, reducing stress and nurturing yourself with activities and people that make you smile and fill you with the joy of being alive.

- Stay in the best shape possible sexually, welcoming touch, exploring tools, toys, attitudes, and experiences. Talk out loud about sex as an elder.

- Give your best to relationships: love your loved ones, appreciate people who help you (even if it's their job), get to know people of different generations, and reach out to strangers.

- Celebrate aging. There are plenty of challenges,

granted, but there are also some wonderful surprises if we are open to them.

WHEN DOES OUR SEXUALITY END?

Why do reporters keep asking me this? I'll let you know if I ever find out.

CHAPTER

18

CONCLUSION

We're sexual beings from the day we're born until the day we die. When I am ninety-five, I will still be a sexual person.

—Joycelyn Elders,
former United States Surgeon General[118]

Sex at our age can be better than ever—though very different! Our responses may be slower, our bodies may not always cooperate with our wishes, and the studly or juicy bodies and attitudes with which we strutted around in the past may be dim memories.

But that just paves the path for a new kind of sexuality—one filled with touch, self-nurturing, and the joy of slow, languid arousal. With creativity, solid information, communication, a sense of humor, and likely a drawer full of sex toys and lubricants, we can delight in our new old sexy selves.

Sexy is an attitude, an acknowledgement of our own sensual nature, which includes acceptance of our aging bodies and our need for touch throughout our lives.

> *What works for me at age fifty-nine is my attitude that sex is natural and fabulous, and that I am capable of great sexual pleasure. It is a daily practice for me, just like meditation or other practices. I think about sex as an integral part of who I am. I keep my brain engaged, enjoy self-pleasure, and am open to exploration with a positive attitude and an open mind. (A good partner helps, too, when available.) I find myself reaping the benefits in and out of a relationship.*

IF NOT NOW, WHEN?

> *If I had been born in the forties, I would have sublimated my same-sex feelings into male bonding, robbed jewelry stores with the guys, and gone home to the wife. If I had been born in the eighties, I may have chosen a guilt-free same-sex lifestyle. But having been born in between, I can honestly say that my complex sexuality has ruined my life. I am an honest but conflicted husband, a secretive father, and my career wasn't what it should have been. I have been celibate for years.*

It's never too late to rediscover—or discover for the first time—how to live passionately, authentically, and fully. I don't mean *only* sexually, but I do see sex (partnered or solo) as an important part of the joy and pleasure that we're capable of at this time of life.

If your life now doesn't bring you joy, what can you change so it will? Even if you're not sure what you need, if you are sure what you *don't* need, I hope you'll make a change.

So many of us stay stuck in lives we don't enjoy and relationships that don't nurture us out of fear of the unknown. I remember deciding to break up with a lover of eight years because I realized how lonely I was when I was with him. "I'd rather be lonely alone than lonely with someone," I decided. Despite the hurt and chaos of a breakup, I regretted only that I hadn't done it sooner. The heart knows.

When I was a college student, I wrote in my journal, "I'd rather regret something I did than something I didn't do." Some of my younger explorations—sexual and otherwise—were vapid and tentative, others were life altering. Some experiences disappointed and embarrassed me, others enriched me and expanded my view of the world and my understanding of myself. My only regrets were when I didn't speak my truth and when I hurt someone I loved. But through trying out different ways of living and loving, I learned what would become my core beliefs about how to live and love.

Looking back, I regret very little. Even when an experience or a relationship turned out to be wrong for me, or when I wished I had behaved in a different way, that's how I grew into the person I am now. We can try on different behaviors (safely, please!) and finally settle into what works for us.

We're never done with that journey. What worked for me at thirty-five was not what worked for me at sixty. Now seventy, I'm questioning and exploring again. We're not stagnant beings—or at least, we can *choose* not to be, and it's never too late to change. The older I get, the more firmly I believe that we need to use the years to go after a meaningful life.

Can that be scary, even at sixty, seventy, or eighty? You bet. But if we're unhappy and we don't make a change now, we'll stay stuck in that unhappiness. If we do make a change, we are at least giving ourselves the opportunity to go after our joy.

BESIDES THE PHYSICAL...

We've confused genital prime with sexual prime.... Your sexual peak has a great deal to do with who you are as a person.... If you're interested in sex with intimacy, there isn't a seventeen-year-old-alive who can keep up with a healthy sixty-year-old!

—David Schnarch, PhD, author of *Passionate Marriage: Keeping Love and Intimacy Alive in Committed Relationships*

Sex has never been just about body parts and how well they work. That's even more important now. The best parts of sex at our age may have nothing to do with how easily or how fast we orgasm. It's about what happens in our brains and our emotions.

Our sexual pleasure grows out of being mature enough to know who we are, what we value, what we can offer ourselves and/or a partner. It's about knowing how to laugh at the unimportant aggravations and fix the important ones. It's about accepting that our bodies may be slowing down, but our ability to enjoy life is not. And that includes sexual pleasure!

> *Desire like this, sexual, roller-coastal, liberating, and mad, does not diminish with age. Wrinkled, stooped, stone deaf, and feeble, you never lose the urge to merge.... The world may no longer take notice of me in my comfortable shoes and control-top knickers, but inside, where it counts, I'm baying at the moon, drinking Love Potion #9, and waiting for Godot—with his fly open.*
>
> —S.S. Fair, "Still Horny After All These Years" in *Desire: Women Write About Wanting*, edited by Lisa Solod Warren

READERS SPEAK UP

Let's finish this book by turning it over to you. Here's what you've told me about how your sexual expression and relationships have become better with age:

> *I am fifty-three years old and my "boyfriend" is fifty-two. We have the most incredible sex! I am a grandma and he is a grandpa, and we tease each other about that after an incredible romp in the hay. My body has gone through a lot of changes, some of which make me self-conscious. My hair is thinning and my breasts have changed: they are very*

large and squishy, and they make me feel old. But those things don't bother my lover! We indulge each other's long suppressed fantasies. I never dreamed that sex would be this way at this age.

* * *

Sex is about communication, love, and trust. The older we get, the more we know about all these things.

* * *

When it comes to sex, a woman over sixty brings so much wisdom, insight, experience, empathy, and sweet gentleness. That is what makes me love and adore her and makes me feel so excited to be in a relationship with her.

* * *

I am a far better partner now than when I was, say, twenty. I don't think I was bad—growing up in the "Our Bodies, Ourselves," "Free to Be You and Me," "ERA NOW!" period, going to college at UC Santa Cruz, I think I was probably a better partner than many. But with experience, practice, and the patience that you get as you age, I think I'm far better now.

* * *

The older you get, the better sex gets. The more experience you have, the more likely you are to know what your body enjoys. The less focus there is on achieving an orgasm, the more focus on enjoying yourself.

Long-term relationships can take you on a never ending journey where something new, exciting, and sensual can be found around every corner. It can be the longest, most exhilarating ride in one's life.

* * *

I have never ceased being lusty. I outlived two husbands, pleasured myself, and joined an online dating service. At sixty-six, I met a man six years my junior. I told him right up front that I was looking for a vital man with a sexy appetite. He was doubtful about getting involved with an older woman. I informed him that I am healthy, strong, and believe in living my life. For me, it was almost love at first sight. He says our relationship is righteous. He believes we have another hundred years to share everything. I tell my new man that I love him every day, constantly.

What would *you* like to share with our community about sex and aging? I hope you'll comment on my blog, www.NakedAt OurAge.com, or write an email to joan@joanprice.com. Let's keep this conversation going.

RECOMMENDED RESOURCES

Note: There are many more fine books and informative websites that I don't have the space to include, and new ones will appear after this book comes out. Let this be just the beginning of your exploration. Please visit www.Nakedat OurAge.com, where I'll post an updated list.

AGING AND SEXUALITY

Ageless Erotica edited by Joan Price (Seal Press, 2013)

Assisted Loving: The Journey Through Sexuality and Aging by Ginger T. Manley (Westview, 2013)

Better Than Ever: Love and Sex at Midlife by Bernie Zilbergeld (Crown, 2005)

Better Than I Ever Expected: Straight Talk about Sex After Sixty by Joan Price (Seal Press, 2005)

Dr. Ruth's Sex after 50: Revving Up Your Romance, Passion & Excitement! by Dr. Ruth Westheimer (Quill Driver, 2005)

Free Fall: A Late-in-Life Love Affair by Rae Padilla Francoeur (Seal Press, 2010)

GreatSexAfter40.com by Michael Castleman, www.GreatSexAfter40. com

MiddlesexMD blog by Barb DePree, MD,www.middlesexmd.com

Naked at Our Age blog by Joan Price, www.NakedAtOurAge.com

Older, Wiser, Sexually Smarter: 30 Sex Ed Lessons for Adults Only by Peggy Brick, Jan Lunquist, Allyson Sandak, Bill Taverner (Planned Parenthood of Greater Northern New Jersey, 2009)

Safer Sex for Seniors www.safersex4seniors.org

Sex After…: Women Share How Intimacy Changes as Life Changes by Iris Krasnow (Gotham Books, 2014)

The Sex Bible for People Over 50: The Complete Guide to Sexual Love for Mature Couples by Laurie Betito, PhD (Fair Winds Press/Quiver, 2014)

Sex & Love for Grownups: A No-Nonsense Guide to a Life of Passion by Sallie Foley (Sterling, 2005)

Sex and the Seasoned Woman: Pursuing the Passionate Life by Gail Sheehy (Random House, 2006)

Sex for Grownups: Dr. Dorree Reveals the Truths, Lies, and Must-Tries for Great Sex After 50 by Dorree Lynn (HCI, 2010)

Sexuality and Aging: Clinical Perspectives by Jennifer Hillman (Springer, 2012)

Sexuality and Aging Consortium at Widener University, Widener University, www.widener.edu/sexualityandaging

"Sexuality in Midlife and Beyond," Harvard Health Publications, published 2013, www.health.harvard.edu/special_health_reports/sexuality-in-midlife-and-beyond

Still Doing It: Women & Men Over 60 Write About Their Sexuality edited by Joani Blank (Down There Press, 2000)

A Woman's Touch: Sexuality Resource Center, www.sexuality resources.com

ARTHRITIS AND SEX

"Relationships, Intimacy and Arthritis," Arthritis Care, published 2011, http://www.arthritiscare.org.uk/PublicationsandResources/Listed bytype/Booklets/main_content/Relationshipsbooklet2011.pdf

BODY IMAGE AND AGING

For Keeps: Women Tell the Truth About Their Bodies, Growing Older, and Acceptance edited by Victoria Zackheim (Seal Press, 2007)

CANCER AND SEXUALITY

Conquer Prostate Cancer: How Medicine, Faith, Love and Sex Can Renew Your Life by Rabbi Ed Weinsberg, EdD, DD with Robert Carey, MD (Health Success Media, 2008)

"Healthy Sexuality After Cancer," A Woman's Touch, published 2011, https://sexualityresources.com/ask-sex-counselor/cancer-survivors-sexuality/healthy-sexuality-after-cancer

Man Cancer Sex by Anne Katz, RN, PhD (Hygeia Media, 2009)

"Penile Rehabilitation after Prostate or Pelvic Surgery or Radiation," A Woman's Touch, published 2011, https://sexualityresources.com/ask-dr-myrtle/mens-issues-and-sexual-problems/penile-rehabilitation-after-prostate-or-pelvic-surgery

Prostate Cancer and the Man You Love: Supporting and Caring for Your Partner by Anne Katz, RN, PhD (Rowman & Littlefield, 2012)

Saving Your Sex Life: A Guide for Men with Prostate Cancer by John P. Mulhall (Hilton Publishing, 2008)

"Sexuality and Relationships for Breast Cancer Survivors & Their Partners," A Woman's Touch, http://www.sexuality resources.com/ask-sex-counselor/relationship-advice/sexuality-and-relationships-breast-cancer-survivors-their

"Sexuality for the Man with Cancer," American Cancer Society, www.cancer.org/acs/groups/cid/documents/webcontent/002910-pdf.pdf

"Sexuality for the Woman with Cancer," American Cancer Society, www.cancer.org/acs/groups/cid/documents/webcontent/002912-pdf.pdf

Sexy after Cancer: Meeting Your Inner Aphrodite on the Breast Cancer Journey by Barbara Musser (SAC Publishing, 2012)

Surviving after Cancer: Living the New Normal by Anne Katz, RN, PhD (Rowman & Littlefield, 2011)

Us Too: Prostate Cancer Support, Education and Advocacy, www.ustoo.org

Woman Cancer Sex by Anne Katz, RN, PhD (Hygeia Media, 2009)

DATING AGAIN

Autumn Romance: Stories and Portraits of Love after 50 by Carol Denker (Books to Believe In, 2014)

Daring to Date Again: A Memoir by Ann Anderson Evans (She Writes Press, 2014)

Getting Naked Again: Dating, Romance, Sex, and Love When You've Been Divorced, Widowed, Dumped, or Distracted by Judith Sills (Grand Central Life & Style, 2009)

Prime: Adventures and Advice on Sex, Love, and the Sensual Years by Pepper Schwartz (William Morrow, 2007)

A Round-Heeled Woman: My Late-Life Adventures in Sex and Romance by Jane Juska (Villard, 2003)

DEMENTIA AND SEX

Freedom of Sexual Expression: Dementia and Resident Rights in Long-Term Care Facilities (video), Terra Nova Films, http://www.terra novaondemand.org/title.cfm?itemcode=FOS

Jan's Story: Love Lost to the Long Goodbye of Alzheimer's by Barry Peterson (Behler, 2010)

Sexuality & Dementia: Compassionate and Practical Strategies for Dealing with Unexpected or Inappropriate Behaviors by Douglas

Wornell, MD (Demos Health, 2013)

A Thousand Tomorrows: Intimacy, Sexuality, and Alzheimer's (video), Terra Nova Films, http://www.terranovaondemand.org/title. cfm?itemcode=ATT

DESIRE

Desire: Women Write About Wanting edited by Lisa Solod Warren (Seal Press, 2007)

Enduring Desire: Your Guide to Lifelong Intimacy by Michael E. Metz and Barry W. McCarthy (Routledge, 2011)

The Heart of Desire: Keys of the Pleasures of Love by Stella Resnick, PhD (Wiley, 2012)

Reclaiming Desire: 4 Keys to Finding Your Lost Libido by Andrew Goldstein and Marianne Brandon, (Rodale, 2004)

Rekindling Desire: A Step-by-Step Program to Help Low-Sex and No-Sex Marriages by Barry McCarthy and Emily McCarthy (Routledge, 2003)

The Return of Desire: A Guide to Rediscovering Your Sexual Passion by Gina Ogden (Trumpeter, 2008)

The Sex-Starved Wife: What to Do When He's Lost Desire, by Michele Weiner Davis (Simon & Schuster, 2008)

Still Sexy After All These Years? The 9 Unspoken Truths about Women's Desire Beyond 50 by Leah Kliger and Deborah Nedelman (Perigee, 2006)

A Tired Woman's Guide to Passionate Sex: Reclaim Your Desire And Reignite Your Relationship by Laurie B. Mintz (Adams Media, 2009)

Wanting Sex Again: How to Rediscover Your Desire and Heal a Sexless Marriage by Laurie Watson (Berkley Trade, 2012)

DISABILITY, CHRONIC PAIN

The Ultimate Guide to Sex and Disability: For All of Us Who Live with Disabilities, Chronic Pain and Illness by Miriam Kaufman, MD, Cory Silverberg, and Fran Odette (Cleis Press, 2003, 2007)

ERECTILE DYSFUNCTION

Coping with Erectile Dysfunction: How to Regain Confidence and Enjoy Great Sex by Michael E. Metz and Barry W. McCarthy (New Harbinger, 2004)
Frank Talk, www.franktalk.org
Intimacy with Impotence: The Couple's Guide to Better Sex after Prostate Disease by Ralph & Barbara Alterowitz (Da Capo, 2004)
"Successful Self Penile Injection: Hints, Questions and Answers," Us Too, www.ustoo.org/PDFs/Injection.pdf
WebMD Erectile Dysfunction Health Center, www.webmd.com/erectile-dysfunction/guide/default.htm

FEMALE SEXUAL PLEASURE

How to Give Her Absolute Pleasure: Totally Explicit Techniques Every Woman Wants Her Man to Know by Lou Paget (Harmony, 2000)
She Comes First: The Thinking Man's Guide to Pleasuring a Woman by Ian Kerner (Harper Collins, 2009)
The Smart Girl's Guide to the G-Spot by Violet Blue (Cleis Press, 2007)
The Ultimate Guide to Cunnilingus: How to Go Down on a Woman and Give her Exquisite Pleasure 2nd ed. by Violet Blue (Cleis Press, 2010)

JOINT REPLACEMENT AND SEX

Recover Sex/Pleasure: Hip Replacement/Knee Replacement by Cynthia Mosher, www.recoversex.com

KINK/BDSM

Basic BDSM Instruction, www.newtokink.com

Kink Academy, www.kinkacademy.com

The New Bottoming Book by Dossie Easton and Janet W. Hardy (Greenery Press, 2001)

The New Topping Book by Dossie Easton and Janet W. Hardy (Greenery Press, 2003)

Passionate U, www.passionateu.com

Playing Well with Others: Your Field Guide to Discovering, Exploring and Navigating the Kink, Leather and BDSM Communities by Lee Harrington and Mollena Williams (Greenery Press, 2012)

The Ultimate Guide to Kink: BDSM, Role Play and the Erotic Edge by Tristan Taormino (Cleis Press, 2012)

LGBT

Dear John, I Love Jane: Women Write about Leaving Men for Women, edited by Candace Walsh and Laura André (Seal Press, 2010)

Finally Out: Letting Go of Living Straight, A Psychiatrist's Own Story by Loren A. Olson (inGroup Press, 2011)

Gen Silent (video), www.stumaddux.com/GEN_SILENT.html

It Gets Better Project, www.itgetsbetter.org

National Resource Center on LGBT Aging, www.lgbtagingcenter.org

SAGE: Services & Advocacy for Gay, Lesbian, Bisexual & Transgender Elders, www.sageusa.org

Sexual Intimacy for Women: A Guide for Same-Sex Couples by Glenda Corwin (Seal Press, 2010)

The Whole Lesbian Sex Book: A Passionate Guide for All of Us 2nd ed. by Felice Newman (Cleis Press, 2004)

LONGTIME RELATIONSHIPS

Bedded Bliss: A Couple's Guide to Lust Ever After by Kristina Wright (Cleis Press, 2013)

Mating in Captivity: Unlocking Erotic Intelligence, by Esther Perel (Harper Perennial, 2007)

Partners in Passion: A Guide to Great Sex, Emotional Intimacy and Long-term Love by Mark A. Michaels and Patricia Johnson (Cleis Press, 2014)

Passionate Marriage: Keeping Love and Intimacy Alive in Committed Relationships by David Schnarch, PhD (W. W. Norton & Company, 2009)

LONG-TERM RESIDENTIAL CARE AND SEX

Sexuality and Aging: Clinical Perspectives by Jennifer Hillman (Springer, 2012)

Sexuality & Long-Term Care: Understanding and Supporting the Needs of Older Adults by Gayle Doll (Health Professions Press, 2011)

MALE SEXUAL PLEASURE

All Night Long: How to Make Love to a Man Over 50 by Barbara Keesling (M. Evans & Co, 2004)

Great Sex: A Man's Guide to the Secret Principles of Total-Body Sex, by Michael Castleman (Rodale, 2008)

How to Be a Great Lover: Girlfriend-to-Girlfriend Totally Explicit Techniques That Will Blow His Mind by Lou Paget (Broadway Books, 1999)

"Pelvic Floor Health for Men," A Woman's Touch, published 2012, https://sexualityresources.com/ask-sex-counselor/educational-brochures/pelvic-floor-health-men

Penis Power: The Ultimate Guide to Male Sexual Health by Dudley S. Danoff, MD, FACS (Del Monaco Press, 2011)

The Ultimate Guide to Fellatio: How to Go Down on a Man and Give

Him Mind-Blowing Pleasure by Violet Blue, 2nd edition (Cleis Press, 2010)

The Ultimate Guide to Prostate Pleasure: Erotic Exploration for Men and Their Partners, by Charlie Glickman and Aislinn Emirzian (Cleis Press, 2013)

MASTURBATION

Getting Off: A Woman's Guide to Masturbation by Jamye Waxman (Seal Press, 2007)

Sex for One: The Joy of Selfloving by Betty Dodson, PhD (Harmony, 1996)

MONOGAMY

The New Monogamy: Redefining Your Relationship after Infidelity by Tammy Nelson, PhD (New Harbinger Publications, 2013)

NONMONOGAMY AND POLYAMORY

The Ethical Slut: A Practical Guide to Polyamory, Open Relationships & Other Adventures by Dossie Easton and Janet W. Hardy (Celestial Arts, 2009)

Loving More, www.lovemore.com

Opening Up: A Guide to Creating and Sustaining Open Relationships by Tristan Taormino (Cleis Press, 2008)

Sex at Dawn: The Prehistoric Origins of Modern Sexuality, by Christopher Ryan and Cacilda Jethá (Harper, 2010)

Swingers Board, www.swingersboard.com

PAINFUL SEX

The Echenberg Institute for Pelvic and Sexual Pain, www.secret suffering.com

Heal Pelvic Pain: The Proven Stretching, Strengthening, and Nutrition Program for Relieving Pain, Incontinence, & I.B.S, and Other Symptoms without Surgery by Amy Stein (McGraw-Hill, 2008)

Healing Painful Sex: A Woman's Guide to Confronting, Diagnosing, and Treating Sexual Pain by Deborah Coady, MD, and Nancy Fish, MSW, MPH (Seal Press, 2011)

International Pelvic Pain Society, www.pelvicpain.org (Find a local provider at http://www.pelvicpain.org/Patients/Find-a-Medical-Provider.aspx)

"Patient Booklets," The National Vulvodynia Association, www.nva. org/new_patient_guide.html

"Patient Education," International Society for the Study of Vulvar Disease, http://issvd.org/patient-education/

"Vaginal Renewal™," A Woman's Touch, published 2014, http://www. sexualityresources.com/ask-dr-myrtle/womens-issues-and-sexual-problems/vaginal-renewal-tm

When Sex Hurts: A Woman's Guide to Banishing Sexual Pain by Andrew Goldstein, MD, Caroline Pukall, PhD, and Irwin Goldstein, MD (Da Capo Press, 2011)

POLYAMORY

See **Nonmonogamy and Polyamory**

PORN

Good Porn: A Woman's Guide by Erika Lust (Seal Press, 2010)
The Smart Girl's Guide to Porn by Violet Blue (Cleis Press, 2006)

SEX, GENERAL

About.com Sexuality, Cory Silverberg, http://sexuality.about.com/

American Savage: Insights, Slights, and Fights on Faith, Sex, Love, and Politics, Dan Savage (Dutton, 2013)

Best Sex Writing 2015 edited by Jon Pressick, (Cleis Press, annual series)

Bonk: The Curious Coupling of Science and Sex by Mary Roach (W.W. Norton, 2008)

The Chemistry Between Us: Love, Sex, and the Science of Attraction by Larry Young and Brian Alexander (Current, 2012)

Sexual Intelligence: What We Really Want from Sex and How to Get It by Marty Klein, PhD (HarperOne, 2012)

SEX FURNITURE

Intimate Furniture, www.intimatefurniture.com

IntimateRider, www.intimaterider.com

Liberator, www.liberator.com

Love Bench, www.DrMarylou.com

Love Bumper, www.lovebumper.com

Tantra Chair, www.tantrachair.com

SEX THERAPISTS DIRECTORY

American Association of Sexuality Educators, Counselors, and Therapists, www.aasect.org

SEX TOYS

The Adventurous Couple's Guide to Sex Toys 2nd ed. by Violet Blue, (Cleis Press, 2013)

Coalition Against Toxic Toys, www.badvibes.org

The Many Joys of Sex Toys: The Ultimate How-to Handbook for Couples and Singles by Anne Semans (Harmony, 2004)

STROKE

"Sex and Intimacy After Stroke," by Jon Caswell, *Stroke Connection*, March/April 2009, pp 12-15, www.nxtbook.com/nxtbooks/aha/strokeconnection_200903/index.php#/14

TANTRA

Great Sex Made Simple: Tantric Tips to Deepen Intimacy & Heighten Pleasure by Mark A. Michaels and Patricia Johnson (Llewellyn, 2012)

ACKNOWLEDGMENTS

I thank you, my community of readers. You confided your concerns, asked intimate questions, shared your stories. I could not have written this book without you. You are the reason I do this work.

I thank the sex educators and authors who contributed their expertise. You have enriched this book, and I'm grateful.

I thank Brenda Knight at Cleis Press for telling me, "We need this book, and you're the one to write it." I thank the whole Cleis Press family for embracing me and the mission of this book.

I thank Randy Austin-Cardona, my research assistant. Your work was invaluable to me.

I thank all of you who join me in talking out loud about senior sex and changing the world, one mind at a time.

ENDNOTES

1. "Characteristics of Women with Body Size Satisfaction at Midlife: Results of the Gender and Body Image (GABI) Study," *Journal of Women & Aging*, 25.4, published 2013, www.tandfonline.com/doi/full/10.1080/08952841.2013.816215#.UmmH3_ljtcY. Quoted in: "Just 12 Percent of Women Over 50 Are 'Satisfied' With Their Bodies," HealthDay, published 2013, consumer.healthday.com/senior-citizen-information-31/misc-aging-news-10/just-12-of-women-over-50-say-they-are-satisfied-with-their-bodies-681275.html. And: "Happy With Your Body? Only 12 Percent of Older Women Are," AARP, published 2013, blog.aarp.org/2013/10/23/happy-with-your-body-only-12-percent-of-older-women-are.

2. "Just 12 Percent of Women Over 50 Are 'Satisfied' With Their Bodies," HealthDay, published 2013, consumer.healthday.com/senior-citizen-information-31/misc-aging-news-10/just-12-of-women-over-50-say-they-are-satisfied-with-their-bodies-681275.html.

3. "Sexuality in Midlife and Beyond," Harvard Health Publications, published 2013, www.health.harvard.edu/special_health_reports/sexuality-in-midlife-and-beyond.

4. "How do female arousal products work?" Planned Parenthood, published 2010,

consensualtext.org/2010/10/what-are-the-new-female-arousal-products-all-about/.

5. Megan Andelloux, via email, January 2014.

6. "Arginine," Mayo Clinic, www.mayoclinic.org/drugs-supplements/arginine/safety/hrb-20058733.

7. "Lube, lube, lube... which one do I choose?" by Megan Andelloux, Women's Web, www.womensweb.ca/health/repro/safesex/lube.php. And: Megan Andelloux, via email, October 2014.

8. Jennifer Pritchett and Sarah Mueller, via email, October 2014.

9. "Some More Info About Flammable Silicone Lubricants" by Charlie Glickman, www.charlieglickman.com/2010/04/07/some-more-info-about-flammable-silicone-lubricants/. And: "Flammable Lube Experiment" (Ask Garnet.blogspot.com), youtu.be/hru402ysXhE.

10. "Exercise Improves Sexual Function In Women Taking Antidepressants: Results From A Randomized Crossover Trial," by Tierney Ahrold Lorenz and Cindy May Meston, *Depression and Anxiety*, published 2013; DOI: 10.1002/da.22208. Quoted in: "Exercise alleviates sexual side-effects of antidepressants in women," Science Daily, published 2013, www.sciencedaily.com/releases/2013/12/131210120700.htm.

11. "Sexual Performance Anxiety," WebMD, www.webmd.com/sexual-conditions/guide/sexual-performance-anxiety-causes-treatments.

12. "Chronic Stress and Sexual Function in Women," by Lisa Hamilton, PhD, and Cindy Meston, PhD, *Journal of Sexual Medicine*, 10:2443–2454, published 2013, onlinelibrary.wiley.com/doi/10.1111/jsm.12249/abstract. And: "3 Tips to Jumpstart Your Libido," by Anna Davies, Prevention.com, www.prevention.com/sex/sex-relationships/how-stress-hurts-your-sex-drive.

13. Ellen Barnard, via email, January 2014.

14. "Things I Have Fished Out of People's Butts," by Mona Moore, Vice, www.vice.com/read/bollocks-to-the-hippocratic-oath-deaths-back-door.

15. "10 Craziest Foreign Objects Found Stuck In A Rectum," by Beverly Jenkins, Oddee, www.oddee.com/item_98446.aspx.

16. CATT™, The Coalition Against Toxic Toys, badvibes.org/. Printed with permission.

17. "Sexual Desire," presentation by Barry McCarthy, AASECT 2012.

18. Larry LeShan, PhD, via telephone, December 2013.

19. "SL Letter of the Day: Peace On The Side," by Dan Savage, Slog, published 2011, slog.thestranger.com/slog/archives/2011/01/18/sl-letter-of-the-day-peace-on-the-side.

20. "Sex, health, and years of sexually active life gained due to good health: evidence from two U.S. population based cross sectional surveys of ageing," by Stacy Tessler Lindau and Natalia Gavrilova, *BMJ*. 340: c810, published 2010, www.ncbi.nlm.nih.gov/pmc/articles/PMC2835854/.

21. "A Study of Sexuality and Health among Older Adults in the United States," by Stacy Tessler Lindau, MD, MAPP, L. Philip Schumm, MA, Edward O. Laumann, PhD, Wendy Levinson, MD, Colm A. O'Muircheartaigh, PhD, and Linda J. Waite, PhD, *New England Journal of Medicine*, 357:762-774, published 2007, www.nejm.org/doi/full/10.1056/NEJMoa067423.

22. "What We Don't Talk about When We Don't Talk about Sex: Results of a National Survey of U.S. Obstetrician/Gynecologists," by Janelle Sobecki, Farr Curlin, Kenneth Rasinski, and Tessier Lindau, *Journal of Sexual Medicine*, 9:1285–1294, published 2012, onlinelibrary.wiley.com/doi/10.1111/j.1743-6109.2012.02702.x/abstract;jsessionid=2AB6EEB2028 4121C8250A75431481ACE.f02t04.

23. "What We Don't Talk about When We Don't Talk about Sex: Results of a National Survey of U.S. Obstetrician/Gynecologists," by Janelle Sobecki, Farr Curlin, Kenneth Rasinski, and Tessier Lindau, *Journal of Sexual Medicine*, 9:1285–1294, published 2012, onlinelibrary.wiley.com/doi/10.1111/j.1743-6109.2012.02702.x/abstract;jsessionid=2AB6EEB2028 4121C8250A75431481ACE.f02t04.

24. *Sexual Intelligence: What We Really Want from Sex and How to Get It*, by Marty Klein, PhD (HarperOne, 2012).

25. "A Study of Sexuality and Health among Older Adults in the United States," by Stacy Tessler Lindau, MD, MAPP, L. Philip Schumm, MA, Edward O. Laumann, PhD, Wendy Levinson, MD, Colm A. O'Muircheartaigh, PhD, and Linda J. Waite, PhD, *New England Journal of Medicine*, 357:762-774, published 2007, www.nejm.org/doi/full/10.1056/NEJMoa067423.

26. *The Sex-Starved Wife: What to Do When He's Lost Desire*, by Michele Weiner Davis (Simon & Schuster, 2008).

27. "Sexual Pharmacology," presentation by Richard Siegel, MS, CST, AASECT 2013.

28. "Sexuality in Midlife and Beyond," Harvard Health Publications, published 2013, www.health.harvard.edu/special_health_reports/sexuality-in-midlife-and-beyond. And: "Can We Talk about Sex? Seven Things Physicians Need to Know About Sex and the Older Adult," by Jeanne Mettner, *Minnesota Medicine*, published August 2013, www.minnesotamedicine.com/Portals/mnmed/August%202013/canwetalkaboutsex.pdf.

29. "Hormone Therapy," American Congress of Obstetricians and Gynecologists (ACOG), published 2013, www.acog.org/-/media/For-Patients/pfs003.pdf?dmc=1&ts=20141107T1646532971.

30. Jacques Rossouw, MD, chief of the Women's Health Initiative Branch within the NHLBI's Division of Cardiovascular Sciences, quoted in "Women's Health Initiative reaffirms use of short-term hormone replacement therapy for younger women," NIH, published 2013, www.nih.gov/news/health/oct2013/nhlbi-17.htm.

31. "Hormone Therapy," American Congress of Obstetricians and Gynecologists (ACOG), published 2013, www.acog.org/-/media/For-Patients/pfs003.pdf?dmc=1&ts=20141107T1646532971.

32. Paul Roberts, pharmacist, via email, January 2014. And: Paul Roberts, via discussion, January 2014.

33. "Hormone Therapy," American Congress of Obstetricians and Gynecologists (ACOG), published 2013, www.acog.org/-/media/For-Patients/pfs003.pdf?dmc=1&ts=20141107T1646532971.

34. "Hormone Replacement Therapy," NIH: National Heart, Lung, and Blood Institute via MedlinePlus, published 2014, www.nlm.nih.gov/medlineplus/hormonereplacementtherapy.html.

35. "Erectile Dysfunction: Testosterone Replacement Therapy," WebMD, www.webmd.com/erectile-dysfunction/guide/testosterone-replacement-therapy.

36. Adapted from "Sex Shouldn't Hurt" by Melanie Davis, Safer Sex for Seniors, published 2012, safersex4seniors.org/assets/SS4S_Sex_Shouldnt_Hurt.pdf. Printed with permission.

37. *Healing Painful Sex: A Woman's Guide to Confronting, Diagnosing, and Treating Sexual Pain* by Deborah Coady, MD and Nancy Fish, MSW, MPH (Seal Press, 2011) pp. 107-111.

38. *Healing Painful Sex: A Woman's Guide to Confronting, Diagnosing, and Treating Sexual Pain* by Deborah Coady, MD and Nancy Fish, MSW, MPH (Seal Press, 2011) pp. 107-111.

39. "Sexuality in Midlife and Beyond," Harvard Health Publications, published 2013, www.health.harvard.edu/special_health_reports/sexuality-in-midlife-and-beyond.

40. National Vulvodynia Association, learnpatient.nva.org.

41. *Naked at Our Age: Talking Out Loud about Senior Sex*, by Joan Price (Seal Press, 2011) chapter 11. And: "Sexuality in Midlife and Beyond," Harvard Health Publications, published 2013, www.health.harvard.edu/special_health_reports/sexuality-in-midlife-and-beyond. And: National Vulvodynia Association, learnpatient.nva.org.

42. "A population-based assessment of chronic unexplained vulvar pain: have we underestimated the prevalence of vulvodynia?" by Harlow and Stewart, *Journal of the American Medical Women's Association*, 58(2):82-8, published 2013, www.ncbi.nlm.nih.gov/pubmed/12744420.

43. "Treatment A Trois: One Center's Approach to Pelvic Pain," presentation by Kimberly Resnick Anderson, LISW, MSSA, CSSP, DST and Amy Senn, PT, Summa Health System's Center for Sexual Health, AASECT 2013.

44. "Self-Help Strategies," The National Vulvodynia Association, learnpatient. nva.org/understanding_vulvodynia_5.php. Printed with permission.

45. Adapted from "Everything You Need to Know About Vulvodynia" by the National Vulvodynia Association, learnpatient.nva.org/maintaining_healthy_relationships_1.php. Printed with permission.

46. *Naked at Our Age: Talking Out Loud about Senior Sex*, by Joan Price (Seal Press, 2011) chapter 11.

47. "Male dyspareunia," by Mathew Oommen, MD and Wayne JG Hellstrom, MD, UpToDate, published 2013, www.uptodate.com/contents/male-dyspareunia.

48. "Orgasmic Pain and a Detectable PSA Level after Radical Prostatectomy," by Michael O'Leary, MD, *Reviews in Urology*. 7.4,240–241, published 2005, www.ncbi.nlm.nih.gov/pmc/articles/PMC1477581. And: "Painful Orgasm After Radical Prostatectomy," *Journal of Sexual Medicine* 10.5, pp. 1417–1423, published 2013, www.issm.info/news/sex-health-headlines/painful-orgasm-after-radical-prostatectomy.

49. "Chronic Pelvic Pain," International Pelvic Pain Society, www.pelvicpain. org/pdf/Patients/CPP_Pt_Ed_Booklet.pdf.

50. "Sex Shouldn't Hurt" by Melanie Davis, Safer Sex for Seniors, published 2012, safersex4seniors.org/assets/SS4S_Sex_Shouldnt_Hurt.pdf.

51. "Keeping your sex life going despite cancer treatment," American Cancer Society, published 2013, www.cancer.org/treatment/treatmentsandsideeffects/ physicalsideeffects/sexualsideeffectsinwomen/sexualityforthewoman/ sexuality-for-women-with-cancer-keeping-sex-life-despite-cancer-treatment.

52. "Cancer treatment for women: Possible sexual side effects," Mayo Clinic, published 2014, www.mayoclinic.com/health/cancer-treatment/SA00071.

53. Presentation by Ellen Barnard, AASECT 2013. And: Ellen Barnard, via email, December 2013.

54. "Penile Rehabilitation after Prostate or Pelvic Surgery or Radiation," A Woman's Touch, published 2011, sexualityresources.com/ask-dr-myrtle/ mens-issues-and-sexual-problems/penile-rehabilitation-after-prostate-or-pelvic-surgery.

55. "Penile Rehabilitation after Prostate or Pelvic Surgery or Radiation," A Woman's Touch, published 2011, sexualityresources.com/ask-dr-myrtle/ mens-issues-and-sexual-problems/penile-rehabilitation-after-prostate-or-pelvic-surgery.

56. Presentation by Anne Katz, AASECT 2013. And: Anne Katz, via email, November 2013.

57. "Can We Talk about Sex? Seven Things Physicians Need to Know About Sex and the Older Adult," by Jeanne Mettner, *Minnesota Medicine*, published August 2013, www.minnesotamedicine.com/Portals/mnmed/August%20 2013/canwetalkaboutsex.pdf.

58. Adapted from "Chronic Medical Conditions and Sex," by Michael Castleman, http://www.greatsexafter40.com/info/medical-issues/sex-chronic-medical-conditio. Printed with permission.

59. Marty Klein, PhD, quoted in "Don't Let Arthritis Ruin Your Sex Life," by Michael Castleman, AARP.com, published July 2013, www.aarp.org/home-family/sex-intimacy/info-07-2013/dont-let-arthritis-ruin-your-sex-life.html.

60. "Joint Replacement Surgery Can Improve Intimacy," by Linda Ruth,

Arthritis Foundation, published 2013, www.arthritistoday.org/news/joint-replacement-better-sex-259-2.php.

61. "Sexual Relations," www.recoversex.com/total-knee-replacement/sexual-relations-after-total-knee-replacement.

62. "Sexual Positioning Following Total Knee Replacement," www.recoversex.com/total-knee-replacement/sexual-positioning-following-total-knee-replacement.

63. "Relationships, Intimacy and Arthritis," Arthritis Care, published 2011, www.arthritiscare.org.uk/PublicationsandResources/Listedbytype/Booklets/main_content/Relationshipsbooklet2011.pdf.

64. "Relationships, Intimacy and Arthritis," Arthritis Care, published 2011, www.arthritiscare.org.uk/PublicationsandResources/Listedbytype/Booklets/main_content/Relationshipsbooklet2011.pdf.

65. "Sex Positions After Joint Replacement," Northern Inyo Hospital, nih.kramesonline.com/HealthSheets/3,S,40019.

66. "Sexuality in Midlife and Beyond," Harvard Health Publications, published 2013, www.health.harvard.edu/special_health_reports/sexuality-in-midlife-and-beyond.

67. "Physicians should counsel patients about sex life after cardiac event: A Consensus Document From the American Heart Association and the European Society of Cardiology Council on Cardiovascular Nursing and Allied Professions," American Heart Association, published July 29, 2013, newsroom.heart.org/news/physicians-should-counsel-patients-about-sex-life-after-cardiac-event.

68. "Myths About Sexual Activity and Heart Disease: Common Misconceptions about the Sexual Impact of Heart Disease and Heart Attack" by Cory Silverberg, 2009, sexuality.about.com/od/sexualhealthqanda/a/myths_about_sex_and_heart_disease_attack.htm.

69. "Sexuality in Midlife and Beyond," Harvard Health Publications, published 2013, www.health.harvard.edu/special_health_reports/sexuality-in-midlife-and-beyond.

70. "Use of Sildenafil (Viagra) in Patients With Cardiovascular Disease," Circulation, 99: 168-177, published 1999, doi: 10.1161/01.CIR.99.1.168, circ.ahajournals.org/content/99/1/168.full. And: "Viagra and Heart Risks," by Michael Haederle, AARP.com, published 2012, www.aarp.org/health/

drugs-supplements/info-01-2012/viagra-and-heart-risks-health-discovery. html.

71. "Sexuality in Midlife and Beyond," Harvard Health Publications, published 2013, www.health.harvard.edu/special_health_reports/sexuality-in-midlife-and-beyond.

72. "Sex and High Blood Pressure," American Heart Association, published 2014, www.heart.org/HEARTORG/Conditions/HighBloodPressure/WhyBlood PressureMatters/Sex-and-High-Blood-Pressure_UCM_451787_Article.jsp.

73. "Stroke," National Library of Medicine, www.nlm.nih.gov/medlineplus/ency/article/000726.htm.

74. "Sex and Intimacy After Stroke" by Jon Caswell, *StrokeConnection*, March/April 2009, pp. 12-15, www.nxtbook.com/nxtbooks/aha/stroke connection_200903/index.php#/14.

75. "Recovery After Stroke: Redefining Sexuality," National Stroke Association, published 2006, www.stroke.org/stroke-resources/library/redefining-sexuality.

76. "Sex and Intimacy After Stroke" by Jon Caswell, *StrokeConnection*, March/April 2009, pp. 12-15, www.nxtbook.com/nxtbooks/aha/stroke connection_200903/index.php#/14.

77. "Erection Changes After 50: The Facts" by Michael Castleman, Psychology Today, www.psychologytoday.com/blog/all-about-sex/201205/erection-changes-after-50-the-facts/.

78. "Sexuality in Midlife and Beyond," Harvard Health Publications, published 2013, www.health.harvard.edu/special_health_reports/sexuality-in-midlife-and-beyond.

79. "Sexuality in Midlife and Beyond," Harvard Health Publications, published 2013, www.health.harvard.edu/special_health_reports/sexuality-in-midlife-and-beyond.

80. "Erectile Dysfunction and Lifestyle Factors," WebMD, www.webmd.com/erectile-dysfunction/guide/lifestyle-factors-linked-to-ed.

81. "Sexuality in Midlife and Beyond," Harvard Health Publications, published 2013, www.health.harvard.edu/special_health_reports/sexuality-in-midlife-and-beyond.

82. "Sexuality in Midlife and Beyond," Harvard Health Publications, published

2013, www.health.harvard.edu/special_health_reports/sexuality-in-midlife-and-beyond.

83. "Successful Self Penile Injection: Hints, Questions and Answers," Us Too, www.ustoo.org/PDFs/Injection.pdf.

84. "Successful Self Penile Injection: Hints, Questions and Answers," Us Too, www.ustoo.org/PDFs/Injection.pdf.

85. "Sexuality in Midlife and Beyond," Harvard Health Publications, published 2013, www.health.harvard.edu/special_health_reports/sexuality-in-midlife-and-beyond.

86. "Sexuality in Midlife and Beyond," Harvard Health Publications, published 2013, www.health.harvard.edu/special_health_reports/sexuality-in-midlife-and-beyond. And: "Men's Forum: Erectile Dysfunction," Kaiser Oakland Urology, mydoctor.kaiserpermanente.org/ncal/Images/Erectile%20Dysfunction_tcm75-139412.pdf. And: "Erectile Dysfunction: Vacuum Constriction Devices," WebMD, www.webmd.com/erectile-dysfunction/guide/vacuum-constriction-devices.

87. *Penis Power*, by Dudley Seth Danoff (Del Monaco, 2011), pp. 114-116.

88. "Erection Changes After 50: The Facts" by Michael Castleman, Psychology Today, published 2012, www.psychologytoday.com/blog/all-about-sex/201205/erection-changes-after-50-the-facts/.

89. "Restoration of Satisfying Sex for a Castrated Cancer Patient with Complete Impotence: A Case Study," *Journal of Sex & Marital Therapy*, 32(5):389-99, published 2006, www.tandfonline.com/doi/full/10.1080/00926230600835346#.UnV8ovljtcY.

90. "The Gray Divorce Revolution: Rising Divorce among Middle-aged and Older Adults, 1990-2010," by Susan L. Brown and I-Fen Lin, Department of Sociology and National Center for Family & Marriage Research, Bowling Green State University, published March 2013, www.bgsu.edu/content/dam/BGSU/college-of-arts-and-sciences/NCFMR/documents/Lin/The-Gray-Divorce.pdf.

91. "The Divorce Experience: A Study of Divorce at Midlife and Beyond," by Xenia Montenegro, AARP, published May 2004, assets.aarp.org/rgcenter/general/divorce.pdf.

92. "10 Best Places for Single Seniors to Retire," U.S.News, published

November 2010, money.usnews.com/money/retirement/articles/2010/11/01/the-10-best-places-for-single-seniors-to-retire.

93. "Sexuality in Midlife and Beyond," Harvard Health Publications, published 2013, www.health.harvard.edu/special_health_reports/sexuality-in-midlife-and-beyond.

94. "A Profile of Older Americans: 2011," Administration on Aging, U.S. Department of Health and Human Services, published 2011, www.aoa.gov/Aging_Statistics/Profile/2011/docs/2011profile.pdf.

95. "A Profile of Older Americans: 2011," Administration on Aging, U.S. Department of Health and Human Services, published 2011, www.aoa.gov/Aging_Statistics/Profile/2011/docs/2011profile.pdf.

96. "A Profile of Older Americans: 2011," Administration on Aging, U.S. Department of Health and Human Services, published 2011, www.aoa.gov/Aging_Statistics/Profile/2011/docs/2011profile.pdf.

97. "Brains Do It: Lust, Attraction, and Attachment" by Helen E. Fisher, Dana Foundation, published January 2000, www.dana.org/Cerebrum/2000/Brains_Do_It__Lust,_Attraction,_and_Attachment/.

98. "My Body Changed. So Did Intimacy," by Joyce Wadler, The New York Times, published October 18, 2013, www.nytimes.com/2013/10/22/booming/my-body-changed-so-did-intimacy.html?_r=0.

99. "Is It Wrong To Want To Please Your Man?" by Walker Thornton, Better After 50, published June 27, 2013, betterafter50.com/2013/06/is-it-wrong-to-want-to-please-your-man/.

100. "National HIV and STD Testing," Centers for Disease Control and Prevention, hivtest.cdc.gov/faq.aspx.

101. "Sexual activity and STD rate up among seniors," CNN Health, published February 2, 2012, thechart.blogs.cnn.com/2012/02/02/sexual-activity-and-std-rate-up-among-seniors/.

102. "Sex, Romance, and Relationships: AARP Survey of Midlife and Older Adults," AARP.com, published April 2010, assets.aarp.org/rgcenter/general/srr_09.pdf.

103. "Study of American Sex Habits Suggests Boomers Need Sex Ed," by Belinda Luscombe, Time Health and Family, published Oct. 4, 2010, healthland.time.com/2010/10/04/study-suggests-boomers-need-sex-ed/.

104. "Older women's attitudes, behavior, and communication about sex and HIV: a community-based study," by Lindau, Leitsch, Lundberg, and Jerome, *Journal of Women's Health*, 15(6):747-53. Published 2006 www.ncbi.nlm. nih.gov/pubmed/16910906. And: "More Midlife (and Older) STDs," by Tiffany Sharples, Time Health and Family, published July 2, 2008, content. time.com/time/health/article/0,8599,1819633,00.html#ixzz2SukOi9lh.

105. "Sexual activity and STD rate up among seniors," CNN Health, published February 2, 2012, thechart.blogs.cnn.com/2012/02/02/sexual-activity-and-std-rate-up-among-seniors/. And: "Sex and the Elderly: STD Risk Often Ignored," by Salynn Boyles, WebMD, published February 2, 2012, www. webmd.com/healthy-aging/news/20120202/sex-and-elderly-std-risk-often-ignored.

106. "Patterns and Correlates of Sexual Activity and Condom Use Behavior in Persons 50-Plus Years of Age Living with HIV/AIDS," *AIDS and Behavior*, 12(6): 943–956, Published November 2008, www.ncbi.nlm.nih.gov/pmc/articles/PMC2575000/.

107. "Government-Backed Group Calls for Universal HIV Testing of Adults, by Alexandra Sifferlin, Time Health and Family, published April 30, 2013, healthland.time.com/2013/04/30/panel-releases-recommendation-for-widespread-hiv-testing/.

108. "HIV/AIDS among Persons Aged 50 and Older," Centers for Disease Control and Prevention, published 2008, www.cdc.gov/hiv/pdf/library_factsheet_HIV_among_PersonsAged50andOlder.pdf.

109. "Oral Sex and HIV Risk," Centers for Disease Control and Prevention, published 2014, www.cdc.gov/hiv/resources/factsheets/print/oralsex.htm.

110. "Sex in Geriatrics Sets Hebrew Home Apart in Elderly Care," by Bryan Gruley, Bloomberg, Published 2013, www.bloomberg.com/news/2013-07-23/sex-in-geriatrics-sets-hebrew-home-apart-in-elderly-care.html.

111. "Promoting Awareness of Sexuality & Sexual Health in the Elderly," presentation by Jeannine Clark, M.S.N. for the Nevada Geriatric Education Center, University of Nevada, Reno, 2010, echo.unr.edu/ess/echo/presentation/6eab576d-72cb-4c17-9e45-f24035efadb0.

112. "Policies and Procedures Concerning Sexual Expression at the Hebrew Home at Riverdale," updated by Robin Dressel and Mildred Ramirez, The Hebrew Home at Riverdale, Revised 2013, www.hebrewhome.org/uploads/ckeditor/files/sexualexpressionpolicy.pdf.

113. "Policies and Procedures Concerning Sexual Expression at the Hebrew Home at Riverdale," updated by Robin Dressel and Mildred Ramirez, The Hebrew Home at Riverdale, Revised 2013, www.hebrewhome.org/uploads/ckeditor/files/sexualexpressionpolicy.pdf.

114. "Policies and Procedures Concerning Sexual Expression at the Hebrew Home at Riverdale," updated by Robin Dressel and Mildred Ramirez, The Hebrew Home at Riverdale, Revised 2013, www.hebrewhome.org/uploads/ckeditor/files/sexualexpressionpolicy.pdf.

115. "Let's Talk about Sex" by Robin Dessel, McKnight's, published 2013, www.mcknights.com/lets-talk-about-sex/article/306264.

116. "Gen Silent: The Statistics," Stu Maddux, stumaddux.com/gen_silent_press_room_files/Gen%20Silent%20stats%20061711.pdf.

117. "National Transgender Discrimination Survey: Report on Health and Healthcare," National Center for Transgender Equality and the National Gay and Lesbian Task Force, Published 2010, transequality.org/PDFs/NTDSReportonHealth_final.pdf.

118. Closing keynote, presentation Joycelyn Elders, Momentum 2012 and CatalystCon West 2013 (She says this often!).

To access the index, please visit my website, www.joanprice.com. *The Ultimate Guide to Sex after Fifty* book page will have a link to an index you can print out.

ABOUT THE AUTHOR

JOAN PRICE (www.joanprice.com) calls herself an "advocate for ageless sexuality." Joan has been writing, speaking, and blogging about senior sex since 2005. Formerly a health and fitness writer (and before that, a high school English teacher!), she switched topics to senior sex with her spicy memoir, *Better Than I Ever Expected: Straight Talk about Sex After Sixty*, written to celebrate the joys of older-age sexuality with her lover and future husband, artist Robert Rice (www.robert riceart.com), whom she met when she was fifty-seven and he was sixty-four.

After hundreds of readers wrote Joan with questions and concerns about their own senior sex life, she wrote *Naked at*

Our Age: Talking Out Loud about Senior Sex, to address the challenges of sex and aging. *Naked at Our Age* was chosen Outstanding Self-Help Book 2012 from the American Society of Journalists and Authors and 2012 Book Award from American Association of Sexuality Educators, Counselors and Therapists. In 2013, Joan conceived and edited the steamy anthology, *Ageless Erotica*. In 2014, she received the Catalyst award for "inspiring exceptional conversations in sexuality."

Although Robert died in 2008, Joan continues on her mission to change society's view of senior sex, one mind at a time. Her blog about sex and aging, www.Naked AtOurAge.com, has received numerous awards from health, aging, and sexuality sites. As a speaker, Joan delights and informs boomer and senior audiences with her helpful, candid, content-packed presentations. She also offers personalized, educational consultations by phone and Skype.

Joan lives in Sebastopol, California, where she also teaches contemporary line dancing, which she calls "the most fun you can have with both feet on the floor." Contact her at joan@joanprice.com.